EARLY YEARS
TEACHING &
LEARNING

3RD EDITION

Denise Reardon,
Dilys Wilson
Dympna Reed

Los Angeles | London | New Delhi
Singapore | Washington DC | Melbourne

Los Angeles | London | New Delhi
Singapore | Washington DC | Melbourne

SAGE Publications Ltd
1 Oliver's Yard
55 City Road
London EC1Y 1SP

SAGE Publications Inc.
2455 Teller Road
Thousand Oaks, California 91320

SAGE Publications India Pvt Ltd
B 1/I 1 Mohan Cooperative Industrial Area
Mathura Road
New Delhi 110 044

SAGE Publications Asia-Pacific Pte Ltd
3 Church Street
#10-04 Samsung Hub
Singapore 049483

Publisher: Jude Bowman
Editor: George Knowles
Production editor: Victoria Nicholas
Editorial assistant: Catriona McMullen
Copyeditor: Elaine Leek
Proofreader: Derek Markham
Marketing manager: Lorna Patkai
Cover design: Wendy Scott
Typeset by: C&M Digitals (P) Ltd, Chennai, India
Printed in the UK

First edition (*Achieving Early Years Professional Status*) published
in 2009. Reprinted in 2009 (once) and 2010 (three times).
Second edition (*Achieving Early Years Professional Status*)
published in 2012. This third edition *Early Years Teaching and
Learning* first published in 2018.

Library of Congress Control Number: 2017963277

British Library Cataloguing in Publication data

A catalogue record for this book is available from
the British Library

ISBN 978-1-4462-9403-1
ISBN 978-1-4462-9405-5 (pbk)

At SAGE we take sustainability seriously. Most of our products are printed in the UK using responsibly sourced
papers and boards. When we print overseas we ensure sustainable papers are used as measured by the PREPS
grading system. We undertake an annual audit to monitor our sustainability.

EARLY YEARS TEACHING & LEARNING

Sara Miller McCune founded SAGE Publishing in 1965 to support the dissemination of usable knowledge and educate a global community. SAGE publishes more than 1000 journals and over 800 new books each year, spanning a wide range of subject areas. Our growing selection of library products includes archives, data, case studies and video. SAGE remains majority owned by our founder and after her lifetime will become owned by a charitable trust that secures the company's continued independence.

Los Angeles | London | New Delhi | Singapore | Washington DC | Melbourne

Learning and discovering are not linear processes but webs
of insane matrices, layers of disparate, unconnected facts
accrued over the years that will suddenly coalesce...

Hannah Rothschild (2015)

CONTENTS

About the Authors and Contributors　　　　　　　　*ix*

Authors' Acknowledgements　　　　　　　　*xiii*

**1 Getting Started – An Introduction to Teaching
and Learning in the Early Years**　　　　　　　　**1**

Denise Reardon

**2 A Principled Pedagogical Approach to Teaching
and Learning in the Early Years**　　　　　　　　**17**

Denise Reardon

3 Early Years Movers and Shakers　　　　　　　　**35**

Denise Reardon, Fatema Haji and Dympna Reed

4 Reflective Practice and Practice-Based Inquiry　　　　　　　　**59**

Dilys Wilson and Ruth Miller

5 High-Quality Early Years Teaching and Learning　　　　　　　　**77**

Denise Reardon

**6 Planning for Effective Teaching and Learning in
the Early Years (EY)**　　　　　　　　**99**

Denise Reardon

**7 Communication, Language and Literacy in
the Early Years**　　　　　　　　**117**

Denise Reardon

**8 Promoting Babies' and Young Children's Physical
and Emotional Well-being**　　　　　　　　**137**

Dilys Wilson

9 **Developing a Creative Approach to Teaching and Learning in the Early Years**   **153**

Denise Reardon and Dympna Reed

10 **Safeguarding and Promoting the Welfare of All Babies and Young Children**   **169**

Dympna Reed and Jennifer Smith

11 **Responding to the Strengths and Needs of All Babies and Young Children**   **187**

Denise Reardon

12 **Undertaking Wider Professional Responsibilities**   **205**

Julie Vaggers

Appendix 1.1: Teachers' Standards. (Early Years) From September 2013. National College for Teaching and Leadership   *219*

Appendix 1.2: Early Years Educator (Level 3): Qualifications Criteria. National College for Teaching and Leadership (2013)   *225*

Appendix 2: EYFS (2017a) Staff: Child Ratios – all providers (including childminders)   *231*

References   *235*

Index   *249*

ABOUT THE AUTHORS AND CONTRIBUTORS

Denise Reardon is an established author who has been successfully involved in early years teaching, training and lecturing for over 30 years. She has taught early years children in nurseries and schools and worked as a Local Authority Early Years Advisory Teacher. She has also been instrumental in leading a wide number of national early years initiatives and programmes spanning both further education (Canterbury and North-West Kent) and the higher education sector (Canterbury Christchurch University). She has successfully written and co-authored foundation, bachelors and Master degrees for early years teachers, educators and practitioners. Her Master's dissertation in Education Leadership explores team working and was used to inform previous publications of this book. Denise has recently retired from being the Early Years Teacher, Programme Director at Canterbury Christchurch University to concentrate on her writing, three early years grandchildren, and now sits on the 'Early Years Teacher' advisory board at Middlesex University and is a member of the world Preschool Association (OMEP), an international non- governmental and non-profit organisation with consultative status at the United Nations and UNESCO. Denise has a particular interest in early years creativity and the evolving role of the Early Years teacher.

Dympna Reed trained as a teacher in Belfast N. Ireland and has taught in a variety of schools in the South East of England since 1969. Many years were spent as an innovative Reception Class teacher in the school where she was a Deputy Head. She was seconded to become a part-time Early Years Teacher Advisor in East Sussex and did a Post Graduate Certificate in Early Years Education at the University of Brighton, focusing on Effective Leadership in the Foundation Stage. She helped to write and deliver a variety of training courses for East Sussex School Improvement Service. A year was spent working for a different Local Authority as an Advisory Teacher and she returned to East Sussex as the full-time Lead Teaching and Learning Consultant for Early Years. This involved working with pre-schools, nurseries, childminders and schools to mentor and support and to offer training in the many new initiatives for the EYFS. Dympna worked as a visiting assessor and mentor atCanterbury Christchurch University for the Early Years Teacher, and Early Years Professional Status programme.

Since retirement she has been involved as a governor of two schools and takes an active interest in Early Years provision. She has five grandchildren ranging in age from new-born to 14 years.

Dilys Wilson has been involved in the early years sector for over 35 years, starting out in London as a teacher in early years settings and schools, before becoming a lecturer in a Further Education College teaching on courses for students training as early years practitioners. In this role, she was involved in reviewing and developing early years training programmes at Levels 2, 3 and 4 to address the constantly shifting training and early years policy context. With the development of Early Years Professional Status in 2006/7 she moved to Middlesex University to lead the programme where she is currently the Early Years Initial Teacher Training (EYITT) programme leader. She has worked closely with the wider early years sector to promote the important role that teachers with Early Years Teacher Status play as leaders of practice with children from birth to five years. Her interest in the emotional factors involved in working with young children and their families informs her approach to teaching and programme development and she has been involved in CPD training for practitioners on supervision and emotional well-being. She has contributed to research publications and conference presentations on a range of early years professional practice issues.

Fatema Haji Since 2006, Fatema has worked as a mentor, tutor and assessor and moderator alongside establishments delivering the EYITT programme across the country. Working across various providers means that she can improve practice for the providers and give advice where necessary. She also works with nurseries across the country to raise their standards for the children. Not only has she improved setting standards by training managers but she has improved Ofsted gradings for the settings. Her expertise lies in observation, planning and assessment. Furthermore, she has worked alongside many Government departments, including OFSTED to raise their profile in the local media across the country. When she is not working or looking after her three young children, Fatema enjoys reading and sports.

Ruth Miller leads the development of work-based learning and accreditation across the School of Health and Education at Middlesex University, and with external partners. With over 20 years of experience supporting diverse learners across Further and Higher Education, she has led the development of innovative work-based learning programmes and apprenticeships, across health, social care, sport and early years in response to workforce development needs. She worked with Skills for Care to develop the Higher Apprenticeship for managers in Social Care. She has a particular interest in providing progression pathways for experienced practitioners through recognition of their prior learning (RPL) and has published case studies showcasing her work with teaching assistants and early years practitioners. She has led significant curriculum development around *practitioner inquiry* and *work-based projects* that develop student's project leadership skills and make a real impact on practice development in the workplace. She also has an interest in developing communities of learning for work-based students and using online technologies for support. She has shared this practice widely at conferences.

Jennifer Smith has had a highly successful career in Education specialising in Primary and Early Years phases. Qualifying in Liverpool, Hertfordshire and Middlesex University with an Honours degree in Education and a Master's degree focusing on Developing Reading Skills, her career progressed from the classroom to senior leadership roles and then into Primary School Headships. Promotion to join East Sussex School's Advisory service brought experience in supporting school leaders to raise standards and responsibility for the Local Authority's Early Years provision and development. Qualification as an Ofsted Inspector of Schools, Head teacher Performance Management Assessor and NPQH Assessor extended her work and experience across the country. Opportunities arose to contribute to DfE consultative group,s and Brighton University development of Early Years Master's level courses further extended her contributions to the world of education. In later years, whilst based at Canterbury Christchurch University, experience was gained in Higher Education as an assessor of EYPS students and Master's level students. She has extensive experience as a school Governor, was a trainer of Governors, and is currently Chair of Trustees for a Multi- Academy Trust of Secondary and Primary Special schools in East Sussex.

Dr Julie Vaggers has recently retired after 19 years as head teacher of a large integrated nursery school and children's centre in Tottenham, Haringey. She has taught in the early years for 33 years. Julie was also a mentor, tutor and assessor for the National Professional Qualification in Integrated Centre Leadership and the Early Years Professional, working with Middlesex University and London Metropolitan University. Julie has constantly lobbied for recognition of the importance of early years and was a member of the All-party Parliamentary Group for Nursery Schools secretariat. She established an Early Years Training centre in Haringey with her early years colleagues. Her research interests include the challenges in early years leadership and the emotional well-being of leaders in the early years. For her PhD she explored how leaders can encourage collaboration across the services. She is particularly interested in cross-sector collaboration and the development of sustainable professional networks that benefit children and families.

AUTHORS' ACKNOWLEDGEMENTS

The authors would like to extend their warmest thanks to the following professionals for their invaluable support and information.

Shaun Allery, Reception Teacher, St Mary Magdalene School, Bexhill

Sir David Bell, President Thomas Coram

Kelly Brooker, Deputy Head and Training Officer at Barnet Early Years Alliance

Sharon Goate, Director First Class Day Nursery

Professor Denise Hevey, Emeritus Professor Northampton University

Abigail Hunt, Artist and Freelance Art Educator, Tate London

Iona School & Nursery, Steiner Waldorf Education in Nottingham, East Midlands

Lourdes Kerr, Early Years Teacher/Childminder

Maureen Lee, Director of Early Years, Best Practice Network

Chris Lewis, Head Teacher; **Guthsna Kahn**, Deputy Head Teacher; and **Debra Watkinson**, Senior Admin Officer, Children's House Nursery School, London

Charlotte Ronnie, Early Years Teacher

Sally Schweizer, Author and retired Steiner School Teacher

Natalie Shuttleworth, Head of School at Torfield School, Hastings, East Sussex

Veronique Vanderschelden, Head Teacher, St Mary Magdalene School, Bexhill

The authors and the publisher are grateful for permission to reproduce the following material in this book:

Chapter 2, excerpt from Finnegan, J. & Lawton, K. (2016) Lighting up Young Brains, Save the Children Fund. Reproduced with permission of Save the Children.

Chapter 3, quotation from Sir David Bell. Reproduced with kind permission.

Figure 4.1 adapted from Kolb, David A., *Experiential Learning: Experience as the source of learning and development, 2nd Edition* © 2015. Reprinted by permission of Pearson Education, Inc. New York, New York.

Figure 4.2 based on Gibbs, G. (1988) *Learning by Doing: A guide to teaching and learning methods. Further Education Unit* (Oxford Polytechnic: Oxford). Reproduced with permission of Oxford Centre for Staff and Learning Development (OCSLD), Oxford Brookes.

Figure 4.3 based on Figure 7.1 in Denscombe, M. (2017) *The Good Research Guide, 6th Edition* (Open University Press/ McGraw-Hill Education). Reprinted with permission of The McGraw-Hill Companies, Inc.

Table 4.1 based on Driscoll, J. (2007) Figure 2.2, The What? Model of Structured Reflection and its relationship to an experiential learning cycle in *Practising Clinical Supervision: A Reflective Approach for Healthcare Professionals, 2nd Edition*, (Bailliere Tindall). Reproduced by permission of Elsevier under the STM Publishers Agreement.

Chapter 5, excerpt from Mathers, S., Singler, R. & Karemaker, A. (2012) Improving Quality in the Early Years: A Comparison of Perspectives and Measures (Oxford: University of Oxford and A+ Education). Reprinted with permission of the authors and the Nuffield Foundation.

Chapter 7, excerpt from Blakemore, S. J. & Frith, U. (2005) The Learning Brain: lessons for education, Blackwell: London. Republished with permission of John Wiley & Sons, and permission conveyed through Copyright Clearance Center, Inc.

Table 9.1 from Katz, L. (2011) 'Current perspectives on the early childhood curriculum', in House, R. (ed.) Too Much, *Too Soon: Early Learning and the Erosion of Childhood*. Stroud: Hawthorn Press. pp.118-30. Reproduced with permission of Hawthorn Press.

1

GETTING STARTED – AN INTRODUCTION TO TEACHING AND LEARNING IN THE EARLY YEARS

DENISE REARDON

Chapter overview

This first chapter seeks to provide a historical overview about the evolving roles of the Early Years Teacher and Early Years Educator (the EYT/E). It explores the concept of teaching and learning for babies, toddlers and young children and why it is so important for the EYT/E to explore a number of seminal early years policies and reviews initiated by previous and current governments and to understand the way they have contributed to the role of the EYT/E today. Seminal research evidence presented in this chapter includes, for example, Field (2010), Marmot (2010), Allen (2011), Munro (2011), Tickell (2011), Nutbrown (2012) and government policy that took place over the last decade. The significant body of evidence (Callanan et al., 2017; OECD, 2017a; Sylva et al., 2010) that suggests the presence of a graduate pre-school teacher has an impact on both the quality of pre-school learning and on child outcomes (social, behavioural and cognitive) will also be explored. The chapter concludes by reviewing the significant transformations that have led to the EYT/E in practice today, tomorrow and in the future.

INTRODUCTION

Teaching babies, toddlers and young children refers to a very precious time in children's lives when all the necessary foundations for well-being, learning and development are made. Children develop rapidly in their early years and a child's experiences between birth and age 5 will have a major impact on their future life chances (OECD, 2017b). Good parenting and high-quality early learning that gives children a broad range of knowledge, skills and understanding, together provide the right foundation for good future progress through school and life (Callanan et al., 2017). From the very first moment a baby enters the world they start developing and learning through their senses. Teachers, parents, carers and other professionals must make sure that early learning experiences are playful, joyful, active, stimulating and safe in order to support each child's early development, care and learning needs. Chapter 6 critically explores ways in which the EYT/E can promote effective learning in the early years. In essence, parents are the child's 'first teacher'. Parents and carers teach their children through everyday activities, for example, the way that they speak and interact with their child, through dressing, feeding, bathing and bedtime routines. Also by making daily chores playful and fun, for example, laying the table, sorting washing, walks outdoors, counting steps and trips to the local shops. These playful, everyday activities are just as much about teaching as learning to read, write and use numbers. To enhance learning, all of these everyday activities should be accompanied by conversation, direct comments related to the task or a running commentary.

 **Point for reflection**

Setting up teaching and play as opposites is a false dichotomy. (Ofsted, 2015a)

• How can play be used to engage early years children in learning?

It is the role of the EYT/E to work hand in hand with the child's parent or carer to promote their learning and development and prepare them for what lies ahead, albeit, starting school or in their personal life. Sadly, the reality is that not all children are treated fairly or experience what they are entitled to. Teaching early years children requires EYT/Es to be vigilant and inclusive in their practice. In England, there are clear mandatory requirements set out in the Early Years Foundation Stage (EYFS) Statutory Framework (2017a), as well as in the Equality Act 2010, to support the needs of all children, including those with Special Educational Needs and Disabilities (SEND) and those at risk of harm and neglect. The significant aspects of safeguarding and children's welfare are critically examined in Chapter 10 of this book. Promoting children's rights and inclusive practice is critically explored in Chapter 11.

Recent social changes have challenged the purpose of early education and the consequences for what is expected of those who work with young children (OECD, 2017a). EYT/ are tasked with making a lasting, positive impact on children's well-being and development, opening young children's minds to new concepts and ideas on a daily basis. Research demonstrates that the quality of early education and childcare provision is substantially raised when practice is led by specialists (Callanan et al., 2017).

There is much to learn about teaching babies and young children from past and present reading, research and initiatives, for example the Macmillan sisters (1860–1931), Maria Montessori (1870–1952), Freidrich Froebel (1882–1952), Reggio Emilia (1950s) and more recently Ferre Lavers and Margy Whally, the Director of The Pen Green Centre for Children and their Families at Corby in England. The fact that many of these ways of working come largely from past generations does not make their opinions any less relevant today. In fact, it makes their work even more valuable because they come from those who have learned much through their years of devotion to teaching young children. Chapter 3, Early Years Movers and Shakers, seeks to critically explore the influences of alternative education systems on teaching and learning in the early years.

All references made in this book to teaching and learning in the early years recognises the fact that teachers, educators, parents and carers all teach young children in their own particular way. In England, the nature of teaching can be affected by the size and type of early years setting, school, service or network that professionals work in, for example, a larger private, voluntary and independent (PVI) setting and children's centres may offer more direct opportunities for EYT/Es to work collaboratively with colleagues, other agencies and parents; whereas if you work as a childminder you may be teaching children all by yourself.

 —— **Point for reflection** ————————————

- How do the qualification levels of early years staff in your school, setting or network compare with the results of the Effective Provision of Pre-school Education (EPPE) study (Sylva et al., 2010) discussed in the OECD Research Brief 'Qualifications, Education and Professional Development Matter' (2017a)? This shows that the key explanatory factors for high-quality ECE are related to staff with higher qualifications, staff with leadership skills and long-serving staff; trained staff working alongside and supporting less qualified staff; staff with a good understanding of child development and learning.

BACKGROUND TO THE PROFESSIONALISATION OF THE EARLY YEARS WORKFORCE

The chapter authors featured in this book feel very privileged to have supported so many early years graduates and practitioners to gain qualifications and develop the necessary professional competencies required to work with young children and their families. Much of our work has been driven not only by a passion for the early years but also were developed during many of the past and present reforms that are critically examined below. It is good to have taken part and witnessed all the research, time, money and expertise that have gone into transforming the early years sector and making it what it is today. Undeniably, the evidence suggests that there is still more that must be done by the EYT/E to make sure that all children get the best start in life. Research led by Sandra Mathers for the Nuffield Foundation looked at provision for disadvantaged 3- and 4-year-olds (Hillman and Williams, 2015). This research showed that, where settings employ specially trained graduates, quality is higher and the gap between settings in disadvantaged and more affluent areas is narrower. Chapter 11 explores this topic in more detail.

Early education and care received considerable attention in England between 1997 and 2010 under a Labour government who pledged to ensure the availability for parents of more childcare places, better quality early education and care, and greater choice and accessibility. During 2006, the first ever legislation specific to early childhood education and care received royal assent. The Childcare Act 2006 places a statutory duty on Local Authorities to take lead responsibility for childcare in partnership with others, to raise quality, improve delivery and achieve better results (see DCSF, 2006). A further priority is to develop more integrated provision that seeks to improve well-being and reduce inequalities. The aspiration to change the early years workforce was initially outlined in *The Children's Plan: Building Brighter Futures* (DCSF, 2007) and *Every Child Matters: Change for Children* (DfES, 2003). Running parallel to this were many early years research initiatives, including the DfES-funded longitudinal study of Effective Provision of Pre-school Education (EPPE; Sylva et al., 2004), which influenced a commitment to providing high-quality, pre-school childcare provision for children, parents, carers and society in general, as recognised in the *Choice for Parents, the Best Start for Children: A Ten-year Strategy for Childcare* (DfES, 2004). The strategy not only championed the development of high-quality childcare provision, but also signalled the notion that working with pre-school children should have as much status as a profession as teaching children in schools and an early years graduate level programme called Early Years Professional Status (EYPS) was introduced to raise the bar.

During 2011, public sector spending cuts became a glaring and unpleasant reality in England, however, at the same time there were increasing calls for the early years services to do better in addressing the needs of children and families with the most complex needs (Goddard and Temperley, 2011). Despite the early years in England being caught up in the financial constraints imposed during a time of austerity, the then Coalition Government (2010–2015) announced its intention to continue to fund those working in the early years sector to achieve graduate level as well as introduce the role of the Early Years Educator. These decisions were mainly influenced by the research evidence presented in the series of seminal reviews, namely: Field (2010), Marmot (2010), Tickell (2011), Allen (2011), Munro (2011) and the Coalition Government's policy statement 'Supporting Families in the Foundation Years' (DfE/DH, 2011), and the Nutbrown Review (2012). Dame Clare Tickell's review of the Early Years Foundation Stage (2011) and the final report of the Evaluation of the Graduate Leader Fund (Mathers et al., 2011) strengthened the case for training graduates by recognising the influence that a well-qualified workforce can have on the quality of provision and outcomes for young children. The key findings of the *Evaluation of the Graduate Leader Fund – Final Report*, commissioned by the government and carried out by the National Centre for Social Research, the University of Oxford and the Institute of Education (University of London), are presented in Box 1.1.

BOX 1.1

Key findings: The Impact of Gaining EYPS: Evaluation of the Graduate Leader Fund – Final Report (July 2011)

- Settings that gained a graduate leader with EYPS made significant improvements in quality for pre-school children (aged 30 months to 5 years) as compared with settings that did not. Gains were seen in overall quality and in a number of individual dimensions of practice, including: positive staff–child interactions; support for communication, language and literacy; reasoning/thinking skills and scientific understanding; provision of a developmentally appropriate schedule; and providing for individual needs and diversity.
- EYPS provided 'added value' over and above gaining a graduate in terms of overall quality and (to a lesser extent) provision to support literacy/language, and planning for individual needs/diversity.
- Improvements related most strongly to direct work with children, such as support for learning, communication and individual needs, reflecting the role of EYPs as 'leaders of practice'. Fewer measurable improvements were seen in the more 'structural aspects' of provision, including the quality of the physical environment, care routines and provision for parents and staff members.

(Continued)

- EYPs were more influential on the quality of practice in their own rooms than on quality across the whole setting. The more time EYPs spent in rooms with children, the greater the impact they had on the quality of provision in that room.
- EYPs are tasked with 'leading practice across the full age range from birth to the end of the Early Years Foundation Stage'. However, in contrast to the positive findings in relation to quality for pre-school children, there was little evidence that EYPs improved the quality of provision for younger children (birth to 30 months). The low number of EYPs working in these rooms means that we cannot draw firm conclusions on the potential impact of EYPS on provision for infants and toddlers. Further research is needed to establish the most effective ways of raising quality for under-3s through workforce development.

Source: www.gov.uk/government/uploads/system/uploads/attachment_data/file/181480/ DFE-RR144.pdf (accessed 29 July 2017)

During 2012, the Nutbrown Review called for new qualification routes to be introduced to the early years workforce. Nutbrown (2012) recommended an early years specialist route to QTS and that all early years staff should have achieved Level 3 qualifications by 2022. This supported research evidence to suggest that qualified professionals leading early years practice will help to raise the status of the sector, increase professionalism and improve outcomes for children. Consequent reforms were introduced through 'More Great Childcare' (DfE, 2013a), which set out the English government's vision to raise the quality of early years provision. As a consequence, the Early Years Initial Teacher Training (EY ITT) and the Early Years Educator (EYE) were introduced during 2013, with the government developing the associated qualification criteria, which are included in Appendix 1 at the end of this book.

Case study 1.1

From a recently qualified Early Years Teacher: April 2017

For me the purpose of me training to become an Early Years Teacher was to further develop and enhance my own practice. In attending the programme, I have massively improved and enriched my early years practice.

My training has helped me to review the teaching and learning in my setting and has developed my ability to implement more robust strategies and ideas. As a result of this, I have seen a leap in children's development. I am much more thorough about ensuring that every area of learning in the EYFS is covered, setting targets and meeting them. My training has made me much more conscientious about ways to support and meet individual children's learning needs.

Since completing the course I have become more confident and assertive in making leadership decisions. I have improved my leadership style and believe that I come across as much more professional to the team and am very meticulous about developing the team. I am much more concerned about building a team that work together. I have learnt to lead by example and as a role-model rather than simply instructing my colleagues what to do. As a result, I have delegated a lot of my work and now encourage the team to come up with their own ideas for developing the setting which many of the team members have eagerly taken on board.

From the parents' perspective, my training has given them confidence in my ability to teach their children and I would agree with them that I have a much greater understanding of the psychology behind what helps children to learn.

I would not have wanted to miss out on becoming an Early Years Teacher.

Early Years Initial Teacher Training introduced in September 2013, was conceived upon the successes of its predecessor, Early Years Professional Status (EYPS). Early Years Teachers in England must meet the same entry requirements as trainee primary school teachers and successful trainees are awarded Early Years Teacher Status (EYTS) once they have demonstrated that they meet the Teachers' Standards (Early Years) (NCTL, 2017). However, it is of concern that Nutbrown (2012) reported that many of those who gained EYPS, the predecessor to Early Years Teacher, became very disillusioned with the lack of parity with those who held Qualified Teacher Status (QTS). At the time of starting to write this chapter, Early Years Teachers in England who meet the requirements of the National College for Teaching and Leadership (NCTL) Teachers Standards (Early Years) (NCTL, 2013) are not awarded QTS and this remains a contentious issue. However, the government's Early Years Workforce Strategy (2017b) proposes consulting on allowing those with Early Years Teacher Status (EYTS) and its predecessor Early Years Professional Status (EYPS) to lead Nursery and Reception classes in maintained schools. With more than 16,000 specialist graduates (DfE, 2017b) now in situ, the quality of the early years workforce in England will undisputedly continue to rise, albeit that the terms and conditions of those teaching across the early years has yet to be fully recognised. The position of the Early Years Workforce Strategy in England is improving, as detailed in Box 1.2.

BOX 1.2

Position of the Early Years Workforce Strategy in England

- The quality of early years provision in England is impressive, with 91% of settings rated by Ofsted as good or outstanding in 2016 compared to 74% in 2012.
- Key to this is a well-qualified workforce with 77% of group-based staff in 2016 holding at least a Level 3 qualification relevant to childcare and 29% at least a graduate status (level 6).
- The gap between the development of disadvantaged children and their peers at age 5 is narrowing, from 19.0 percentage points in 2013/14 to 17.3 percentage points in 2015/16.

Source: Adapted from the Early Years Workforce Strategy (DfE, 2017); www.gov.uk/government/publications/early-years-workforce-strategy (accessed March 2017)

Historically, it is widely acknowledged, that the number of graduates working in early years settings, outside schools, was very low, particularly in the private, voluntary and independent (PVI) sectors. Traditionally, it was the requirement for those leading practices in the early years to be qualified up to Level 3, many of whom would have gained a National Diploma or an NVQ from awarding bodies such as CACHE (Council for Awards in Children's Education) or BTEC Edexcel. In order to attain an early years graduate status, practitioners need to not only gain a degree but also demonstrate that they meet a set of national standards. The standards form the basis for the assessment and accreditation to Early Years Teacher ITT. Table 1.1 illustrates the key differences between Early Years graduate training programmes delivered in England between 2006 and 2017. Notably there has been an apparent shift, firstly, in the number of standards required to be met by those participating in the associated training routes and secondly the shift from an end of programme setting visit used to assess the outcome for the participant, to the ongoing observation and target setting that mirrors other phases of ITT training.

PEDAGOGICAL PRACTICE

The aspiration to create a highly skilled early years workforce in England is starting to come to fruition. It was initially based on research evidence – for example, amongst other studies, the DfES-funded longitudinal study of Effective Provision of Pre-school Education (EPPE; Sylva et al., 2004). The study highlighted the importance of providing good-quality stable early education and care experiences for early childhood social, behavioural, emotional, psychological, physical

Table 1.1 Key differences between the graduate level Early Years programmes delivered under the CWDC and Teaching Agency (2006-2012), the EYT/E (NCTL, 2013)

Early Years Professional (CWDC) 2006-2012	New Era Early Years Professional (TA 2012-2013)	Early Years Teacher (NCTL) from 2013
All students who joined a pathway on or prior to January 2012, **assessed against 39 national standards** through a Setting Visit at the end of their programme	All students who joined a pathway on or after September 2012, **assessed against 8 national standards** through a Setting Visit at the end of their programme	All students joining pathways on or after September 2013 **assessed against 8 national standards** through ongoing observation and target setting of their practice
Training Routes: • **Validation** (3 months) for those holding a degree • **Short** (6 months) for those holding a degree requiring additional experience • **Long** (15 months) for those holding a Foundation degree working in an early years setting • **Full** (12 months) for those holding a degree, not working in an early years setting	**Training Routes:** • **Graduate Practitioner** Pathway (GPP, 6 months) • **Undergraduate Practitioner Pathway** (UPP, 12 months) • **Graduate Entry Pathway** (GEP, 12 months) • **Undergraduate Entry Pathway** (UEP, 24 months)	**Training Routes:** • **Graduate entry** - for degree holders with limited experience with children and who are not currently working with them • **Graduate employment** - for degree holders currently working in an early years setting • **Undergraduate entry** - for those taking an early childhood degree, who may or may not be currently working in an early years setting • **Assessment only** - for graduates with substantial experience across the 0 to 5 age range who also have knowledge of Key Stage 1 and 2 in schools
GCSE English and Maths required **on completion** • enhanced background checks by the Disclosure and Barring Service (CRB/DBS)	GCSE English and Maths required **on entry** • enhanced background checks by the Disclosure and Barring Service (DBS)	GCSEs (A* to C) in English, Maths and a science subject **on entry** • **passes in** numeracy and literacy **skills tests** • enhanced background checks by the Disclosure and Barring Service (DBS)

and cognitive development and for their well-being now and in their futures. More recently, EPPE findings (Sylva et al., 2010) confirm that the higher the staff qualifications, the more developmental progress children make in the pre-school period and that there is a growing body of evidence that children who are given a strong start in their development, learning and well-being will have better outcomes when they grow older.

Photo 1.1 Trainee Early Years Teacher engaged in high-quality pedagogical practice

The previous editions of this book highlighted the fact that for children to achieve better outcomes, they need to be afforded high-quality childcare provision that fosters secure relationships and offers an appropriate learning environment with high-quality teaching and learning experiences. The EPPE research into Effective Pedagogy in Early Learning (Sylva et al., 2010) and the Study of Pedagogical Effectiveness in Early Learning (SPEEL; Moyles et al., 2002) offer an evaluation tool to promote effective early years practice which resonates nicely with today's practice. The tool is outlined in Figure 1.1; it encourages those using it to consider not only the workforce, but also the issue of pedagogical practice, content and the environment.

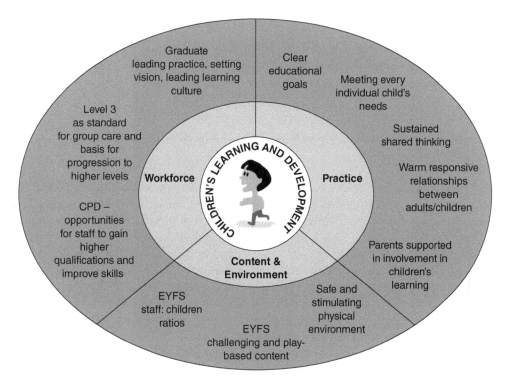

Figure 1.1 Quality Audit Tool.

(*Sources*: Department for Children Schools and Families PowerPoint presentation, EYFS; Effective Provision of Pre-School Education Research into Effective Pedagogy in Early Learning; Study of Pedagogical Effectiveness in Early Learning reproduced in Moyles et al., 2002)

Early Years Teachers and Educators in England must keep themselves up to date with any national and local statutory and non-statutory frameworks that they work within. They are also advised to reflect on their ability to work collaboratively with other professionals in order to mentor and empower other early years colleagues to deliver the best possible outcomes for children. Chapter 12 on 'Undertaking Wider Professional Responsibilities' examines this area in more detail.

 Points for reflection

- What current policy, legislation and statutory frameworks, including the EYFS, apply to your role?
- How do you support and mentor colleagues to understand how current policy legislation, and statutory frameworks, including the EYFS, impacts on the lives of children and their families and at the same time applies to them?

(Continued)

- Identify the way you have shaped and supported the implementation of a recent policy within your:
  - School/setting
  - Teaching and early years practice

REFLECTIVE PRACTICE

Developing reflective practice skills for the EYT/E are of paramount importance (see Chapter 4). Reflective practice encourages those working with young children to examine what they do in a critical and analytical manner. Reading and research undertaken as part of the EYT/E programmes supports them to challenge the practice in their settings and develop a clear understanding about why they do what they do. The EYT/E needs to have a clear understanding of the reasons why they teach in an age-appropriate manner. They must develop the ability to reflect and recognise how their role improves the learning ability and life-chances of the children in their care and the way that it maximises their ability, experiences and opportunities. Chapters 2 and 9 examine the pedagogical nature of the EYT/E role and ways to creatively teach in an age-appropriate manner.

 — **Ideas for practice**

To become a reflective EYT/E, you must always analyse and evaluate the everyday practice in your school, setting or network and make any necessary adjustments to ensure improvements. Moss (2008: xvi, in Reed and Canning, 2012) advocates that you can do this by:

- Making reflective practice an integral part of your own professional identity.
- Developing a culture of teaching and learning community in your school, setting or network, that encourages individuals to actively listen and respond to the thoughts and experiences of children, colleagues and other professionals.
- Thinking ... 'critically and creatively' developing 'beyond the role as worker – as technician'.

RE-IMAGINING THE EARLY YEARS

A significant amount of research, government policy reforms, interventions and initiatives have gone into constructing the role of the EYT/E in England, and equally so, defining ways to effectively promote children's outcomes, safety, welfare, health, learning and development. The importance of a highly skilled and qualified early years workforce cannot be disputed, as supported by the research already presented in this chapter, namely Nutbrown (2012), EPPE (Sylva et al., 2010), the OECD (2017a,c) and Callanan et al. (2017), all indicating that well-educated, well-trained professionals are key factors in providing high-quality teaching and learning experiences with the most favourable cognitive and social outcomes for children. Whilst we have come this far in England, in a review into the future of EY training and qualifications in England, Osgood et al. (2016) call for a concerted effort across the EY sector, from advocacy groups, employer organisations, unions, training providers, academics and every single member of the early years workforce, to push for a re-imagin(in)g of the child, the setting and the worker in an attempt to fully recognise the child in society and those that are responsible for their education and care.

CONCLUSION

The aim of this chapter has been to offer an insight into the changes and reforms that have shaped and contributed to the construction of the EYT/E qualifications in England and how important it is to have a highly educated and skilled work-force. Whilst the focus has been on the English system, it must be acknowledged that much of the content of the English education system is transferable to other educational contexts, both here in the UK and internationally. Succeeding chapters in this book have been written to critically examine the pedagogical role required of the EYT/E, working across a diverse range of early years settings. Case studies featured in the body of this book refer to individual children as child X even though it is not the same child featured. The authors featured in this book are in support of certain common themes woven across each of the succeeding chapters, for example, the importance of promoting a holistic play-based EY curriculum; becoming a reflective practitioner; listening to the voice of the child; the promotion of safe and inclusive practices; celebrating children's achievements; working with parents, carers and other professionals to create a team around the child; each of these themes in their own right is critical to the success of the EYT/E in the future.

 Key points

- From the very first moment a baby enters the world they start developing and learning through their senses.
- There is much to learn about teaching babies and young children from past and present pioneers, reading, research and initiatives (see Chapter 3).

(Continued)

- Teachers, educators, parents and carers all teach young children in their own particular way.
- To become a reflective EYT/E, you must always analyse and evaluate the everyday practice in your school, setting or network and make any necessary adjustments to make improvements.
- The higher the staff qualifications, the more developmental progress children make in the pre-school period.
- Children who are given a strong start in their development, learning and well-being will have better outcomes when they grow older.
- There needs to be a concerted effort across the EY sector to push for a re-imagin(in)g of the child, the setting and the worker.

FURTHER READING

Hallet, E. (2016) *Early Years Practice for Educators*. London: Sage.

This book will help to extend your knowledge and understanding of early years practice.

Miller, L. and Hevey, D. (2012) *Policy Issues in the Early Years*. London: Sage.

This book offers an in-depth insight into some of the most significant issues affecting early years education.

Pugh, G. and Duffy, B. (2013) *Contemporary Issues in the Early Years*, 6th edn. London: Sage.

This book provides a critical examination of the essential issues in early years policy and practice.

Reed, M. and Canning, N. (2012) *Reflective Practice in the Early Years*. London: Sage.

This book expands on the necessity to engage in reflective practice.

USEFUL WEB RESOURCES

Graham Allen MP, Early Intervention: The Next Steps.
www.gov.uk/government/publications/early-intervention-the-next-steps–2

This 2011 independent report provides more information about how intervention in children's earliest years can eliminate or reduce costly and damaging social problems.

Frank Field, The Foundation Years: Preventing Poor Children Becoming Poor Adults.
http://webarchive.nationalarchives.gov.uk/20110120090141/http://povertyreview.independent.gov.uk/media/20254/poverty-report.pdf

This report published in 2010 provides more information about the Independent Review on Poverty and Life Chances.

Dame Clare Tickell, The Early Years: Foundations for Life, Health and Learning.
www.gov.uk/government/uploads/system/uploads/attachment_data/file/180919/DFE-00177-2011.pdf

This review published in 2011 looks into the impact of the Early Years Foundation Stage (EYFS) on children's learning and development, and on early years practitioners.

Department for Education (DfE), Statutory Framework for the Early Years Foundation Stage: Setting the Standards for Learning, Development and Care for Children from Birth to Five.
www.foundationyears.org.uk/files/2017/03/EYFS_STATUTORY_FRAMEWORK_2017.pdf

The mandatory framework for all early years providers in England from 3 April 2017.

Foundation Years
www.foundationyears.org.uk web

This weblink provides a broad range of information developed by government, professionals and the voluntary and community sector and is continually updated with the latest news, information and resources.

Early Years Educator (Level 3) Qualification Criteria
www.gov.uk/government/publications/early-years-educator-level-3-qualifications-criteria

This document outlines the assessment criteria and minimum qualification content requirements for Level 3 Early Years Educators set out by the National College for Teaching and Leadership in 2013.

Teachers Standards (early years)
www.gov.uk/government/publications/early-years-teachers-standards

This site features 'best practice' standards for early years teachers set out by the National College for Teaching and Leadership in 2013.

TACTYC Occasional Paper 9 – Early Years Training and Qualifications in England: Issues for policy and practice (Professor Jayne Osgood, Dr Alex Elwick, Dr Leena Robertson, Dr Mona Sakr and Dilys Wilson, Centre for Education Research and Scholarship, Middlesex University)
http://tactyc.org.uk/wp-content/uploads/2016/06/Occasional-Paper-9-V5-PDF.pdf

This paper reviews the range, determination and future of early years training and qualifications.

Moss, Peter (2006) 'Structures, understandings and discourses: possibilities for re-envisioning the early childhood worker', *Contemporary Issues in Early Childhood*, 7 (1).

http://journals.sagepub.com/doi/pdf/10.2304/ciec.2006.7.1.30

Please see – This paper reviews the range, determination and future of early years training and qualifications.

OECD, Early Childhood Education and Care

www.oecd.org/edu/school/earlychildhoodeducationandcare.htm

This site will extend knowledge of the work of the OECD to help support countries in reviewing and redesigning policies to improve their early childhood services and systems.

 **Online resources**

Visit https://study.sagepub.com/education to find a selection of scholarly journal articles chosen to support each chapter.

2

A PRINCIPLED PEDAGOGICAL APPROACH TO TEACHING AND LEARNING IN THE EARLY YEARS

DENISE REARDON

Chapter overview

This chapter focuses on ways to develop a principled pedagogical approach to teaching and learning in the early years (EY). The pedagogical nature of teaching will be examined within the context of exploring definitions and descriptors of a teacher as pedagogue. Whilst many of the initiatives discussed will be of particular interest to teaching within the English context, colleagues working across the UK and in other parts of the world may also find the chapter enlightening. Significant aspects of EY pedagogical practice will be explored within the confines of any of the English national policies, guidelines, and statutory and non-statutory frameworks that are in place. A feature of this chapter includes examining recent developments in child neuroscience and why this makes it even more important for Early Years Teachers and Educators (EYT/Es) to adopt a strong principled pedagogical approach to their early years teaching. The chapter features realistic case studies, covering the observation of a trainee EYT and examines the full spectrum of developing a principled pedagogical approach to teaching in the early years from pedagogy to practice and from principles to professional identities. The EY landscape continues to shift rapidly which makes it even more important for EYT/Es to adopt a strong pedagogical, principled approach to their teaching and learning if they are to be successful in their careers.

INTRODUCTION

The title Early Years Teacher/Educator (EYT/E) are relatively new to the early years sector. Teaching the EY curriculum across the UK is very fragmented, and England, Scotland, Wales and Northern Ireland have all developed their own approach. Unlike the English, Scottish and Northern Irish, the Welsh Foundation Stage is designed for children 0–7 years. Although there are a number of approaches in the UK, we can all learn from each other's vast pool of research, experience and good practice.

In order to become a nationally recognised teacher in England, Scotland, Northern Ireland or Wales, you will most certainly have to meet a set of nationally recognised standards and follow a nationally prescribed curriculum. Those currently studying to become an EYT/E in England are required to teach and to have a breadth and a variety of experience in schools and Early Years settings. The EYT/E is required to teach children from different backgrounds and across the 0–5 age range, as well as gaining experience of different approaches to teaching in the National Curriculum Key Stage 1. For the purpose of this chapter, I have decided to refer to the Early Years Teacher and Educator (NCTL, 2013) and to the English Early Years Foundation Stage (EYFS) (DfE, 2017a), however, the subject matter may also be relevant to roles being followed elsewhere, both across the UK and in other parts of the world.

QUALIFICATION AND TITLE

Recent early years developments in England called for 'the establishment of an Early Years specialist route to qualified teacher status to bring the profession more in line with teaching' (Nutbrown, 2012: 45). To begin with many professionals, myself included, struggled with the name 'teacher'. This was mainly due to the fact that like so many others my teaching is firmly grounded in the belief that early years children learn through play and a fear that early years teaching would gravitate to a more formal approach to learning. Much of my rationale for a play-based approach in the early years is influenced by the work of many eminent educationalists, psychologists, researchers and practitioners, and the array of literature that has been written about how young children learn through play and the role adults perform to support early development and learning. Early years teaching in England and elsewhere is historically influenced in particular by the work of Susan Isaacs and the Macmillan sisters, and the 'enduring influence of Frobel, Montessori and Steiner' (Goouch, 2010: 3). Chapter 3, 'Early Years Movers and Shakers' examines the early pioneers of Early Childhood Education and Care (ECEC) and how they have influenced ECEC practice today.

The qualifications and titles of childcare workers both here in the UK and internationally differ greatly from country to country and from service to service.

In Denmark, Finland, Germany and Norway a 'pedagogue' is someone who is trained to take a wider view of early learning and care. In England, the qualification level and title for Early Years Teachers and Educators relates to the skills set and knowledge that is recognised for them to work across the early Years sector in England.

 Points for reflection

How does your practice relate to the following:

- Good understanding of child development and learning
- Ability to develop children's perspectives
- Ability to praise, comfort, question and be responsive to children
- Leadership skills, problem solving and development of targeted lesson plans
- Good vocabulary and ability to take on board children's ideas

These skills and staff traits have been identified as being vital in facilitating high-quality practice in the OECD (2017a) report 'Encouraging Quality in Early Childhood Education and Care'.

The OECD (2017a) report recognises that 'it is not the qualification per se that has an impact on child outcomes but the ability of better qualified staff members to create a high-quality pedagogic environment that makes the difference' (Elliott, 2006; Sheridan et al., 2009). There is strong evidence that enriched stimulating environments and high-quality pedagogy are fostered by better qualified staff; and better-quality pedagogy leads to better learning outcomes (Litjens and Taguma, 2010)'.

At the time of writing this chapter, the DfE (2017c) announced that it will be consulting on allowing those with Early Years Teacher Status, and its predecessor Early Years Professional Status (EYPS), to lead Nursery and Reception classes in maintained schools. Professor Nutbrown's call for 'clear and intelligible roles, responsibilities and status, which is understood across the sector' (2012) is coming to fruition. She believed that in reforming and changing the title of the Early Years Teacher from its predecessor the Early Years Professional (EYP) and introducing the role of Early Years Educator would 'raise the status of the sector, increase professionalism and improve quality'. A bespoke set of nationally recognised standards (please see Appendix 1) was introduced for both roles in England by the National College for Teaching and Leadership (NCTL) (2013) to be met by all those aspiring to enter the profession.

PEDAGOGY, TEACHING AND PLAY

To reframe a myth that teaching and play are two distinct entities, the Ofsted (2015a) survey *'Teaching and Play in the Early Years – a Balancing Act?'* defined the elements of early years practice that made up teaching, believing that 'Teaching should not be taken to imply a "top down" or formal way of working'. Signs of significant elements of good practice associated with effective teaching are:

- Assess what children know, understand and can do, taking into account children's interests and dispositions to learning and use this information to plan children's next steps in learning and monitor their progress.
- Interact with children during planned and child-initiated play and activities.
- Communicate and model language, showing, explaining, demonstrating, exploring ideas, encouraging, questioning, recalling, providing a narrative for what they are doing.
- Facilitate and set challenge.
- Provide resources and equipment.
- Pay attention to the physical environment.
- Provide daily structure and routines that establish expectations.

Photo 2.1   Children cooking in a high quality learning environment

Teaching early years in England can mean teaching within preschool education in a maintained school, free school and academy or within a private, voluntary or independent (PVI) EY setting. Forming a principled pedagogical approach to your teaching relates to how you teach babies and young children in any school or EY setting combined with valuing any learning and experiences that the children bring from their family and their community at large.

Seeking a definition for pedagogical practice in the early years is not new; there are many definitions of effective pedagogy, for example in the DfES-sponsored study of effective pedagogy in the early years, Siraj-Blatchford et al. (2002) expressed the view that effective pedagogy is both 'teaching and the provision of instructive learning environments and routines'. More than 20 years ago, Bruner (1996: 64) said that 'Modern pedagogy is moving increasingly to the view that the child should be aware of her own thought processes, and that it is crucial for the pedagogical theorist and teacher alike to help her to become more meta-cognitive, to be aware of how she goes about learning and thinking as she is about the subject matter she is studying'. The Study of Pedagogical Effectiveness in Early Learning (SPEEL) (Moyles et al., 2002) supported a belief that excellent practitioners can – and should – be involved in the drive for understanding existing pedagogy and ultimately raising standards for teaching and learning. Box 2.1 identifies the SPEEL descriptors of Pedagogy – Practice – Principles and Professional Dimensions.

BOX 2.1

Descriptors of Pedagogy – Practice – Principles and Professional Dimensions

PEDAGOGY is both the behaviour of teaching and being able to talk about and reflect on it. Pedagogy encompasses what practitioners actually DO and THINK and the principles, theories, perceptions and challenges that inform and shape it. It connects the relatively self-contained act of teaching and being an Early Years educator, with personal, cultural and community values (including care), curriculum structures and external influences. Pedagogy in the Early Years operates from a shared frame of reference (a mutual learning encounter) between the practitioner, the young child and his/her family.

PRACTICE is all that the pedagogue does within the teaching and learning context on a daily, weekly and longer-term basis to promote effectiveness. Practice includes planning, evaluating and assessing children's play and other learning experiences both indoors and outdoors. Practice is the application of practitioners' qualities, knowledge, thinking and underpinning principles and involves making both conscious and intuitive judgements. Practice is flexible,

(Continued)

based on establishing and maintaining effective relationships through anticipating, observing, interpreting and evaluating the actions and behaviours of children and other adults. Practice represents the fluent performance of a complex and dynamic interaction, involving communication with and between children and adults, including parents.

PRINCIPLES underpin practice and are based upon informed knowledge and theories of early childhood development, education and care, including management and organisational factors. Principles are at the heart of practitioners' values and beliefs. They are the ideological base for practitioners' thoughts and actions and are reflected in their visions, aims and goals. Practitioners who are reflective and on-going learners, recognise that principles are capable of adaptation and change in the light of further evidence.

PROFESSIONAL DIMENSIONS: Effective Early Years practitioners are those who possess particular professional qualities, knowledge and thinking which they bring to their role. Professional qualities are attributes and skills both brought to, and developed within, the role of the effective Early Years pedagogue and are underpinned by a sense of self-efficacy. Professional knowledge – intuitive and explicit – is that understanding which practitioners have and employ to develop a wide range of learning experiences for young children (including those within the Curriculum Guidance for the Foundation Stage [DfES, 2000]). Professional thinking includes the ability to reflect on practice and to make informed decisions through well-conceived examination and analysis of pedagogy. It involves the thinking practitioner in articulating and evaluating practice and a continuous striving to improve. Professionals have a positive disposition to learn and are capable of extending themselves professionally.

Source: Moyles, J., Adams, S. and Musgrove, A. (2002) SPEEL: The Study of Pedagogical Effectiveness in Early Learning

 Points for reflection

Take a look at Case Study 2.1 which illustrates an observation undertaken by a university Link Tutor on a trainee Early Years Teacher in England. Try to identify:

a. Ways in which the student demonstrated her competencies against any nationally prescribed standards relevant to your programme of study.
b. Any descriptors of Pedagogy – Practice – Principles and Professional Dimensions featured in Box 2.1.

Case study 2.1

Trainee Early Years Teacher delivering a Language Session to children aged 3 to 4 years

Observation Notes

Throughout your planned activity you promoted the characteristics of an effective learning environment and were responsive to the children's feelings and moods.

The materials you provided encouraged them to engage their listening and observation skills effectively. You communicated sensitively to all the children and demonstrated a great rapport with them. There were lovely examples of how you valued their input, used active listening skills, emotional intelligence and high levels of interpersonal skills to direct their responses. When a child was reticent you took cues from them and followed their lead, allowing them to think and communicate in their own time. You also engaged in sustained shared thinking with the children, e.g. you modelled how to extend their thinking about each of the sounds by asking simple open and closed questions encouraging problem solving. You were able to guide the children to think about mathematical concepts for example, matching sounds to pictures, counting and colour recognition through your use of mathematical language.

It was clearly evident from observing you teaching the children today that there are high levels of mutual respect between you and the children. The feedback you provided encouraged positive learning dispositions such as resilience, confidence and independence.

You planned appropriately challenging opportunities for group learning drawing on a sound knowledge of children's prior attainment. This encouraged the children's awareness of each other within a group situation and your expectations for them to learn through social interaction demonstrated your secure knowledge and understanding of child development with reference to the young children's age group.

From my observation of your practice today, during the planned activity and generally in the toddler room, you have made an effective contribution for ensuring that:

S1

- The activity planned was relevant to the children
- Your planning was challenging to the children's development and learning
- You engaged positive group management and behaviour strategies
- Children were aware of purpose of the activity/learning opportunity
- You communicated high expectations as appropriate to groups of children and individual children

(Continued)

- Your professional behaviour and role-modelling was exemplary
- You demonstrated enthusiasm for a range of creative learning opportunities
- You challenged inappropriate behaviour and comments, demonstrating anti-biased and anti-discriminatory practice

S2 – You:

- Demonstrated your knowledge of attachment theory and the benefits this brings
- Showed excellent communication skills with the children aged 4–5 years, listening actively using emotional intelligence
- Responded to the child with non-verbal/pre-verbal skills to support his developing language
- Demonstrated quality interactions with the children using sustained shared thinking
- Showed awareness of social and emotional factors and cultural and linguistic factors e.g. the child who has English as a second language
- Gave a clear introduction and development of ideas
- Questioned, building on answers given to expand children's thinking and reflect on their learning
- Engaged in effective use of plenary activities to reflect on learning

S3 – Planning documents

- The session plan and resources provided examples of your ability to design opportunities for learners to develop the Early Years aspects of CLL learning and development, however reference to the EARLY YEARS FS is not always clear
- Planning took into account children's needs and interests, however these need to be linked to the EARLY YEARS FS
- Observation
- You demonstrated a sufficiently secure grasp of the concepts, ideas and principles of the Early Years Foundation Stage, however these were not implicit in your planning and need to be strengthened

S4 – You:

- Set challenging objectives
- Showed an increasingly varied approach to assessment and group work
- Designed a session that built on children's interests
- Included session planning that showed some knowledge and understanding of teaching requirements in the EYFS; this needs strengthening
- Demonstrated how you can promote a love of learning and stimulate children's intellectual curiosity
- Demonstrated how Early Years Teachers can lead and support other practitioners in the development of different observational techniques
- Demonstrated enthusiasm for the activity

S5 – You:

- Demonstrated in lesson, different approaches to different children, e.g. in questioning, in discussion
- Gave appropriate feedback to individuals according to their strengths and needs
- Engaged and retained the active participation of children
- Managed the children's group to support inclusion

STATUTORY EXPECTATIONS

Teaching within a national framework such as the English Early Years Foundation Stage (EYFS) (DfE, 2017a) is not without criticism, Goouch (2010) goes as far as saying that it 'promotes teaching and learning to ensure children's "school readiness", may often result in a literal translation into practice by conscientious people anxious to be correct in their work'. The EYFS (DfE, 2017a) has successively been developed over the years and now embraces the inclusion of the Reception year. Teachers leading practice in the Reception year are sometimes far removed from their pedagogical principled-based early years' colleagues and may be seen as hot-housing children for Year 1. Balancing the enormous pressure placed on EYT/Es to meet nationally defined targets can sometimes seem overwhelming and yet 'arguably the single most important target, often overlooked seems to be to really know and understand the children in their care' (Goouch, 2010).

Teaching babies and young children must be situated within teacher–child relationships and foster 'emotional engagement, alertness, reflective presence, respect, engagement in critical reflection, and dialogue' (Dalli et al., 2011). Based on this, EYT/Es need to adopt 'a physical and emotional presence, active listening processes, and an ability to orient oneself towards the relationship with the child and the child's experience'. Teaching in the EYFS in a pre-school setting can be very different from teaching National Curriculum Key Stage 1 and 2 in schools. The Foundation Stage in England offers a bespoke pedagogical curriculum for the under-5s. Across Europe the approach to teaching and learning is very different. In England children now start school as early as 4 years old but in other European countries children do not start formal schooling until they are 6 or 7 years old.

In England, the EYT/E's national standards (NCTL, 2013) align nicely with the EYFS (DfE, 2017a), for example EYT/Es are tasked with teaching the EYFS three prime areas of learning and development, which are Communication and Language, Physical Development, and Personal, Social and Emotional Development. In addition there are four specific areas, through which the three prime areas are strengthened and applied: these include Literacy, Mathematics, Understanding of the World and Expressive Arts and Design.

PEDAGOGY AND THE BRAIN

Recent development in neuroscience enlightens early years specialists, teachers, educators and parents that in the early years children's brains are particularly receptive to learning but as they grow older their brains do not process information at the same phenomenal rate. 'The science is clear, in the first few years of life, a child's brain develops rapidly, driven by a mix of experience, environment and genes' (Finnegan and Lawton, 2016). This means EYT/Es designing pedagogical teaching and learning opportunities that build on babies' and young children's developmental milestones and current level of understanding if they are to give them a love of learning and a strong start to a lifelong journey of learning.

 Points for reflection

Stop and consider the ramifications of the following neuroscience research on your EY teaching and learning?

From birth to age two babies and young children's brains go through a period of rapid development and growth

- During the first two years of life the brain displays a remarkable capacity to absorb information and adapt to its surroundings.
- A fully-grown adult brain has an estimated 86 billion neurons, the majority of which are already formed in the womb (Herculano-Houzel, 2009; Goswami, 2015).
- By age one, the size of a child's brain is already 72% of adult volume on average and by age two it has grown to 83% of an adult's volume on average (Knickmeyer et al., 2008).
- At age two, the connections that are being formed in a child's brain are happening about twice as fast as in an adult's brain (Stiles and Jernigan, 2010).

Between the ages three to five the brain starts to process information in more efficient and complex ways

- From age three, a child's brain begins a phase called 'synaptic pruning'. This is a period in a child's life where the brain becomes more efficient and more complex through refining the networks that were formed during the first two years.
- At age three a child's brain is estimated to be about twice as active as an adult's brain (Brotherson, 2009).
- At age five a child's brain uses almost twice as much energy as an adult's brain to support brain development (Kuzawa et al., 2013).

- This period from age three to five is also critical for children's language skills. A child's language skills develop rapidly during the first few years of life: On average, a child's vocabulary expands from 55 words at 16 months, to 225 words at 23 months to 573 words at 30 months (Goswami, 2015).

Source: Save the Children report 'Lighting Up Young Children's Brains' (Finnegan and Lawton, 2016)

Teaching well-designed pedagogical educational programmes involves careful planning based on a sound awareness of the curriculum area, an excellent knowledge of the child/children's developmental stages and their needs. Fundamentally, teaching within the EYFS (DfE, 2017a) or any other early years framework requires pedagogues, Early Years Teachers and Educators to ask themselves 'How do I make an impact on the children's learning and development? The activity featured in Table 2.1 gives you the opportunity to reflect on this question. I once posed this question to a graduate entry student who previously worked as a forensic scientist; she compared teaching to Professor Edmund Lockard's exchange principle, that every contact leaves a trace. 'Lockard's exchange principle, refers to the transfer of trace evidence like fibres, soil, dust and hair, from one person or location to anyone or thing that contacts it.' Using Lockard's exchange principle within the context of teaching early years defines the presence of the teacher or pedagogue and the child being in contact with each other, nuggets of wisdom shed from one to be picked up by the other. This transfer has the potential to work both ways, for example, skilful observations of the child/children's learning and development will greatly increase the significance of planning for the next steps in the child/children's learning and development.

Certain aspects of early years teaching is all about developing life skills such as feeding, washing hands, going to the toilet, developing positive relationships with each other and adults, embracing new challenges and experiences, learning to talk and express themselves, developing a 'can do attitude' and positive disposition to learning. Children in the early years requires EYT/Es to develop a thorough understanding about the variety of ways in which children learn, grow and develop, it is not all about sitting children down to impart a body of knowledge. It is all about skilfully planning age-appropriate daily experiences, activities and routines. Developing a sound understanding of the curriculum area to be delivered is essential, for example research into effective teachers of numeracy has shown that the most effective teachers of primary mathematics are those who believe that it is important to help children to see the links and connections between different mathematical ideas, different representations of mathematics and children's existing methods and understandings. Teaching is based on dialogue between the teacher and the child and between children to ensure that these connections are highlighted (Taylor and Harris, 2013).

Table 2.1 Reflective activity

EYFS (2017a) Prime Areas of Learning and Development	How do I provide opportunities for children to:	What impact does this have on children's learning and development?
Communication and language	• Experience a rich language environment? • Develop their confidence and skills in expressing themselves? • Speak and listen in a range of situations?	
Physical	• Become active and interactive learners? • Develop their co-ordination, control and movement? • Understand the importance of physical activity? • Make healthy choices in relation to food?	
Personal, Social and Emotional	• Develop a positive sense of themselves and others? • Form positive relationships and develop respect for others? • Develop social skills? • Learn how to manage their feelings? • Understand appropriate behaviour in groups? • Have confidence in their own abilities?	
The specific areas, through which the prime areas are strengthened and applied		
Literacy	• Link sounds and letters? • Begin to develop pre-reading and pre-writing skills? • Develop a phonological awareness? • Learn to read and write? • Ensure access to a wide range of reading materials (books, poems, and other written materials)? • Ignite their interest in the written word, stories and other media?	
Mathematics	• Develop and improve skills in counting? • Understand and use numbers? • Calculate simple addition and subtraction problems? • Describe shapes, spaces, and measures?	
Understanding the world	• Make sense of their physical world and their community? • Provide opportunities to explore, observe and find out about people, places, technology and the environment?	
Expressive arts and design	• Explore and play with a wide range of media and materials? • Share their thoughts, ideas and feelings through a variety of activities in art, music, movement, dance, role-play, and design and technology?	

In a similar vein the teaching of early phonics, reading and writing can be fostered during storytelling and rhyme time activities by drawing children's attention to the letter shapes and sounds. Goouch and Lambirth (2011: 86) believe that by 'Simply linking the first letters of the children's name to the appropriate page in the book, allows children to feel confident about letter sound relationships'. Chapter 7 examines the topic of teaching communication, language and literacy in more detail.

 Ideas for practice

Pedagogical principles for quality teaching are set out in the Ofsted Early Years Inspection Handbook (2015, updated 2017). They include:

- Setting consistently high expectations of what each child can achieve, including the most able and the most disadvantaged.
- Having a secure understanding of the age group.
- Having relevant subject knowledge that is detailed and communicated well to children.
- Gathering assessment information that is based on:
    o what children already know, understand and can do
    o parents' and previous providers' views.

- Using assessment information to:
    o plan appropriate teaching and learning strategies
    o identify children who are falling behind in their learning or who need additional support
    o enable children to make good progress and achieve well.

- Engaging with parents to:
    o support their child's learning and –
    o understand how their child should progress
    o how their child is doing in relation to their age
    o what their child needs to do to progress.

- Promoting equality of opportunity and recognition of diversity.
- Support children to acquire the skills and capacity to develop and learn effectively, and to be ready for the next stages in their learning, especially school.

EYT/Es must develop their understanding to provide activities and learning opportunities for children to play, explore, investigate, experience things and 'have a go'. Involve children in active learning, problem solving and rejoicing at their achievements. Children need to be encouraged to think critically, develop their own ideas, make links between ideas, and develop strategies for doing things: your role is to make it happen!

The Early Years Inspection Handbook (Ofsted, 2015, updated 2017) makes it quite clear that 'there is no expectation for teachers to conform to a "one-size-fits all" mentality'. By definition, the EYT/E, like parents and carers play a crucial role in the formative years of a child's learning and development. Weisman (2012) suggests that the teacher's role is 'much more conductor than composer'. The children that you teach are at the beginning of their learning and development, steering a 'love of learning' is one of the best gifts you can bestow. According to Whitebread (2015: 25), an effective EYT/E will need to 'consider not only their own inter-personal style as a teacher, and not only the learning activities they will devise and provide for the children, but also the ethos within which they and the children will live and work'.

Photo 2.2 Early Years Educator fostering a love of reading in a home environment

Given the transformation that has taken place over the past decade to professionalise the pedagogical status of those working with young children, both here in the UK and Internationally, it is far too early to give a clear-cut definition of an Early Years Teacher or Educator in England or any other teacher to that effect. Weisman (2012) believes that a precise definition of effective teaching is 'elusive' and uses Ernest Hemmingway's analogy of teaching as 'a moveable feast' because 'wherever you go for the rest of your life, it stays with you …'. We all have experience of teachers that have made an impact on our lives, some good, some not so good. Hopefully your teaching will be remembered by the children in your care.

 Key points

- The most effective teachers possess strong pedagogical principles.
- From birth to age 2 the brain goes through a period of rapid development and growth and between age 3 and 5 the brain starts to process information in more efficient and complex ways.
- A teacher's role is more that of a conductor than a composer.
- Teaching is a 'moveable feast' because 'wherever the child goes for the rest of their life, it stays with them'!
- Ofsted does not have a preferred approach to teaching or play.
- Teach children through age-appropriate play activities; purposeful play allows children to grow and develop.
- In teaching, one size does not fit all!
- The best teaching must have a strong element of fun, wonder and excitement.

FURTHER READING

Edgington, M. (2004) *The Foundation Stage Teacher in Action: Teaching 3, 4 and 5 Year Olds.* London: Sage.

This book includes an extended section on leadership, on managing the foundation stage and ways to involve the team in monitoring and evaluating Foundation Stage practice.

Waller, T. and Davis, G. (2009) *Early Childhood.* London: Sage.

This book will help you explore all the major themes in early years education and care.

Goouch, K. and Lambirth, A. (2011, 2nd edn 2017) *Teaching Early Reading and Phonics: Creative Approaches to Early Literacy.* London: Sage.

The authors in this book show how important it is to ensure that EY children acquire a wide range of reading strategies, while also setting out practical 'pointers' which will enable EYT/Es to translate the theory into effective practice.

Taylor, H. and Harris, A. (eds) (2013) *Learning and Teaching Mathematics*. London: Sage.

This book is grounded in the latest research about how EY children become effective learners, in mathematics.

Whitebread, D. and Coltman, P. (eds) (2015) *Teaching and Learning in the Early Years*, 4th edn. Abingdon: Routledge.

This book advocates that the EY curriculum must start with the children, their needs and their potential and that the best teaching must have a strong element of fun, wonder and excitement.

USEFUL WEB RESOURCES

Study of Early Education and Development

www.gov.uk/government/collections/study-of-early-education-and-development-seed

This significant study (SEED, 2015, updated 2017) features research about the current childcare and early education model in England.

Department for Education (DfE), Statutory Framework for the Early Years Foundation Stage: Setting the Standards for Learning, Development and Care for Children from Birth to Five.

This framework is mandatory for all early years providers in England from 3 April 2017: maintained schools; non-maintained schools; independent schools; all providers on the Early Years Register; and all providers registered with an early years childminder agency.

www.foundationyears.org.uk/files/2017/03/EYFS_STATUTORY_FRAMEWORK_2017.pdf

Ofsted *Early Years Inspection Handbook*

This handbook (issued 2015, updated 2017) is used by Ofsted inspectors when inspecting early years providers.

www.gov.uk/government/publications/early-years-inspection-handbook-from-september-2015

Lighting Up Young Brains

This study from the Save the Children Fund looks at the science behind young children's brain development and shows how parents, carers and early years workers can support this process.

www.savethechildren.org.uk/resources/online-library/lighting-young-brains

Teaching and Play in the Early Years – A Balancing Act?

This survey by Ofsted published in 2015 explores perceptions of teaching and play in the early years.

www.gov.uk/government/publications/teaching-and-play-in-the-early-years-a-balancing-act

The OECD (Organisation for Economic Co-operation and Development)

The OECD conducts analysis and develops new data in early childhood education (ECEC) to provide valid, timely and comparable international information to help support countries review and redesign policies to improve their early childhood services and systems.

www.oecd.org/edu/school/earlychildhoodeducationandcare.htm

 **Online Resources**

Visit https://study.sagepub.com/education to find a selection of scholarly journal articles chosen to support each chapter.

3

EARLY YEARS MOVERS AND SHAKERS

DENISE REARDON, FATEMA HAJI AND DYMPNA REED

Chapter overview

Early Childhood Education and Care (ECEC) has witnessed tremendous changes over the past centuries. This chapter considers how many of the pioneering ECEC visionaries framed today's practice. The chapter begins by exploring how 17th- and 18th-century philanthropists, anthropologists and psychologists were influenced by historical events and society's poor attitude to children and childhood. The way these earlier visionaries influenced the work of 19th-century early years reformers and many of the progressive approaches to ECEC during the first and second half of the 20th century that brought about new insights and possibilities is also explored in this chapter. Much of what the ECEC pioneers discovered in the past is still very relevant today and has been developed and refined to suit the times we live in. The chapter concludes by identifying a number of 20th- and 21st-century ECEC visionaries who stand on the 'giant' shoulders of their predecessors.

EARLY YEARS APPROACHES AND METHODOLOGIES

Approaches and methodologies to Early Years Care and Education (ECEC) 'are wide and varied and are influenced by the philosophy which underpins the pedagogy and organisation of the setting' (Curtis et al., 2014: 26). During the past 400 years, radical psychologists, anthropologists, educationalists and researchers have had a major influence on the theory and practice of ECEC globally. As early as the 18th century, Rousseau (1712–1778) asserted that 'children were born good and were tainted by the influence of those around them' (Curtis et al., 2014), meaning that children are significantly influenced by environmental factors, their peers, people they encounter, society and its conventions. This chapter presents an overview of some of the approaches and methodologies offered to Early Years Teachers and Educators (EYT/Es).

THE FOUNDERS OF INFANT CHILD CARE

Robert Owen, 1771–1858

The forefather of the infant school

The children attending Robert Owen's Infant School at New Lanark in Scotland were 'children of the Industrial Revolution' (Mukherji and Dryden, 2014: 147). His concerns were about the appalling working conditions and exploitation of child labour as factories rapidly expanded. In his role as the partner and manager of a cotton mill, he actively improved the living and working environments for the mill workers and set up a school for their children.

His principled and pedagogical approach provided factory workers' children with an education that fostered their curiosity and interests nurtured by images, artefacts and real-life conversations (Whitbread, 1972). Challenged by evangelical views of saving children's souls and indoctrinating them into Christianity, he believed children did not need to recite the Bible or books, experience corporal punishment or listen to harsh words spoken to them. He believed children needed to experience 'a wealth of sensory experiences' (Curtis et al., 2014: 147).

Owen's philosophies were deeply rooted in giving children the opportunity to engage in physical activity, sing, dance and march with vigour both indoors and outdoors. Owen was influential in setting up the first infant schools that catered for children up to the age of 6, taking some of his pedagogical theories and beliefs from Pestalozzi and Froebel, each one sharing a conviction that ECEC must be based on warmth and real-life experiences, a theory that is well respected today.

Ideas for practice

Robert Owen set up community schools which were offered to 'every child above one year old' but in reality, children started at 2-3 years. In them he insisted there be real affection between the teacher and the taught.

- How do you display 'real affection' between you and the children in your care?

Friedrich Froebel, 1782–1852

The inventor of the kindergarten

Prior to the establishment of the first kindergarten in Germany during 1837, there had been no formal education for children under the age of 7. Kindergarten, which literally means the 'children's garden', reflected Froebel's ideas that voluntary play is a necessary element in educating the whole child, allowing him [sic] to use all his imaginative powers, trying out different ideas and physical movements to explore his interests.

Although the concept of play was known to be beneficial, Froebel was the first to put it into action. He believed 'play is the highest expression of human development in childhood, for it alone is the free expression of what is in a child's soul'. He did not agree that play is merely preparation for adult life. However, he regarded the role of the adult as crucial in helping children to learn. For the EYT/E this means being an equal partner in the child's play and learning, similar in nature to communicating with each other.

The exploration of the links between a setting and home were also mentioned in his book *Mother Songs, Games and Stories*, which was published in 1844 and was used as a tool in the kindergarten to link the school to the child's home life.

The German state (Prussia), although initially motivated by the desire to foster unity through a common language, began to feel threatened by children becoming free-thinkers rather than 'entry-level workers' and a ban was placed on kindergartens in 1851, a year before Froebel's death. But the impact of Froebel's work on play for children meant the great educator's legacy had become widespread internationally, through papers, pamphlets, visits and books, so that his pioneering theory of play based on first-hand experience spread world-wide.

Photo 3.1   Heuristic play materials in a Steiner setting

 —— **Ideas for practice** ———————————————————

To gain an insight into the principles and pedagogy of a Frobelian environment, compare these elements with how you organise the environment in your practice.

A Frobelian environment should:

- be physically safe but intellectually challenging, promoting curiosity, enquiry, sensory stimulation and aesthetic awareness;

- combine indoors and outdoors, the cultural and the natural;
- provide free access to a rich range of materials that promote open-ended opportunities for play, representation and creativity;
- demonstrate the nursery to be an integral part of the community it serves, working in close partnership with parents and other skilled adults;
- be educative rather than merely an amusing or occupying time; promote interdependence as well as independence, community as well as individuality and responsibility as well as freedom.

Source: Weston, 2002: 115

Captain Thomas Coram, 1668–1751

Founder of one of the first children's charities

Captain Thomas Coram was a philanthropist who created the London Foundling Hospital in Lamb's Conduit Fields, Bloomsbury, and London. He was sent to sea aged 11 and never received proper education. He returned from sea to be shocked at seeing children abandoned or dying on the streets of London. He began a campaign to create a home for abandoned children in 1720, by enlisting the support of leading members of the aristocracy. Early supporters of Thomas Coram's work included the composer George Frideric Handel, the artist William Hogarth and later the author Charles Dickens. His legacy, to develop new approaches to childcare and education informed by developments in child psychiatry, and the importance of children's emotional well-being and a secure loving family through adoption and early years care and parenting, continues today.

Thomas Coram often spoke of the scandal of 'invisible children' by which he meant vulnerable children who were actually there for all to see – on the streets or even in the gutter – but went ignored and effectively unseen. His 17 year struggle to establish what was the first children's charity in Britain is the inspiration for today's Coram because the struggle to give all children the best possible start in life continues. There are many thousands of 'invisible' children in Britain today – they may not be abandoned or in the gutter, but they often live out of sight and out of mind and are perhaps just as vulnerable. But Coram thrives and is acutely conscious of the challenges that still exist. (Sir David Bell, President of the children's charity 'Coram', 7 September 2017)

Over the centuries, more than 25,000 children's lives were saved by the Coram foundation with his legacy living on to create better life-chances for children through championing their rights and advocacy, ensuring that laws and policies reflect the 'voice of the child' whilst at the same time offering support and training to the agencies, teachers and professionals who work with them. Coram is now 278 years old and of great significance is the work done today to protect the rights of child refugees, migrant children and young people to help keep them safe regardless of their ethnicity, immigration status or nationality. The Coram charity continues today from the same historic site, Coram Fields, with a children's play area that refuses entry to adults unaccompanied by children.

Photo 3.2 A toddler playing at Coram's Fields

Johann Heinrich Pestalozzi, 1746–1827

The father of pedagogy

Pestalozzi was a Swiss social reformer and educator and his ideas led to great educational reforms in Europe in the 19th century. Like Coram, he was particularly concerned about the poor and he wanted to ensure their right to learn and be educated. He is often known as the 'Father of Pedagogy': 'It is John Pestalozzi who has been described as the starting point for modern educational theory and practice' (Green and Collie, 1916: 1, cited in Mukherji and Dryden, 2014: 145). He believed that education should be a branch of knowledge in its own right, with a child-centred active approach based on the needs and interests of the child.

He emphasised the importance of the use of direct exploration of the natural world, training the child in a sensorial way through the use of personal observations and judgements.

Both Montessori and Piaget were greatly influenced by his teachings and pursued his belief that 'life for the young child should be happy and free and education in self-control should be gradual and careful'. He established schools for children and also to train teachers, the most famous of which was at Yverdun in Switzerland.

 Ideas for practice

Making personal observations and judgements

> Observation is the formal term for one of the most important aspects of day-to-day professional practice when working with children of all ages. It is how we find out the specific needs of individual children by carefully looking, listening and noting the activities of a child or group of children. (www.westsussex.gov.uk/media/5555/effective_poa_and_planning.pdf)

- Observe a child or group of children exploring the natural world. Watch and listen and take notice of what you see and hear!

20TH-CENTURY INFLUENTIAL PEDAGOGUES

Susan Isaacs, 1885–1948

Observing children in their natural environments

In 1907, Isaacs trained as a teacher of young children (5- to 7-year-olds) at the University of Manchester and after qualifying she further graduated in 1912 with a first-class degree in Philosophy and then trained as a psychoanalyst at Cambridge, dedicated to the teachings of Freud.

From 1924 to 1925 Susan Isaacs ran the Malting House School, set up by the eccentric Geoffrey Pyke, as an experimental educational institution and ideas explored in this school have remained influential up until the present day. Eventually she became Head of the Department of Child Development at the Institute of Education in London.

Isaac's main theory was around the importance of observing a child, recording data and analysing the data to plan with the child. This common theme runs through the EYFS (DfE, 2017a), with the importance of the key worker to record the child's development, plan for next steps and share with other professionals.

Using observation, Isaacs noted the interests of children and allowed experiential learning to further children's quests for constructing their own knowledge and understanding. She claimed that children should be able to express their feelings openly and needed the freedom to explore, take risks and learn through play. Her research on observations formed the basis of her books *The Nursery Years* (1929), *Intellectual Growth in Young Children* (1930), in which she charts the children's explorations of both their inner and outer worlds. In the current EYFS (DfE, 2017a), observations are to be regarded as the most powerful of all the methods we have available when working with children. Observation, assessment and planning all feed into one another and contribute to our knowledge about the child. Chapter 6 explores the nature of the Assessment and Planning Cycle within today's context.

Photo 3.3 Socio dramatic play outdoors

Isaacs' book *The Educational Value of the Nursery School* (2013 [1937]) expressed a passionate belief for nursery education, believing that attending a nursery school should be a natural part of a child's early life. It was a place that should both mirror the family through love and warmth, as well as offering new and exciting opportunities and resources that might not be available at home.

Isaacs' creative use of the outside space at the Malting House School, Cambridge, will be familiar to early years settings, who are using their outdoor areas effectively, as is expected in the EYFS (DfE, 2017a). It offers opportunities for doing things in different ways than when indoors, by giving children first-hand contact with the natural world in order to explore, use their senses, take risks and be physically active and exuberant, using their 'super-ego' – her word for the child's enduring need for self-expression.

Susan Isaacs was influenced by Froebel in relation to the value of play, in particular, imaginative play. Her view that play should be truly open-ended and child-centred and that free-flow play would enable children to produce high-level thinking is backed up by research carried out in Russia by Lev Vygotsky (1896–1934) and published in 1962 (Social Development Theory).

Isaacs' view that a child's social world shapes their development is relevant today, with the impact of children's exposure to popular culture and new technologies. According to the Technology and Play Report (2015: 9), 31% of under-5s have an iPad and their average use is 1 hour and 19 minutes on weekdays and 1 hour and 23 minutes at weekends.

 Points for reflection

Isaacs' view that a child's social world shapes their development is greatly discussed today with the impact of children's exposure to popular culture and new technologies.

- How many children in your school/setting have access to an iPad?
- How long do they spend on it per day?
- What are they viewing?

The McMillan sisters (Rachel, 1859–1917, Margaret, 1860–1931)

Pioneers of children's health and well-being

The McMillan sisters were leading activists in the struggle to improve the health and well-being of children living in poverty and industrial regions. They believed hungry and/or sick children cannot learn and they 'led the way in promoting free school meals and medicals' (Pound, 2011: 27), with the provision of the School Meals Act being passed in 1906.

Influenced by the work of Pestalozzi, Froebel and Steiner, they believed that teachers should be trained to work directly with children and in partnership with their families, a theme that is extremely relatable today.

In 1914 the sisters opened the first Open-Air Nursery School and Training Centre in Peckham, London, with an emphasis on young children using their imagination, giving them space and time, freely available outdoor play and boundless movement and music. The Rachel McMillan Open Air Nursery, in Deptford, London, operates today, and is credited with influencing early years education across the world.

 ——— **Point for reflection** ————————————————

The McMillan sisters' theory that economically and socially disadvantaged children and their families need support is still as evident today. Watch this YouTube clip of the McMillan Open Air Nursery during 1951 and compare it to your school or setting today:

www.youtube.com/watch?v=V4jDyKPHuzg

Rudolph Steiner, 1861–1925

Experiential education and developing the 'whole child'

Rudolph Steiner's theories were based around a movement called Anthroposophy, giving children's creative, spiritual and moral needs as much attention as their intellectual needs. Steiner founded his first school in 1919 for the children of the Waldorf-Astoria factory workers. Steiner's education offered healing throughout the post-war period 'by providing a creative and unhurried learning environment where children could find the joy of learning and experience the richness of childhood' (Steiner Waldorf School Fellowship, n.d.). Steiner put his principles into practice by giving equal attention to the physical, emotional, intellectual, cultural and spiritual needs of each child, working in harmony with their personal development.

He believed that the first seven years of life are the most important for a child. Chapter 2 explores recent developments in neuroscience and the way that babies and young children absorb learning. Children in the early years learn greatly about themselves and their environment, mostly through imitation. Research undertaken by Bandura (1977) confirmed this, by showing that copying or imitating others is instinctive to young children.

Furthermore, Steiner believed that in the early stages of life, education works with the child's natural innate rhythms to develop a strong body with good motor skills, and a healthy diet. Diet has become a major discussion in the UK with, for example, Jamie Oliver campaigning for better children's health and well-being through good food, especially in school (see Jamie's Food Revolution, www.jamiesfoodrevolution.org). Chapter 89 explores babies and young children's physical development and healthy eating.

Steiner schools place much emphasis on creativity, with drawing, imaginative story-telling, painting, music, movement, poetry, modelling and drama used in all subjects. They also value physical movement and children participate in traditional games, sports, gymnastics and drama productions. In the 'Kindergarten' section of the school, children learn solely through play and hands-on activities and children find their own learning in situations through free play. They are not encouraged to read or write until the end of the first 'life-period', when the milk teeth are lost: 'with the change of teeth the inner etheric forces … are freed and we carry on the free thought that begins to assert itself from the seventh year onwards' (Steiner, 1928, quoted by Sheen [n.d.]), The Steiner approach does not concern itself with school readiness but more so 'readiness for life' (House, 2011: 182).

 Idea for practice

Young children in a Steiner setting learn 'emotional self-regulation in a quite unselfconscious way' (House, 2011: 10). This approach harmonises with Guy Claxton's work (2002) on 'unconscious learning' and 'building learning power'. Access this link to watch his YouTube clip www.youtube.com/watch?v=WIYRhoWtoiM

- How do you provide Steiner's 'creative and unhurried learning environment' and 'unconscious learning' in your setting?

Maria Montessori, 1870–1952

Self-directed activity and choices for children

Another highly prominent early 20th-century educationalist was Maria Montessori, born in Italy in 1870. Working as an Italian doctor in special education, she upheld learning as a process that cannot be determined by a child's age but a process that is determined by the rate and speed at which a child can acquire one skill before moving on to another. Her work was influenced by Seguin, Froebel, Pestalozzi and Rousseau.

Curtis et al. (2014: 109) consider Montessori schools to be 'child centred and holistic, emphasising children's natural curiosity and personal development'. A Montessori classroom is designed around three key points: the teacher, the child and the environment. Each child works at his own pace, and any help from other children happens spontaneously. There's no pressure from teachers to work faster, and as teachers offer guidance for building on skills as needed it allows for as much freedom of choice, movement and self-expression in 'structured and planned settings' (Curtis et al., 2014) with child-sized resources and furniture.

 Ideas for practice

Montessori's philosophy encourages teachers to observe children, foster their independence in a prepared environment, and then observe them again and adapt the environment to meet the needs of the child.

- Compare the EYFS (DfE, 2017a) 'four guiding principles' with Montessori's and Steiner's ideologies in Table 3.1.

Table 3.1 Steiner and Montessori Ideologies

EYFS Four guiding Principles (DfE, 2017a)	Steiner (1923)	Montessori (1966)
Unique Child	'We do not educate the child for the age of childhood; we educate him for his whole earthly existence.'	'This fashioning of the human personality is a secret work ... All that we know is that he has the highest potentialities, but we do not know what he will be. He must "become incarnate" with the help of his own will.'
Positive Relationships	'There are three primary virtues which we must develop in the child: gratitude, love and responsibility. These three virtues are the foundation on which the whole social life is built.'	'Little children between three and six years of age have a special psychology. They are full of love. They are only without love if they are ill-treated. If they are badly treated their real nature is altered. They are full of love themselves and need to be loved in order to grow.'
Enabling Environment	'In order to become true educators, the essential thing is to be able to see the truly aesthetic element in the work, to bring an artistic quality into our tasks, such as the creation of play materials.'	'This fashioning of the human personality is a secret work ... All that we know is that he has the highest potentialities, but we do not know what he will be. He must "become incarnate" with the help of his own will.'

EYFS Four guiding Principles (DfE, 2017a)	Steiner (1923)	Montessori (1966)
Learning and Development	'To a healthy child, playing is not only a pleasurable pastime, but also an absolutely serious activity. Play flows in real earnest out of the child's entire organism.'	'The child who concentrates is immensely happy; he ignores his neighbours or the visitors circulating about him. For the time being his spirit is like that of a hermit in the desert; a new consciousness has been born in him – that of his own individuality.'

Sources: Steiner Waldorf Foundation (2009); Montessori Schools Association (2008)

P.B. Ballard, 1929

The practical infant teacher

In 1929, Dr P.B. Ballard edited a series of six illustrated volumes to support the work of infant teachers. They were called *The Practical Infant Teacher*. He identified 'a guide to the most modern methods of teaching and the happy occupations of children in nursery and infant schools'. Ballard was a prolific writer of theory and curriculum books in the years before the Second World War. The editor notes written in 1929 are still of profound value to the EYT/E today.

Loris Malaguzzi, 1920–1994

Self-guidance, exploration and discovery

Loris Malaguzzi was the pedagogical leader of the Reggio Emilia approach to early years education. He held a philosophical belief that all children are competent and capable thinkers and learners as well as creative communicators and conversationalists.

The Reggio Emilia approach in Northern Italy 'grew out of a desire to recover after the Second World War' (Curtis et al., 2014: 27). People felt that their children were in need of a new way of learning. Malaguzzi and the parents believed that during children's early years of development they are gifted with 'a hundred languages' through which they can express their ideas. The Reggio Emilia approach is teaching how to use these symbolic languages (e.g. painting, sculpting and drama) in everyday life. The programme is based on the principles of respect, responsibility and community through exploration and discovery in a supportive and enriching environment, based on the interests of the children through a self-guided curriculum.

The Early Years Teacher and Educator role within the Reggio Emilia approach involves working as co-practitioner as the role of the practitioner is fundamentally to be that of a 'learner' alongside the child. In the Reggio approach, you become a practitioner–researcher, a resource and guide offering your experience to the children. Within Reggio Emilia settings the practitioners are committed to reflection about their own teaching and learning, and great attention is given to the look and feel of the classroom. The environment is considered to be the 'third teacher'.

High levels of expression are reached by Reggio Emilia children; they use many forms of symbolic representation, particularly the graphic arts, which in turn are documented by the pedagogical staff and the children themselves. Small groups of children work together, very often with an adult all around the educational setting, which has been organised so as to facilitate social, cognitive, verbal and symbolic representations.

 Ideas for practice

- Read Malaguzzi's 'One Hundred Languages of Children' poem about the multitude of ways in which children can express their ideas, thoughts, feelings and frustrations on this weblink: www.nurseryworld.co.uk/nursery-world/news/1100324/languages-children
- Reflect on the ways that you may include dancing, dreaming, playing, questioning, singing, reasoning, imagining, listening, laughing, crying, loving, painting, sculpting, exploring and experimenting in your teaching.
- Find out more about the work of Malaguzzi and his legacy on this weblink: www.routledge.com/posts/9621

The HighScope approach, 1931 – current

Learning through materials, people and ideas

The HighScope approach to ECEC identifies and builds on children's strengths, interests and abilities. Influenced by Piagetian principles, the HighScope approach is intended to be used as an 'open framework' that can be adapted to the specific needs of the children. The principles are based on a belief that children (aged 0–5 years) learn best through active experiences with people, materials, events and ideas, rather than through direct adult-initiated and structured activities. HighScope practice promotes a belief to others that children learn best while pursuing their personal interests and goals, and that they should be encouraged to make choices about materials and activities throughout the day.

Case study 3.1

An observation from an EYT of children aged 3–4 years, engaged in the HighScope 'plan, do and review' method

PLAN - At the start of the session the teacher provided the children with big books illustrating activities to choose from. The children looked through the big books and planned what they would like to do, some with their peers, others choosing to work autonomously.
DO - The children divided up and sought the necessary resources to set up their activities. The children explored their activities while asking and answering questions, solving problems and interacting with their peers and other practitioners.
REVIEW - At the end of the morning the teacher held a plenary session and the children spoke about what they had done, sharing any paintings, drawings, models or artefacts made with their peers before tidying away.

Ideas for practice

In the HighScope approach teachers and educators are seen as 'partners who support the children's play and learning through active exploration and problem solving' (Curtis et al., 2014: 231). Organise a teaching session, setting aside 5-10 minutes for a small-group discussion and let the children choose and plan what they would like to do. Allow 15-25 minutes for the children to engage freely in their chosen activity and make sure that you act as their equal partner to support and extend their play and learning. Reconvene with the children for a further 5-10 minutes to review and listen to what held their interest and why, as well as what they have discovered and learnt. Celebrate their achievements!

Professor Ferre Laevers, 1950 – current

Measuring children's well-being and involvement

Professor Ferre Laevers founded the Experiential Education (EXE) philosophy to assess the degree of 'emotional well-being' and the level of 'involvement' of the children in an early years setting/school. As an Early Years Teacher or Educator, you can use the EXE model to observe the child's development and interactions with the learning environment. It can help you to become aware of the strengths and weaknesses in your provision through:

- assessment of the actual levels of well-being and involvement of the babies, and young children;
- the analysis of observations undertaken;
- the selection and implementation of actions to improve quality.

 Ideas for practice

- Find out more about the EXE philosophy by accessing this weblink: https://vorming. cego.be/images/downloads/Ond_DP_IntroductionExpEduc.pdf
- Reflect on the EXE 'Ten action points' featured below to find out how you can make the care and education of the children you teach more effective through well-being and involvement.

EXE – Ten Action Points

1. Rearrange the classroom in appealing corners or areas
2. Check the content of the corners and replace unattractive materials by more appealing ones
3. Introduce new and unconventional materials and activities
4. Observe children, discover their interests and find activities that meet these orientations
5. Support ongoing activities through stimulating impulses and enriching interventions
6. Widen the possibilities for free initiative and support them with sound rules and agreements
7. Explore the relation with each of the children and between children and try to improve it
8. Introduce activities that help children to explore the world of behaviour, feelings and values
9. Identify children with emotional problems and work out sustaining interventions
10. Identify children with developmental needs and work out interventions that engender involvement within the problem area.

Source: 'Making care and education more effective through wellbeing and involvement: an introduction to Experiential Education,' Ferre Laevers, Research Centre for Experiential Education, University of Leuven, Belgium. Available at https://vorming.cego. be/images/downloads/Ond_DP_IntroductionExpEduc.pdf (accessed 17 November 2017)

The EXE model can be used to review and assess the impact of the environment on children's play. It supports making changes to the learning and play environment from practitioner-oriented to child-oriented. Re-arranging the physical environment and resources can support children's learning, allowing children to use their initiative and select freely and independently from a wide selection of purposeful and meaningful activities appropriate to their individual needs.

The birth of the National Childminding Association in Britain, 1979 – current

Over forty years ago, Denise Hevey (current day Professor Emeritus at the University of Northampton) was instrumental in founding the National Childminding Association (NCMA). Her own child was in the care of an excellent childminder when her local authority was setting up groups to discuss the first BBC programme for childminders called 'Other People's Children'. With her childminder's agreement, they went to the first meeting and naively asked why local childminders had not been told about their entitlement to free milk in parity with nurseries and infant schools. She was astonished to be told that the forms would be too complicated for childminders to fill out! She wrote to *The Guardian* to express her concern that childminders had no national voice. She was overwhelmed by the response from childminders, parents and some local authority (LA) workers also appalled by the situation.

Brian and Sonia Jackson's study (1979) identified that large numbers of young children were being cared for in poor circumstances with inconsistent regulation and minimum support from their LA in the North of England. Brian Jackson's previous attempt to set up a representative group foundered because it was perceived to be dominated by LA interests.

 Ideas for practice

- Look at the excerpt taken from an Ofsted 'good practice' example of childminder Nicola Phillips, which illustrates how far the status of childminding has come since its inauguration.
- Reflect on the way that the childminder featured in the 'good practice' excerpt teaches.
- How does it resonate with the way that you teach children to improve their communication and language development?

Nicola's success in teaching children to improve their communication and language development is grounded in her having excellent knowledge of what children in her care can do. She prioritises speaking and listening throughout each day. Key aspects that result in her highly effective early years practice are:

(Continued)

- giving full attention to what children are saying and what they are playing with
- good quality assessment that accurately demonstrates the pace of children's development
- a comprehensive knowledge of what each child needs to make further progress
- inventive resources that are often created from everyday things
- giving children opportunities to explore the natural outdoor environment
- play-filled days that meet children's emotional and physical needs as well as improving their communication.

Source: Teaching young children to develop their communication skills: Nicola Phillips, childminder (Ofsted, July 2015), available at www.gov.uk/government/publications/teaching-young-children-to-develop-their-communication-skills (accessed 12 September 2017)

Te Whāriki

A woven mat for all to stand on

Te Whāriki or 'Woven Mat' is used as a metaphor for the New Zealand (NZ) ECEC curriculum (Ministry of Education, New Zealand Government, 1996, revised 2017). It acknowledges children's uniqueness as learners, their ethnicity and their rights in NZ society. The revised curriculum (2017) is based on societal changes, shifts in policy and the vast array of educational research around curriculum, assessment, pedagogy and practice. At the heart of Te Whāriki, teachers in ECEC settings weave together the principles and strands featured in Box 3.1, in collaboration with children, parents and the community, to create a local curriculum for their setting. Implicit in this way, the curriculum or Te Whāriki is a metaphor that describes a woven mat for all to stand on!

BOX 3.1

Te Whāriki or Woven Mat: Principles and Strands (2017)

Principles

- Whakamana – empowerment
- Kotahitanga – holistic development
- Whānau tangata – family and community
- Ngā hononga – relationships

Strands

- Mana Atua - well-being
- Mana Whenua - belonging
- Mana Tangata - contribution
- Mana Reo - communication
- Mana Aoturoa - exploration

 Ideas for practice

Teachers working in the Te Whāriki ECEC curriculum accept that:

- Learning is a journey that begins before birth and continues throughout life.
- Each part of the education system has a responsibility for supporting children (and the adults they become) on this lifelong journey of exploration.

They support children by:

- Affirming their identity and culture.
- Connecting with and building on children's funds of knowledge.
- Having positive expectations of children's learning.

Consider how the NZ Te Whāriki ECEC curriculum (2017) resonates with your teaching.

Source: www.education.govt.nz/early-childhood/teaching-and-learning/te-whariki/ (accessed 27 October 2017)

CONCLUSION

Many of the 'Early Years Movers and Shakers' featured in his chapter designed their ECEC pedagogy, philosophies and approaches due to the social and political context of their time. Miller (2002, in Mukherji and Dryden, 2014: 230) believes that 'Most philosophers and development psychologists come from a modernist perspective where childhood is seen as a unique stage of life', while a postmodern perspective understands the impact of gender, class, race and the environment a child grows up in. Many of these eminent individuals were very influenced by each other and some in disagreement with one another; however, it cannot be denied that each one in their own right has been extremely instrumental in transforming ECEC.

To conclude, Table 3.2 recognises the names of some of the best-known educationalists from the early and mid-20th century. It identifies those key theories which established their names in the child education and psychology world. Their influence and that of their predecessors in previous centuries still has a major impact on today's teaching and learning.

Table 3.2 Key educationalists and theorists of the 20th century

Name and dates	Key principles and theories
Jean Piaget 1896-1980 (Switzerland)	**Theory of cognitive development** <ul><li>Schemas</li><li>Assimilation and accommodation through play</li><li>Genetic epistemology</li></ul>
Anna Freud 1895-1982 (daughter of Sigmund Freud, Austria and UK)	**Child psychology** <ul><li>Children who had experienced abandonment, trauma or extreme neglect are traumatised</li><li>Children develop through distinct developmental phases and develop defence mechanisms</li></ul>
Jerome Bruner 1915-2016 (USA)	**Constructivist theory** <ul><li>Modes of representation: Enactive (0-1 yr), Iconic (1-6 yr), Symbolic (7 yr onwards)</li><li>He opposed Piaget's notion of readiness.</li><li>Focus on the 'spiral curriculum' and 'discovery learning'</li></ul>
Lev Vygotsky 1896-1934 (Russia)	**Zone of Proximal Development** <ul><li>Created by free-flow and imaginary play</li><li>Scaffolding theory</li><li>Language development</li></ul>
Melanie Klein 1882-1960 (Austria)	**Child analysis** extending Freud's theories of the unconscious mind <ul><li>Early Oedipus complex</li><li>Roots of the superego</li><li>'Paranoid-schizoid position' followed by 'depressive position' in infants</li></ul>
John Dewey 1859-1952 (USA)	**Instrumental theory of truth and the philosophy of pragmatism** <ul><li>Knowledge is personal and helps the child to adapt to new situations and to achieve full potential</li><li>Education breaks down barriers and forges links in a social institution, enabling us to use skills for the greater good</li></ul>
Donald Winnicott 1896-1971 (UK)	**Object relations theory and 'good enough' parent theory** <ul><li>True self, false self and the transitional object</li><li>Concept of the 'holding environment'</li><li>Play is the key to the development of true self</li></ul>

Name and dates	Key principles and theories
John Bowlby (1907-1990)	**Theory of attachment (monotrophy)** • Infants and their mothers have a biological need to stay in close contact • Maternal deprivation could result in long-term consequences for the child

Modern living educationalists and 'giants'* who influence practitioners, government departments, university researchers today, and are known world-wide through their publications and education theories are as follows:

Lesley Abbott, Angela Anning, Tina Bruce, Guy Claxton, Tricia David, Mary Jane Drummond, Anne Edwards, Sally Goddard-Blythe, Vivian Gussin Paley, Vicky Hurst, Vicky Hutchin, Helen Moyett, Janet Moyles, Cathy Nutbrown, Marjorie Ouvry, Sacha Powell, Linda Pound, Iram Siraj, Kathy Sylva, Colwyn Trevarthen, Margy Whalley, David Whitebread, Marian Whitehead.

These are a few of many and are listed in alphabetical order, not in order of merit. Should you wish to pursue further knowledge of these significant educationalists, an Internet search will be very rewarding.

*Sir Isaac Newton said, 'If I have seen further it is by standing on the shoulders of giants'.

Approaches to ECEC combined with statutory curriculum frameworks present a highly complex set of issues to be discussed, debated, or disputed. The way that you approach ECEC in your teaching is subject to a vast array of political, economic, social and technological (PEST) demands (see Table 3.3), and yet the first years of a child's life are so crucially important, you dare not to get it wrong!

Table 3.3 PEST

Political	Economic
• Changes in government • Curriculum frameworks and policies • Child welfare and safeguarding • LA policies • Current legislation • Future legislation • Regulatory bodies and processes • Ofsted regulations	• Effects of recession • Cost of childcare • Government and LA initiatives, support and contributions • Local needs and the economy • Parental needs, support and contribution • SEN funding • Free entitlement/EY funding
Social	**Technological**
• Refugees, immigrants and asylum seekers • Family demographics, attitudes and views • Social factors • Cultural, religious, ethnic factors, influences and events • Ethical issues • Language barriers	• ICT e-safety, policy and practice – staff and children • Technology legislation and policy • Broadband access, costs, availability to staff and children and access to ICT resources • Competency of ICT user staff and children • Social networking policy, liaison with parents • Parental consent and views

—— **Ideas for practice** ────────────────────────────────

Having read about the different approaches to ECEC, which ones or aspects of ones would you like to put into practice, being mindful of any external factors that you are not able to change but have the potential to affect your teaching?

Please use the PEST analysis template in Table 3.3 to help you review each approach against what's happening in today's ECEC world.

 —— **Key points** ──

Many of the visionaries in this chapter:

- Recognised that the first seven years of a child's life are the most important.
- Developed a unique pedagogical belief and promoted this to others.
- Introduced contemporary methods of working based on sound research evidence.
- Introduced practices to promote the child's love of learning.
- Emphasised that playful experiences takes shape in many forms.
- Identify that children learn through self-initiated free play in an exploratory environment.
- Recognise that observation contributes to our knowledge about the child.
- Did not always agree with each other over the best approaches to learning and development.
- Contributed significantly to ECEC today and continue to do so.

There are far more world-wide visionaries to be studied, however the scope of this chapter prohibits writing about them all.

FURTHER READING

Curtis, W., Ward, S., Sharp, J. and Hankin, L. (2014) *Education Studies – an Issues Based Approach*, 3rd edn. London: Sage.

Chapter 3, 'Approaches in the early years: issues and reflections', asks the reader to consider research and possible approaches when devising ECEC.

Giardiello, P. (2013) *Pioneers in Early Childhood Education*. Abingdon: Routledge.

The book explores the influences that shaped the ideas, values and beliefs of Rachel and Margaret McMillan, Maria Montessori and Susan Isaacs, and how they relate to quality ECEC today.

House, R. (2011) *Too Much, Too Soon*. Stroud: Hawthorn Press.

Chapter 12, 'The Steiner Waldorf Foundation Stage – "To everything there is a season"' (Lynne Oldfield), unpicks the Waldorf 'unhurried' approach to ECEC from the structure of the day, the presentation of activities, the nurturing of the child to the assessment of school readiness.

Chapter 15, 'Challenging the Reggio Emilia approach with relational materialist thinking and an ethics of possibilities' (Hillevi Lenz Taguchi), considers looking at future ECEC possibilities rather than questioning what was, what is and what should be.

Mukherji, P. and Dryden, L. (2014) *Foundations of Early Childhood – Principles and Practice*. London: Sage.

Chapter 8 of this book explores the influencing factors of the historical background to ECEC.

Pound, L. (2011) *Influencing Early Childhood Education: Key Figures, Philosophies and Ideas*. Maidenhead: Open University Press.

This book explores key 19th-century ECEC movements to progressive ideas of the 20th century.

Schweizer, S. (2006) *Well, I Wonder: Childhood in the Modern World*. Rudolf Steiner Press.

This book introduces the Steiner approach, with an emphasis on children's need of daily rhythm, movement and play.

Weston, P. (2002) *The Froebel Education Institute: the Origins and History of the College*. University of Surrey Roehampton.

This book looks at the story leading to the foundation of the Frobelian College.

USEFUL WEB RESOURCES

Coram

www.coram.org.uk

Froebel Educational Institute

www.froebel.org.uk

HighScope

www.highscope.org

Montessori Schools Association

www.montessori.org.uk/msa

Reggio Children Identity and Approach

www.reggiochildren.it/identita/reggio-emilia-approach/?lang=en
www.scholastic.com/teachers/articles/teaching-content/pioneers-our-field-loris-malaguzzi-founder-reggio-emilia-approach

Steiner Waldorf School Fellowship

www.steinerwaldorf.org.uk

 Online resources

Visit https://study.sagepub.com/education to find a selection of scholarly journal articles chosen to support each chapter.

4

REFLECTIVE PRACTICE AND PRACTICE-BASED INQUIRY

DILYS WILSON AND RUTH MILLER

Chapter overview

This chapter looks at professional reflection as an integral part of the development of quality early years practice. It encourages EYT/Es to examine their personal values and beliefs about early years pedagogy so that they can articulate a vision and use reflection as a tool to guide the improvement of their practice. Theories relating to professional reflective practice are explored and models of reflection are introduced to help practitioners become more aware of the stages involved in the reflective process. The chapter illustrates how these reflective tools can be used to guide the EYT/E to reflect on and analyse the challenges and treasures arising out of daily professional practice. Practice-based inquiry and work-based projects are then introduced as a way of systematically improving areas of practice identified for development through professional reflection. The project cycle illustrates the processes, similar to the models of reflective practice already introduced, that EYT/Es can follow to plan, implement and evaluate aspects of early years practice based on the improvement and development needs of the specific setting. This approach to leading change is discussed from the perspective of the 'insider' who understands the context of the early years setting is directly involved in the change process alongside other stakeholders.

INTRODUCTION TO REFLECTIVE PRACTICE

Teaching babies and young children is always varied and interesting but often challenging and perplexing. Ways of working such as the Key Person approach (see Chapter 8) offer organisational structures for supporting children and their families through the initial transition from home to the early years setting and onwards as they embark on their learning journeys. Working in teams with other teachers and early years practitioners can be enriching and constructive but also at times difficult and frustrating (see Chapter 12). These aspects of the EYT/E (Early Years Teacher and Educator) role often involve strong feelings and require regular monitoring and self-management. Reflective thinking (see Chapter 1) is therefore necessary and the term reflective practice is used as a way to formalise the importance of engaging in professional review.

The EYFS (DfE, 2017a: 10) Statutory Framework states that practitioners 'must reflect on the different ways children learn when planning and guiding children's activities' with an assumption that reflection is embedded in practice. The Good Practice in Early Education Report (Callanan et al., 2017) places 'an open and reflective culture' as a theme seen to be present in early years settings that consistently demonstrate good practice. Reflective practice can therefore be viewed as a necessary component for the professional development of the EYT/E and a factor influencing the early years setting's capacity for improvement. The Ofsted Self-Evaluation Guidance for Early Years settings (Ofsted, 2015c) includes a prompt to 'consider the impact' on the children of the policies and teaching practices based on:

- The quality of teaching, learning and assessment.
- Personal development, behaviour and welfare.
- Outcomes for children.

To 'consider the impact' of their teaching and the effectiveness of the provision, the EYT/E will need to engage in reflection both individually and as a team to make sense of how the provision can be tailored to meet the needs of each unique child and cohort of children and their families.

GETTING STARTED: BELIEFS AND VALUES

Although the terms referred to in practice guidance such as 'an open and reflective culture' (Callanan et al., 2017: 15) provide a description of an expected way of working, there is little specific guidance about how this should be implemented. We all process the experiences that we have in different ways and this also applies to our expectations for the way we work with children and their families. We inevitably draw on our own values and beliefs based on our previous experiences of being a child in a family or being a parent, or rooted in the knowledge base of the professional training programme we have experienced. The EYT/E and the teams they work with also need to consider the shared ethos and the values that underpin their collective practice. This self-awareness of our own beliefs and values about our professional identity is an important first step for embarking on reflective practice. Reflecting on our personal perspectives and articulating them to colleagues helps to establish the 'open and reflective culture' referred to as a characteristic of good practice in the SEED report (Callanan et al., 2017).

 Ideas for practice

Pen Green Centre for Children and Families have developed a whole team approach called Making Children's Learning Visible (MCLV). The approach aims to establish 'a way of working which involves parents and practitioners engaging with each other in dialogue and jointly reflecting on their pedagogy and the ways in which they support and facilitate children's learning, both in the home and in the setting.'

The first strand of the programme involves the staff team working together to agree the image of the child that they would like to promote for all of the children in their setting.

1. Make a list of the characteristics you value most for the learning and development of the children you teach.
2. Do you think that your colleagues share your views?
3. Consider ways of developing a shared 'image of the child' in your early years setting.

You can read more about MCLV in the book *Using Evidence for Advocacy and Resistance in Early Years Services: Exploring the Pen Green research approach* (Mckinnon, 2013).

MODELS OF REFLECTIVE PRACTICE

There are many models and tools available to support the reflective process and although it is not possible to consider them all, the examples discussed here provide a good starting point. Donald Schön (1983) has contributed enormously to the debate about the way that professionals respond to work situations and make working decisions about what to do next based on their familiarity with their roles and professional responsibilities. Schön explored the difference between 'reflection-in-action' and 'reflection-on-action'. These ideas can be applied easily to early years practice as EYT/Es constantly 'reflect-in-action' when they need to react and respond in a flexible way based on the children's shifting needs or interests. This can include a combination of what Schön called 'tacit knowledge', by reacting to situations in an intuitive way, or 'professional artistry' which recognises that experienced EYT/Es will be able to draw on their professional expertise when responding to unplanned events or incidents. Bolton's 'hawk in the mind constantly circling, watching and advising on practice' (2010: 33) provides a clear illustration of this kind of reflective process. The ability to then 'reflect-on-action' enables the EYT/E to review afterwards how they responded to the situation and what they learned from it. The subsequent reflection process unpicks the difference between an intuitive response which may not be consciously applied, and recognition that through reflection, 'professional artistry' can be captured and applied again.

Many models of reflective practice use circular or spiral designs to illustrate the different stages of the reflective process and pose questions to guide reflective thinking. Kolb's (2015) experiential learning cycle (Figure 4.1) provides one such model, which focuses firstly on the actual experience of professional practice, which he refers to as 'concrete experience'. The next part of the cycle is 'reflective observation', where the practitioner can take a step back and think about their experience of what happened.

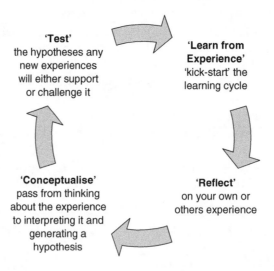

Figure 4.1 Kolb's learning cycle

Source: Adapted from Kolb (2015)

For the EYT/E this stage involves the process that Schön (1983) described as 'reflection-on-action' where there is a thinking distance between the practice and the evaluation of it. The process of 'abstract conceptualisation' comes next in the cycle where the reflective observation is processed further by drawing on knowledge and understanding of children's learning and development and seen through the lens of the pedagogical approach used in the setting. Each stage of the cycle feeds into the next and the process encourages ongoing development and improvement. The final stage of 'active experimentation' then returns to the starting point and a repetition of the cyclical process can then take place based on the next 'concrete experience' of practice.

Another very straightforward model to use that is easy to remember is Driscoll's (2007) 'What?' model. The steps in this process are:

1. What?
2. So what?
3. Now what?

This is similar to the stages in Kolb's model that lead forward to the next stage in the reflective practice cycle. Driscoll also suggests a series of helpful questions to ask to encourage further probing at each stage. The 'What?' stage helps to clarify the experience or incident or event that needs to be thought about with the focus on the actions and reactions of all involved. The EYT/E will be familiar with the daily examples arising from their observations of children or interactions with parents or colleagues that would be useful for them to stop and think about. At the 'What?' stage the EYT/E may consider making descriptive written notes or talking through what happened as a useful starting point. This clarification leads to the 'So what?' stage where the initial experience can be thought about in more detail. Driscoll suggests taking note of the feelings that accompany the reflection and exploring if they were troubling in any way. The insights that arise from this probing will highlight aspects that need to be reflected on and analysed further. The third step is 'Now what?', which leads to thinking about what possible actions could be taken and what the best option might be to move forward. This can be developed further by considering the effectiveness of the action that was taken and any personal and professional learning arising from it.

 —— **Ideas for practice** ————————————————

Use Driscoll's 'What?' model to explore an example from your practice that has been playing on your mind.

Table 4.1 Driscoll's 'What?' model

What?	Write some descriptive notes about your example
So what?	Explore the context, reflect on your feeling and thoughts: • At the time • Now • What was good or positive? • Did anything trouble you? • Did others experience it differently?
Now What?	Make a list of the actions you will take

Source: Based on Driscoll, J. (2007: 45)

Drawing attention to the feelings that are experienced during a particular incident or interaction is a valuable component of the reflective process. Gibbs' (1988) reflective cycle builds on both Driscoll's 'What?' model and Kolb's four-stage reflective cycle model (Figure 4.1) by using six circular stages to guide the reflective process as illustrated in Figure 4.2.

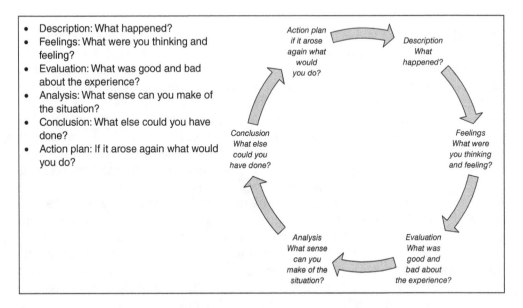

- Description: What happened?
- Feelings: What were you thinking and feeling?
- Evaluation: What was good and bad about the experience?
- Analysis: What sense can you make of the situation?
- Conclusion: What else could you have done?
- Action plan: If it arose again what would you do?

Action plan if it arose again what would you do?

Description What happened?

Feelings What were you thinking and feeling?

Evaluation What was good and bad about the experience?

Analysis What sense can you make of the situation?

Conclusion What else could you have done?

Figure 4.2 Gibbs' reflective cycle

Source: Based on Gibbs (1988)

Gibbs' model is commonly used by health and social care professionals as it recognises that in these helping professions, professionals need to think about their emotional responses to their work so that they can acknowledge the link between their feelings, their thinking and their behaviour. Working in early years settings with young children and their families can also be emotionally draining at times and it can be helpful to realise that the way we feel can be a useful reflective tool. The questions Gibbs poses in his reflective cycle (Figure 4.2) can be used effectively to structure examples of practice discussed during reflective supervision (see Chapter 8) which can be helpful in supporting the EYT/E with the emotional impact of their work and ways of making sense of the positive as well as the more challenging aspects of their roles.

The reflective mirror metaphor

The use of a mirror as a metaphor for reflection illustrates the different perspectives that can be seen from looking in a mirror and how this could be applied to viewing your practice. The metaphor also provides an invitation to imagine new possibilities linked to the image reflected in the mirror or to go 'through the mirror' (Bolton, 2010) where an infinite number of interpretations can be considered.

Table 4.2 The Metaphorical Mirror

Type of mirror	Reflective practice example
Bathroom mirror You look in this mirror when you get up and make a quick decision to do nothing or to make yourself more presentable	You are busy setting up the outdoor area and you think: 1. I'll leave the same play materials in the sand which is good enough for today OR 2. Although it will take longer to prepare, I'll put some diggers, blocks and builders' hats next to the sand as the children were really interested yesterday in watching what was going on at the building site across the road.
Full-length mirror You use this mirror to see a full picture of yourself , e.g. when trying on a new outfit	You have spent a lot of time changing the home corner to a vet's surgery. Standing back, you are more aware of the whole room: • You notice that the book area looks a bit dull and could include more books about animals and people who help us. • You wonder how the mark making area could be enlivened to enhance the play in the vet's surgery.
360° mirror Using this mirror, you can see yourself from all angles and have a view that you don't regularly see	You have been introducing a new letter and sound as part of a whole class phonics session for a class of 4- and 5-year-olds. Two practitioners have joined you to support the involvement of all the children. • At the evaluation meeting afterwards, each of you has a different perspective on the children's engagement and learning. • Getting feedback from others helps you to identify the children who are confident and others who need more support.
Driver's mirror This mirror means that you can check to see what is behind you before moving ahead	The mother of a child who is in the process of settling into the toddler room is about to leave him quickly without saying goodbye while you read him a story. • Based on your previous experience of settling children in, although saying goodbye can upset them, you know that helping the child to manage to acknowledge that mummy is leaving is better for the settling in process in the long run.
Wing mirrors These mirrors help you to see what is behind you or out of view from another mirror	You are aware that one child often seems to be at the centre of disputes between children and it has got to the point where some practitioners and children now expect her to be the instigator. • You raise this at a team meeting and agree to take it in turns to observe her at all times during the nursery session to gain a better understanding of what is going on. • The feedback from your shared observations shows that the child intervenes to help children who are upset but her enthusiastic actions are often misinterpreted.

(Continued)

Table 4.2 (Continued)

Type of mirror	Reflective practice example
Magnifying mirror You use this mirror when you need to examine something up close	You are troubled by a conversation you had with a parent who insisted that their child should not be allowed to sleep during the day as it was difficult getting him to go to bed at night time. As his key person you are aware of how tired he gets during the day and how this affects his behaviour. • You decide to talk to the parent and see if you can work out some strategies to support both the child and the parent's need for rest. • You share the challenges you have been experiencing during supervision. • Your supervisor asks you to review the sleep and rest policy and share your suggestions at the next staff meeting.
Funfair mirrors These mirrors give you a surprising viewpoint as they distort what you usually see in a mirror	The older babies often squeeze together to look through the gate to the outdoor area to watch the older children playing. The baby room team believes that the routine they have organised for the babies to play outside when the other children go inside is better for the babies as it keeps them safe. • Although there are regular observations of the babies, their interest in the older children has not been seen by the practitioners. Some of the children are looking out for older siblings. • A trainee notices this immediately when she starts her placement and she puts into words what the babies might be telling her. • This helps the team to see what they hadn't noticed before.
Shop windows You can see your reflection in a shop window as you move past	During a busy lunchtime with the children you suddenly hear yourself repeatedly telling children to 'hold the water jug carefully', 'remember to wash your hands'. You become aware that you have not had a friendly conversation with any of the children and you take stock for a moment so that you can begin to tune into a child who has been trying to tell you something.

Source: Adapted from Bassot (2016: 16, 17)

 Points for reflection

Bassot (2016) cautions that the 'metaphorical mirror' (Table 4.2) can get steamed up or become dirty and that time needs to be put aside to clean and polish it!

• Choose one of the mirrors and reflect on an example from your practice.
• Use the stages of Gibbs' reflective cycle to reflect on your example.
• How helpful have you found each model in helping you to polish your reflective mirror?

PRACTICE-BASED INQUIRY

Reflection will often identify areas of practice that need development, uncover gaps in provision or areas of dissatisfaction. There are also new policy directives and outcomes from Ofsted reports that identify and 'drive' the need for change or development. As leaders of practice in settings it is the role of the EYT/E to critically evaluate and shape new areas of practice.

Professional standards such as the Teachers' Standards (Early Years) and the Early Years Educator qualifications criteria (see Appendix 1) in England, provide a clear expectation for EYT/Es to take responsibility for taking a leadership role in 'shaping and supporting good practice' (NCTL, 2013). The Leadership Qualities Framework (National Skills Academy for Social Care, 2014) provides a more detailed breakdown of the leadership characteristics for health and social care professionals in similar front line and operational roles, using the following seven dimensions:

1. Demonstrating personal qualities: developing self-awareness; managing yourself; continuing professional development; acting with integrity.
2. Working with others: developing networks; building and maintaining relationships; encouraging contribution; working with teams.
3. Managing services: planning; managing resources; managing people; managing performance.
4. Improving services: ensuring the safety of people who use services; critically evaluating; encouraging improvement and innovation; facilitating transformation.
5. Setting direction: identifying the contexts for change, applying knowledge and evidence; making decisions; evaluating impact.
6. Creating the vision: developing the vision for the organisation; communicating the vision; influencing the wider service vision; embodying the vision.
7. Delivering the strategy: framing, implementing, developing and embedding the strategy.

What is a practice-based inquiry or a work-based project?

Practice-based inquiry (PBI) and work-based projects can help EYT/Es to systematically inform and undertake evidence-based practice development in early years settings. You will notice and may be relieved that this chapter focuses on PBI rather than 'research methods'. Research is often done by outsiders looking in on the work setting, keeping objective, not getting directly involved and seeking to find some universal truths that can be applied to many settings. PBI, however, is carried out by 'insiders' within the workplace, investigating issues that are pertinent to their own setting and action planning development specific to their particular needs. Being an insider has huge advantages, such as already being very knowledgeable about the setting, the staff and any issues. However, the EYT/E engaging in PBI needs to be conscious of potential subjectivity, ethical conduct and purposively invite a range of viewpoints. Practitioner inquiry needs to be systematic and it is about exploring or evaluating aspects of practice directly relevant to the setting. The inquiry may be part of a work-based project that leads to improving specific policies and teaching practices or provision and will often result in useful outcomes for the early years setting. It is about inquiry applied to action (Costley et al., 2010). For the EYT/E PBI or work-based project outcomes could be to implement a new teaching strategy, update and develop policies and procedures, introduce new learning resources or to support the professional development of the staff team. A work-based project is 'a systematic and organised effort to investigate a specific problem that needs a solution' (Sekaran, in Gray, 2014: 3).

The PBI or work-based project cycle

PBI and work-based projects still need to be systematic, rigorous and ethical so that subsequent development is evidence-based and not haphazard. It is helpful to structure any inquiry and development work around a project cycle.

Workman (2007) offers the following four-point project approach:

1. Planning
2. Doing
3. Outcomes
4. Review

This is mostly aligned to the methodological approach of Denscombe's (2017) model of action research, shown in Figure 4.3. Action research is a cyclical approach, similar to the models of reflective practice discussed earlier. As the project develops, later stages are influenced by the outcomes of earlier stages. Reflecting, analysing and monitoring changes that have been implemented are key practices for the EYT/E to develop.

Planning

It is important for the EYT/E to understand that practice development does not occur just for the sake of it. It is driven by many internal and sometimes external influences. We call these 'drivers for change' and they both provide the reason or rationale behind a PBI or a work-based project and they can be used effectively to help 'drive' the change forward.

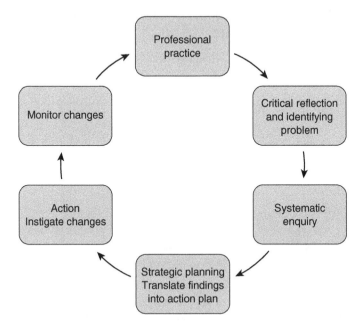

Figure 4.3 Denscombe's model of action research

Source: Denscombe (2017)

 **Points for reflection**

Look at Table 4.3. Consider what *drives* change in your setting.

Table 4.3 Drivers of change

External drivers	Internal drivers
Government initiatives, policies and/or practice guidance	Children's progress, attainment and outcomes
OFSTED inspection reports	Parent feedback
New research, ideas on best practice	An incident

— 🔍 —— **Case study 4.1** ————————————————

Planning a PBI into the use of Information Communication Technology (ICT) resources in my EY setting

1. Identify an important change or innovation that you need or would like to make in your own early years setting/school.

    I am interested in how Information and ICT can be used to promote all of the EYFS Areas for Learning and Development and provide opportunities for children to develop the Characteristics for Effective Learning.

2. Describe the issue, problem or opportunity as you currently see it:

    In my nursery, we have started using a new assessment tracker which highlighted that there were limited resources in the nursery for the children to use to develop their ICT skills. During a discussion at a team meeting the staff team indicated that they were experiencing problems recording base line data on ICT for their key children.

3. Discuss why this development is necessary – this is your rationale:

    The staff team are unsure of how to make use of the ICT resources in a way that is compatible with their pedagogical beliefs. They are concerned about the overuse of ICT and how it might inhibit communication, language and social interaction.

4. What is the aim or aims of the planned change/innovation?

    *   *To evaluate the Information Communication Technology (ICT) area in my setting;*
    *   *To research and develop the ICT resources that are available for children to use in my nursery setting;*
    *   *To pilot the use of the new ICT resources and integrate their use across a range of activities;*
    *   *To model the use of ICT resources to children and staff to support their knowledge, understanding and confidence in using them.*

5. As you develop the detail of your project you will need to break down your aims into specific objectives. Objectives are what you will need to achieve in order to meet your overall aim and are written almost like tasks to complete. They are particularly relevant in a project that aims to develop outputs. Objectives need to be specific and achievable.

Specific objectives:

- *Research current theoretical perspectives and practice guidance on ICT in the early years;*
- *Complete an audit of the ICT resources available in the nursery;*
- *Share my findings with the staff team and agree plans;*
- *Develop and integrate the use of ICT resources across learning activities - especially the use of tablets;*
- *Pilot a 'defunct technology' area in the nursery where children can explore and take apart a range of non-operational resources;*
- *Review children's progress in their ICT skills and gain feedback from staff.*

6. What ethical issues should you be aware of?

- *Staff feelings about the changes and being embarrassed about their competencies;*
- *Exposing children to ICT safely, e.g. ICT safeguarding, policy and practice;*
- *Seeking children's consent.*

Doing the PBI or work-based project

The methodology of a PBI or work-based project is pragmatic. You need to ask yourself:

- Is this the best method of inquiry for my purpose and appropriate in my setting?
- How will these project activities help me to meet my objectives?
- Am I conducting my PBI ethically?

You need to keep focused and not get side-tracked. It is often not necessary at this stage to gather new data through primary research methods such as question-naires or interviews as these are more appropriate at the evaluation stage. Rather your time is better spent making best use of secondary information (that already exists) and existing opportunities for discussion and feedback.

- **Literature review**: systematically reviewing current thinking and practice guidance on a particular area.
- **Documentary analysis**: examining documents for a specific purpose, e.g. comparing your local policies and procedures with national guidelines.
- **Baseline audit**: analysing tracking data for a specific purpose, e.g. to establish trends or gain an accurate summary of the situation to help plan and inform targeted developments.

- **Practice forums**: once you are ready to gain feedback and suggestions from others first make best use of existing forums by using staff team meetings, parent meetings and wider practitioner forums that you may be a part of. These are all a rich source of 'data' and ideas upon which to plan practice developments.

ETHICAL ISSUES

Whatever method you use to explore, gain feedback or evaluate practice, this needs to be done ethically. This means that your inquiry needs to be done for 'good' and not cause any participants (such as staff, parents or the children) any harm or distress. Participants also need to give their informed consent to any inquiry activities you want them to be involved in. If you are proposing to observe children this may require gaining consent from their parents. You also need to consider how any feedback you gather is kept confidential and anonymous. Your organisation may have their own procedures that you need to follow so seek advice before embarking on a PBI.

 Ideas for practice

You may wish to consider using a Fishbone diagram (Figure 4.4), also called cause and effect analysis, to help you to identify the root causes of a problem, especially when there could be multiple or complex causes.

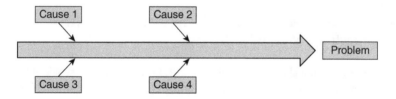

Figure 4.4 Fishbone diagram

1. Identify what the problem is and place it at the head of the 'fish'.
2. To form the 'fish bones', think about what the main causes of the problem might be, e.g. the environment, resources, team working.
3. Discuss the main causes and break them down into smaller 'fish bones' to identify other contributing factors.
4. Having worked out what the problem is and what the likely causes are, decide what you can do about it.

Leading change through PBI

In order to successfully lead the PBI or work-based project EYT/Es will need to bring their colleagues with them. During the planning stage, it is important to consider how best to communicate the need for change and encourage a shared vision and teamwork. Depending on the focus of the project this might also involve the children and parents/carers. Getting everyone involved in analysing what needs to change and in contributing to improvement ideas helps to develop shared responsibility for practice development and a will to make new developments work.

 **Case study 4.2**

Implementing the use of ICT resources

Having an action plan was very beneficial as it meant I could break down the stages into smaller more manageable steps. Also, distributing tasks to staff worked well. Such as, I asked staff to talk about using the iPad safely in circle time with the children. I reminded them the day before and asked the lead teacher to write a reminder on the notice board. The second part of my project was setting up the defunct technology area. This was a new provision in the setting which involved some problem-solving along the way. For example, after we first introduced the activity we realised we needed more screwdrivers of different sizes. So, I went and bought some that evening. I was then not based in the classroom that the activity was set up in so the practitioners in there took over and fed back to me with any issues. One practitioner took the initiative to add hand drills and more screws, another practitioner asked the caretaker to look for more defunct materials. I set up a defunct technology box so that all of the practitioners could access it easily to set up when they wanted to. This collaborative team effort meant that problems were solved quickly.

However, EYT/Es still need to be prepared for resistance to change and to consider ways to overcome this resistance (see Chapter 12). It is important to take time to listen to the views of others including their worries and fears. Make sure that everyone understands why the change is necessary and reduce misunderstanding of what the change will involve.

Outcomes of a PBI or work-based project

The outcomes of the project will be based on the ideas and evidence that have been gathered systematically in the inquiry stage. They will depend on the original aims and objectives and may just be recommendations or new resources or systems that may need to be developed. It is important to consider and action-plan how new ideas or outputs resulting from a PBI or work-based project will be shared, disseminated, implemented and evaluated.

REVIEW: HOW TO EVALUATE YOUR OUTCOMES

Evaluation is to assess the *effectiveness* of something, e.g. an innovation, intervention, policy, practice or service (Robson, 2011). Evaluation of practice is important to provide the evidence base for development, justify expenditure, to highlight achievements and to support accountability (to stakeholders).

Photo 4.1 Children working together on a computer program

In the ICT Case Study the plan was to evaluate the outcomes through a pilot of the use of the new ICT resources and the defunct technology area. Robson (2011) stresses the need to consider how the worth or value of something will be assessed, for example, what methods will be appropriate and what criteria will be used. There were two aspects to the planned evaluation of the use of the ICT resources, firstly by reviewing children's progress and secondly gaining feedback from staff. The first required a careful measurement of children's progress using their assessment tracking data and observations of them interacting with the new resources to review their progress.

The Case Study example set clear criteria against which to 'measure' progress. The second part of the evaluation was to gain feedback. This may require a more qualitative and exploratory method such as a semi-structured discussion through interviews or a meeting/focus group with particular staff. So, the methods chosen for evaluation need to be appropriate. Again, ethical principles need to be followed.

The findings from the initial evaluation may well lead to modification of new developments or further action planning before the change is adopted more widely. Setting-wide evaluation of a new development may follow over a longer period before the overall aim is achieved. New demands may need further developments. And so, the cyclical process of systematic reflection, inquiry, action and review is ongoing.

 Key points

- Learning from experience is based on a capacity to reflect.
- Seeing ourselves from different perspectives supports reflective learning.
- Models of reflection provide useful prompts to guide the reflection process.
- Practice-based inquiry arises out of reflective practice.
- Practice-based inquiry and work-based projects need to be conducted ethically.
- Improving practice is cyclical – there is always a step further.

FURTHER READING

Bassot, B. (2016) *The Reflective Practice Guide: An Interdisciplinary Approach to Critical Reflection*. Abingdon: Routledge.

This book brings together the theories and models of reflection in use across professional and academic boundaries.

Bolton, G. (2010) *Reflective Practice*. London: Sage.

Bolton discusses a range of ways to develop reflective practice that encourages professional creativity.

Denscombe, M. (2017) *The Good Research Guide*, 5th edn. Maidenhead: Open University Press.

Practical guidance is provided in this book on how to engage in small-scale research projects.

Palaiologou, I. (2012) *Ethical Practice in Early Childhood*. London: Sage.

This text discusses the importance of conducting research that is ethical with young children.

Lindon, J. and Trodd, L. (2016) *Reflective Practice and Early Years Professionalism*. London: Hodder Education.

This comprehensive book uses the early years practice context to discuss theories and models of reflective practice.

Roberts-Holmes, G. (2011) *Doing Your Early Years Research Project: A Step by Step Guide*. London: Sage.

A helpful guide with an early years focus on planning, designing and implementing a research project.

USEFUL WEB RESOURCES

Early Education – The British Association for Early Childhood Education

www.early-education.org.uk

This website provides information on current early years research, practice issues and policy.

Leadership Qualities Framework

www.skillsforcare.org.uk/Leadership-management/Leadership-Qualities-Framework/Leadership-Qualities-Framework.aspx

The Skills for Care website provides information on the leadership attitudes and behaviours needed in social care.

 **Online resources**

Visit https://study.sagepub.com/education to find a selection of scholarly journal articles chosen to support each chapter.

5

HIGH-QUALITY EARLY YEARS TEACHING AND LEARNING

DENISE REARDON

Chapter overview

The chapter aims to help the reader develop a broad understanding of the term 'high-quality' teaching and learning in the Early Years (EY) and why it is so hard to pin down a universal definition. The chapter encourages the reader to critically question and explore the perceptions of a wide range of stakeholders, for example trainee EYT/Es, teachers, EY practitioners, parents, carers, children themselves, the community at large, governments and Local Authorities (LA) etc. The concept of Quality Assurance (QA) in the early years is examined by looking through the lens of a number of approaches designed to ensure the quality of EY practice. For the sake of simplicity, the term 'quality improvement' (QI) is used in this chapter to represent a number of approaches that view quality as a continuous process to encourage the EYT/E to question what quality is and help them achieve it by encouraging them to adopt a self-reflective and involved approach. The reader is given the opportunity to question and interrogate a broad range of ways to measure the quality of EY teaching and learning, for example, government QI (quality improvement) schemes such as Ofsted, which is the Office for Standards in Education, Children's Services and Skills. This is the independent, non-ministerial government department responsible for inspecting and regulating early years provision and registered childcare, under sections 49 and 50 of the Childcare Act 2006 in England. There is also a range of early years QI environmental rating scales and Local Authority QI schemes. Key research reports that have potentially influenced government policy guidance, frameworks and models of effective practice both here in the UK and internationally are featured in this chapter alongside viewpoints elicited from a number of influential actors that have made it their life work to focus on improving the quality of early years teaching and learning both in the UK and across the globe. The chapter concludes by asking the reader to question and reflect upon their own personal accountability for the delivery of 'high-quality' EY teaching and learning and the way that their practice has the potential to influence children's transition to school, progress through school and beyond into lifelong learning.

INTRODUCTION

The depth and breadth of the EYT/E's training and continuous professional development will support their teaching and the way that they reflect upon their own practice in order to affect QI in their school/setting. The EYT/E's personal practice must be deep-rooted in a secure understanding of high-quality Early Child Care and Education (ECE), child development and research-informed sources such as national policy, legislation and non-statutory frameworks and guidance. As a result, the EYT/E can justify to colleagues, parents and/or carers the rationalisation for their teaching, and their school/setting early years' policies and practice.

Whilst it may seem obvious that children need 'high-quality' teaching and learning experiences, it takes time for an EYT/E to develop their practice and understanding of what 'high-quality' teaching and learning actually means to them. It is the expectation that the EYT/E should be able to create, maintain and improve on their teaching in order to support children's learning and development in the long term. Their role must be viewed as a continuous journey based on a cycle of research, planning, implementation, reviewing and analysis involving children, parents and professionals. In practice, their role is to facilitate high-quality teaching and learning experiences with quality interactions between themselves and the children in their care, in stimulating indoor/outdoor environments with suitable equipment and resources. But before they can do this they need to be grounded in the knowledge skills and understanding that are pertinent to their role.

 —— **Points for reflection** ─────────────────

The quality of teaching and the way it impacts on the learning and development of children in England is a Key Focus of the Ofsted (2015b) Common Inspection Framework.

Ofsted's definition of outstanding quality teaching is:

- The quality of teaching is consistently of a very high quality.
- Practitioners have a clear understanding of how children learn.
- Children are provided with rich, varied and imaginative experiences.
- Practitioners complete assessments that are precise, fully focused, monitored and used to move the children on in their learning.
- Children consistently demonstrate Characteristics of Effective Learning.

Ideas for practice

High-quality provision in ECE may be secured by EYT/Es that are confident in:

Working together – Identify examples of working with colleagues or other professionals to support a child or children's learning and development.

Engaging with mums, dads and families – Give examples of times that you have engaged with parents or carers to support children's learning and development.

Understanding the importance of pedagogy and child development – How do you demonstrate your knowledge of this to your colleagues, parents, carers and other professionals?

Ensuring high expectations for children to realise the best outcomes – Provide examples to show how you have ensured high expectations of a child who achieved a best outcome.

Delivering high-quality practice and teaching that make a difference on a daily basis to children's outcomes – Demonstrate how you deliver or plan to deliver high-quality teaching that makes a difference to children's outcomes on a daily basis.

At the time of writing this chapter, the push towards the delivery of high-quality ECE both here in England and across the globe is receiving a considerable amount of attention. Two significant English research-informed studies that have the potential to influence the quality of the EYT/E's practice in the long term include the government's longitudinal Study of Early Education and Development (SEED, 2015, updated 2017), which is following 8,000 2-year-olds from across England through to the end of the National Curriculum Key Stage 1 (KS1) in an attempt to discover the critical features of high-quality ECE and how they may help to give children the best start in life. The second study, *Improving Quality in the Early Years: A Comparison of Perspectives and Measures* (Mathers et al., 2012) compares Ofsted inspections grounded in the Early Years Foundation Stage (EYFS) with other quality assessments such as the Early Childhood Environment Rating Scale (ECERS-R, Harms et al., 2005) and the Infant Toddler Environment Rating Scale (ITERS-R, Harms et al., 2006) and the revised ECERS-E (Sylva et al., 2010), as well as a range of other quality assurance schemes.

OFSTED VIEW OF QI

Examples of leading early years QI is offered in *Achieving and Maintaining High-Quality Early Years Provision – Getting It Right the First Time* (Ofsted, 2013). For the EYT/E, the report highlights the importance of them engaging in self-evaluation, reflective practice and the scrutiny of their own practice and that of others using a variety of sources, for example, feedback from Local Authority (LA) advisors; colleagues working in early years networks, settings/schools; and through the use of a range of quality assurance schemes. The most effective settings surveyed in the Ofsted report employed at least one teacher, with six settings employing at least one Early Years Professional (EYP), the predecessor to the EYT/E, and five settings having Early Years Professionals holding relevant early childhood studies (ECS) degrees.

 —— **Points for reflection** ———————————————

How many of the features of strong QI leadership featured below do you engage in and by what means?

- The ability to role-model good teaching with explanation of the theories behind your practice
- Encourage active membership of national early years organisations and professional associations
- Promote adult interactions with children in order to make the greatest impact on their learning
- Extend children's learning, developing their language, feeding in new vocabulary and challenge their thinking by emphasising the importance of listening carefully and thinking about the best time to intervene rather than just jump in
- Share frequent assessment information about children's progress with parents and encourage staff and parents to work together to help children to achieve
- Be clear about which aspects of teaching need improvement, encourage staff to reflect on the quality of their input, address any misunderstandings swiftly and use modelling and scaffolding, discussion, training and support to enhance good practice
- Plan fine-tuned activities based on what you want children to learn, making regular, and accurate use of quality observations moderated by others and assessments that identify the needs of individual children and groups who are most at risk of falling behind
- Track and regularly scrutinise the accuracy of assessments to ensure that activities are matched well to the learning needs of all the children.

Based on *Achieving and Maintaining High-Quality Early Years Provision – Getting It Right the First Time* (Ofsted, 2013).

QUALITY OUTCOMES

The relationship between the quality of early years education and outcomes that may arise from children's attendance in early childhood education (ECE) is considered by Hopkins et al. (2010: 5), who suggest that 'possible outcomes for children includes outcomes for parents, such as gaining employment; or outcomes for society, such as when early years providers also provide services for the whole community'. There is a growing body of evidence in support of 'the long-lasting benefits of early childhood education and care for children's development, together with the complementary benefits for parents and society' (OECD, 2017d). This correlation between children experiencing quality early years experiences and better social and economic prospects prompts governments to investment in early childhood education (ECE), which is a good thing!

In England, an EYT/E works within the Quality Assured (QA), EYFS (DfE, 2017a) curriculum framework which is designed to provide 'quality and consistency in all early years settings, so that every child makes good progress and no child gets left behind' DfE (2017a: 3). Ofsted will judge the quality and standards of the school/settings that the EYT/E works in. The EYT/E working in a school/setting that is eligible to deliver the free early education entitlement must be inspected by Ofsted, with inspections generally occurring on a 3-year cycle.

 Points for reflection

How do you support your school, setting or early years service to meet the descriptors that Ofsted (2015, updated 2017) use in the *Early Years Inspection Handbook* for outstanding teaching, learning and assessment, which are:

- Practitioners have high expectations for all children
- Teaching is consistently of a very high quality
- Practitioners use their expert knowledge of the EYFS and how children learn to provide rich, varied and imaginative experiences for them
- High-quality observations inform accurate assessment that includes all those involved in the child's learning and development
- Provision is planned meticulously and based on regular assessment of children's achievement
- Parents are engaged in their children's learning in the setting and at home
- The exceptional range of resources and activities provided reflect and value the diversity of children's experiences
- The extremely sharp focus on helping children to acquire the EYFS Prime Areas of Learning gives children a strong foundation.

It is not unusual for members of the early years workforce to feel anxious about Ofsted inspection. To help dispel common misconceptions about the inspection process Ofsted have produced a guide called *Early Years Inspections: Myths* (Ofsted, 2017), in order to reduce any concerns that the early years workforce may have about inspection. It is in the EYT/E's best interest to read such guides and understand that inspection is part of the QA process and that it is designed to help them raise the standard of the ECE in their school/setting.

Photo 5.1   High-Quality Outdoor learning in an urban setting

'Following the introduction of the free entitlement to early education in 1998, Ofsted has been responsible for inspecting the quality of education provided by all establishments eligible to deliver this, including those in the private and voluntary sectors' (Hopkins et al., 2010: 20). It is important for the EYT/E to know that Ofsted inspectors seek out evidence to evaluate *'what it is like to be a child in the provision'* (Ofsted, 2015, updated 2017: para. 144; emphasis added). In making their judgements about an early years school/setting, inspectors will consider whether the standard of education and care that is being offered is 'good or whether it exceeds good and is therefore outstanding. If it is not good, inspectors will consider whether it requires improvement or is inadequate' para. 144). Additionally, Ofsted will make a judgement about the effectiveness of the arrangements for safeguarding children in the EYT/E's school/setting.

Points for reflection

In England, during an Ofsted inspection, the inspector(s) will focus on the areas featured below and reflect on the impact that your teaching and provision makes across each of the areas listed:

- The progress all children make in their learning and development relative to their starting points and their readiness for the next stage of their education including, where appropriate, readiness for school
- The extent to which the learning and care that the setting provides meet the needs of the range of children who attend, including disabled children and those who have special educational needs
- Children's personal and emotional development, including whether they feel safe and are secure and happy
- Whether the requirements for children's safeguarding and welfare have been fully met and there is a shared understanding of and responsibility for protecting children
- The effectiveness of leadership and management in evaluating practice and securing continuous improvement that improves children's life chances.

Description of Ofsted outcomes

Grade 1: Outstanding

An outstanding school/setting that is highly effective in delivering outcomes that provide exceptionally well for all its children's needs.

Grade 2: Good

A good school/setting that is effective in delivering outcomes that provide well for all its children's needs. Pupils are well prepared for the next stage of their education, training or employment.

Grade 3: Requires improvement

A setting/school that requires improvement is not yet a good setting/school, but it is not inadequate and will receive a full inspection within 24 months from the date of this inspection.

Grade 4: Inadequate

A setting/school that has serious weaknesses is inadequate overall and requires significant improvement and will receive regular monitoring by Ofsted inspectors.

Special measures

A school/setting that is failing to give its pupils an acceptable standard of education with leaders, managers or governors not demonstrating that they have the capacity to secure the necessary improvement in the school will receive regular monitoring by Ofsted inspectors.

Source: Adapted from *Ofsted Early Years Inspection Handbook*, Ofsted (2015, updated 2017)

The findings of Mathers et al. (2012) also suggest that members of the LA workforce who support early years settings/schools to raise their standard of provision, believe that some managers are 'able to "sell" themselves and their setting much more than others which ... result[s] in better grades', also reported by Campbell-Barr and Leeson (2016). Interestingly, Mathers et al. (2012) suggest that LA workers perceive Ofsted grades awarded to many of the early years schools/settings that they support do not reflect their views and that in many cases it is much higher than they believe is deserved. Ofsted inspections, while a vital part of the quality improvement process for the EYT/E, 'cover only the minimum national standards, only take place over one day, once every three years, and put settings in one of only four broad categories of quality' (Reardon, 2013: 69), this is also confirmed by Mathers et al. (2012) and Campbell-Barr and Leeson (2016).

PREPARING FOR OFSTED

The EYT/E must reflect on the support that they have received from their LA, or any other colleagues to help them prepare for inspection. The EYT/E does not necessarily need to produce the Ofsted self-evaluation form (SEF) prior to inspection (Ofsted, 2015, updated 2017), however they are advised to be prepared to discuss the practice in the setting with the inspector. The EYT/E can show how the setting/school has improved since the last inspection by sign-posting evidence in the form of any written reports or notes of meetings held with LA advisors, in addition to the use of any quality assurance tools such as Early Childhood Environment Rating Scale (ECERS), the Infant Toddler Environmental Rating Scale (ITERS), or the Sustained Shared Thinking and Emotional Well-being (SSTEW) Scale for provision for 2–5-year-olds (Siraj et al., 2015), or indeed any other quality assurance measures used by the EYT/E, setting or school. Inspectors will ask the EYT/E and other staff about the quality of care and activities they provide, and how well the setting is meeting the learning needs of all children, so it is best to be prepared!

Ofsted (2017) says that it does not want to see a particular level or type of paperwork during an inspection. The EYT/E should use whatever approach to paperwork suits them, however it needs to be quality paperwork, very well presented and easily read. Some settings/schools are going over to digital recording; umpteen sticky notes does not hack it any more!

Each inspection is unique and inspectors will only ask the EYT/E to produce evidence that they consider appropriate to support their observation of teaching and learning. A list of paperwork that Ofsted may be interested in is listed in the Early Years Inspection Handbook (2015, updated 2017); however, it is very unlikely that an inspector will ask the EYT/E to produce all of these documents during an inspection.

 ── **Ideas for practice** ─────────────────────────────

In the research brief *Improving Quality in the Early Years* (Mathers et al., 2012), focus groups held with parents, providers and local authorities revealed:

- *Ofsted grades are too broad to provide a detailed measure of quality in childcare settings, and are best used alongside other existing quality assessments* – What 'quality assessment' tools do you use in addition to Ofsted findings to assess the quality of teaching and learning in your school/setting?
- *Ofsted ratings are currently used by many local authorities to determine which nurseries and preschools receive government early years funding for free childcare provision* – How are free childcare places allocated to your setting/school?
- *Many parents consulted felt that Ofsted reports did not provide all the information they needed to make a decision about choosing a childcare setting* – What information do you provide to parents to supplement the school/setting Ofsted report?

The EYT/E's attention to the findings in the research brief *Improving the Quality in the Early Years* (Mathers et al., 2012) informs them that their LA early years workforce will make a decision about any level of support or intervention required based on the EYT/E's school/setting Ofsted inspection results. The research brief also indicates that many LA workers believe that Ofsted does not 'capture a rich and full picture of quality'. One reason is that there is only a limited time on the day of the inspection for Ofsted inspectors to capture a 'snapshot' of the practice. The EYT/E must draw on practice-based evidence on the day of the inspection in order to discuss the quality of provision with the inspector. It is vitally important for the EYT/E not to create a smokescreen in an endeavour to stop inspectors capturing what the quality in the school/setting is really like.

HIGH-QUALITY ECE

The EYT/E's academic research and reading will very likely lead them to the highly significant work of Professor Iram Siraj and her colleagues, which over the past two decades has focused on improving the quality of ECE and has influenced much of today's practice. Of particular interest to the EYT/E, her work includes the following studies, amongst many others:

- *Effective Provision of Pre-School Education (EPPE)* (1996–2001, co-authored with Sylva, Melhuish and Sammons) – the first major longitudinal study, funded by the Department for Education and Employment (DfEE) to focus specifically on the effectiveness of ECE by tracking the development of 3,000 children in various types of pre-school education settings.
- *EPPE 3–11 study* (2003–2008, co-authored with Sylva, Sammons, Melhuish and Taggart) – funded by the Department for Children, Schools and Families (DCSF) to follow the same cohort of children from the original EPPE study.
- The *Effective Pre-school, Primary Project (EPPSE)* (2003–2014, co-authored with Sylva, Melhuish, Sammons and Taggart) – funded by the DCSF and the Department for Education (DfE), provided an additional extension to the EPPE study in order to follow the same cohort to the end of Key Stage 3 (age 14).
- *Researching Effective Pedagogy in the Early Years (REPEY)* (2002, co-authored with Sylva) – published by the Department for Education and Skills (DfES), studied 12 settings from the EPPE project, each chosen because their children had made excellent or good developmental progress over the pre-school period. The REPEY study developed the concept of Sustained Shared Thinking (SST).
- *Effective Pre-school, Primary and Secondary Education (EPPE/EPPSE 3–14)* (1996–2016, co-authored with Sylva, Melhuish, Sammons and Taggart) – funded by the Department for Children Schools and Families (DCSF) and the Department for Education (DfE). A major European longitudinal study that investigated the effectiveness of pre-school education and care in terms of children's cognitive and social-emotional development across different phases of education (pre-school, primary and secondary education) in England.
- *Sustained Shared Thinking and Emotional Well-being scale (SSTEW)* (2015, co-authored with Melhuish and Kingston) – funded by the Department for Education (DfE), considered adult–child interactions alongside the planning and organisation of learning spaces, to provide a deeper focus on the adult role.

EPPSE key findings

- Children who had experienced early years education gained higher English and Mathematics GCSE results and were more likely to have achieved five or more GCSEs at grades A*–C.

- Children who had experienced high-quality pre-school education were better at self-regulation, social behaviour and less inclined to hyperactivity.
- Children who had experienced high-quality pre-school settings were more likely to follow a post-16 academic path.

BENEFITS OF PRE-SCHOOL EDUCATION

The Institute for Fiscal Studies used EPPSE data to predict the future economic returns to society of investing in early years education. The study found that:

- Attending a pre-school setting increased educational attainment with the resulting increase in lifetime earnings that benefited the Exchequer.
- Attending a high-quality pre-school setting had an estimated lifetime earnings benefit to the individual of £26,788 and £35,993 for an average household.
- These increased earnings translate into a benefit to the Exchequer of £8,090 per household.

Wider effects of the EPPSE findings

- The EPPSE findings have been widely disseminated across the world and have been cited in reports by UNICEF and UNESCO;
- The EPPSE study changed thinking and practice in pre-school entitlement, pedagogy, and curriculum and teacher education in the UK;
- In the UK, the findings led to free provision of high-quality pre-schooling for all three- and four-year olds. This has been extended to free entitlement of the poorest 40% (approximately 260,000) [of] two-year olds.

Source: Adapted from The Effective Pre-School, Primary and Secondary Education project (EPPSE). www.ucl.ac.uk/ioe/research/featured-research/effective-pre-school-primary-secondary-education-project (accessed April 2017)

TRANSFORMATION OF ECE

The 'EPPE methods and findings have already transformed the nature of early years research as well as the architecture of early years services in diverse countries' (University of Oxford, 2017). The EYT/E can see that the policy focus on quality ECE has drawn significantly on the findings of the EPPE/EPPSE studies, which both identify various elements of process quality as being related to better outcomes. For example, when looking at the quality of adult–child verbal interactions, the authors found that more 'sustained shared thinking' was observed in settings where children made the most progress.

QI TOOLS AND PROCESSES

Mathers et al. (as cited in Hillman and Williams, 2015: 28) consider two dimensions of quality: 'structural factors' and 'process factors'. Mathers et al.'s structural factors include staff qualifications, adult/child ratios, the size of the provision and the type and amount of resources. Process factors focus on the interactions with children and families, the appropriateness of resources as well as characteristics of leadership and management. A wide variety of QI tools are available for the EYT/E to use to evaluate the quality of their ECE provision in order to improve on it and for research purposes. Chapter 4 on reflective practice and research-based inquiry provides more detailed information on the use of reflective tools and models to explore and initiate new ways of working.

In its survey of providers, the National Audit Office (NAO, 2016) found that despite Ofsted data being used by local authorities to identify settings with poor provision, they found other sources of information more useful in their quality assessments of providers. 'Defining quality is contentious ...' Hopkins et al. (2010: 64) found that 'Ofsted scores for early years settings did not predict children's later outcomes, however other QA schemes were able to do so'. While it is not possible to summarise all QI tools in this chapter, Box 5.1 provides examples of QI tools used by local authorities and ECE providers in England, and in other countries.

BOX 5.1

Examples of QI Tools (other than the ECERS/ITERS/SSTEW assessments)

Essex County Council enabling environment audit

Essex County Council has developed several templates for its schools to use when evaluating the learning environment in the Early Years Foundation Stage (EYFS).

Its enabling environment audit contains eight questions for settings to consider, along with space to note effective practice.

The questions include:

- Does planning reflect the interests and developmental needs of the children?
- Do children have daily access to a well-resourced indoor and outdoor environment?
- Do children appear happy, relaxed and confident in their environment?

Source: Essex County Council, http://dnn.essex.gov.uk/eycp/Resources.aspx (accessed 27 October 2017). Enabling environment audit (Word doc file) downloadable at http://bit.ly/2dRpTQn

Improving the learning environment in EYFS settings: The National Strategies (2008)

In 2008, the National Strategies produced a guidance document on improving the learning environment in EYFS settings, which is now archived (DCSF, 2008b). Although information in this document may not be in line with current policy, EYT/Es may find it useful in forming their own assessments. It features a learning environment audit, based around developing the indoor and outdoor environments, on pages 46–49.

Questions for the overall indoor environment include:

- Is the setting bright, well-organised and inviting to walk into?
- Are the resources and working areas clearly labelled – with words, pictures or real objects where appropriate?
- Do the resources reflect all families and cultures?

It also has questions for the outdoor environment, which cover areas such as whether:

- The area is well organised, inviting and challenging
- There are opportunities for children to be physical
- There is a number line and height chart

Source: http://webarchive.nationalarchives.gov.uk/20130404005529/https://www.education.gov.uk/publications/eOrderingDownload/DCSF-00669-2008.pdf (accessed 27 October 2017)

Lancashire County Council (LCC) Self-evaluation Tool

LCC EYFS toolkit for early years providers includes a self-evaluation tool, which can help the EYT/E and practitioners to highlight and celebrate successes ... and also to identify areas to develop.

There are sections on the environment on pages 3, 12 and 13. For example, you may wish to consider whether the resources in your school/setting are:

- **Focusing**: there are insufficient appropriate resources for play and storage
- **Developing**: there are sufficient appropriate resources for routine care and play
- **Establishing**: appropriate, high-quality resources which are developmentally appropriate and labelled

Source: www.lancashire.gov.uk/corporate/web/viewdoc.asp?id=8538 (accessed 27 October 2017)

(Continued)

OFSTED: Inspecting Registered Early Years Providers: Guidance for Inspectors (2015, updated April 2017)

Ofsted's Early Years Inspection Handbook describes the main activities inspectors undertake when they conduct inspections of early years providers in England under sections 49 and 50 of the Childcare Act 2006. The handbook also sets out the judgements inspectors will make and on which they will report.

Source: www.gov.uk/government/publications/school-inspection-handbook-from-september-2015 (accessed 27 October 2017)

The National Strategies | Early Years: Every Child a Talker: Guidance for English Language Lead Practitioners

Every Child a Talker (ECAT, DCSF, 2008c) offers resources that can help the EYT/E to:

- raise children's achievement in early language
- improvise the EYT/E skills and knowledge
- increase parental understanding and involvement

Source: www.foundationyears.org.uk/wp-content/uploads/2011/10/ecat_guidance_for_practitioners_12.pdf (accessed 27 October 2017)

The Bristol Standard

The Bristol Standard is a self-evaluation framework which can help the EYT/E to develop and improve the quality and effectiveness of their provision through an annual cycle of reflection. The self-evaluation framework is organised into ten dimensions to:

- support the process of continuous quality improvement
- evaluate one area at a time in a manageable way

Source: www.bristol.gov.uk/resources-professionals/bristol-standard (accessed 27 October 2017)

The National Quality Improvement Network (NQIN)

NQIN offers a forum to share best practice, policy and research updates between national and local networks and provides a focus on quality improvement.

Source: www.ncb.org.uk/what-we-do/our-priorities/early-years/our-early-childhood-unit (accessed 27 October 2017)

Professor Ferre Laevers: Process-Orientated Monitoring System

This approach encourages the EYT/E to use an instrument developed by a team based at the Research Centre for Experiential Education (Leuven University – Belgium) under the supervision of Dr Ferre Laevers. It is based on a conceptual framework that has been developed during the last decades in the context of innovative work in pre-school, primary, secondary and higher education. It uses two indicators of quality in this 'experiential' approach: 'well-being' and 'involvement'. Well-being refers to feeling at ease, being spontaneous and free of emotional tensions and is crucial to secure 'mental health'. Involvement refers to being intensely engaged in activities and is considered to be a necessary condition for deep-level learning and development.

Access this weblink to view Professor Ferre Laevers' Process-Orientated Monitoring System in practice: www.youtube.com/watch?v=SzZu_FI5_lc (accessed 15 November 2017)

There is a wide range of quality measurement tools and frameworks that the EYT/E can use to assess the quality of the ECE in their school/setting. Each one can be used to enhance provision at the same time as providing evidence of the school/setting performance. However, the EYT/E needs to be mindful of any quality assurance schemes that may be operating in the school/setting that they are based in. Many of those working across the early years sector express concerns about the number and variety of quality assurance schemes that are available, and ones that they adopt are sometimes not endorsed by central government in England today.

The best-known research-based QI tools include:

- **ECERS-R** (Harms et al., 2005) – designed to evaluate the quality of provision for children aged between 2½ and 5 years
- **ITERS-R** (Harms, et al., 2006) – designed to evaluate the quality of provision for children from birth to 2½ years

Both ECERS-R and ITERS-R can be used by the EYT/E to evaluate the following dimensions of quality:

- **Space and furnishings** (e.g. room layout, accessibility of resources, display)
- **Personal care routines** (e.g. welfare requirements such as health and safety and provision for sleeping)
- **Language and reasoning** (e.g. supporting children's communication, language and literacy development; critical thinking)
- **Activities** (e.g. provision of an exciting and accessible learning environment, resources to support specific types of play)

- **Interaction** (e.g. supervision, support for social interactions)
- **Programme structure** (e.g. opportunities for children to access their own curriculum, planning schedules/routines to meet children's needs)
- **Provision for parents and staff** (e.g. partnership with parents, staff training and development)

ECERS-R and ITERS-R are designed to measure the quality of provision in an early years setting/school as well as any associated improvement in quality over a period of time. An extension to the ECERS-R, an ECERS-Extension (ECERS-E) (Sylva, Siraj-Blatchford et al., 2010) was designed as part of the EPPE project. An example featuring an outline of this QI tool is illustrated in the case study below.

 Case study 5.1

An ITERS-R Audit Undertaken by an Early Years Teacher

Context

I observed what the staff did when they took the babies outside, and linked this to my widespread reading around the six areas of learning in the EYFS (Early Years Foundation Stage). These focus on providing more sensory experiences and developing the babies' acquisition of language skills. The EYFS says that staff should aim to take children outside at least once a day.

I administered the ITERS over a number of days and where appropriate in discussion with the room leaders, to ensure that I could fully understand and assess the setting's environment and the babies' needs. Using ITERS was effective as it enabled me to assess the quality of the provision.

When I fed back the findings of the ITERS audit, I was very happy with the initial comments and agreed actions to be undertaken by the practitioners to the suggestions/improvements I recommended. These included:

- ensuring a high level of supervision with regards to health and safety;
- providing a sheltered place to lay a rug on the grass for babies to be placed upon;
- giving babies the opportunity to crawl into sand pits and water, under supervision;
- letting babies explore the indoor and outdoor environment;
- singing with the babies outdoors and indoors;
- providing resources for babies to grasp, to pull themselves up onto and for low-level climbing to occur;
- providing objects outdoors that are 'bigger' than those provided inside;
- allowing babies to take 'safe risks';

- selecting books for the book area and monitoring their use as babies at this age range do have a tendency to 'mouth' the corners! Soft material and hardback books are best, and staff need to be prepared to throw them out and buy new ones when they become damaged.

There was an improvement to the interactions and communications with babies. Over time I witnessed that, for example, some of the practitioners began rolling the ball to some of the babies and were commenting on the sounds that objects being tapped together make. I placed highlighted photocopies of what needs to be actioned to achieve excellence all round so that the practitioners and room leaders can use these as a self-evaluation/development tool.

 Points for reflection

What are your views on these findings from provider focus groups in the *Improving Quality in the Early Years* study by Mathers et al.:

ECE providers believed Ofsted Inspections are not enough on their own to drive QI.

Some providers acknowledged they were more likely to engage in QI processes to get a good grade to attract parents.

Providers thought that the Ofsted report did not help parents to decide which settings to send their child to as the language was clinical and did not give a true impression of their setting.

There was widespread scepticism about whether Ofsted inspections could capture a true picture of the quality of their settings due to the limited time inspectors were able to spend observing their staff.

Those who managed settings in disadvantaged areas felt that the Ofsted inspection process often did not recognise the additional barriers they faced in delivering high-quality provision.

Some providers used alternative methods for communicating the quality of their setting to parents, for example a plaque on the wall showing they had successfully completed a local quality assurance scheme.

Source: Adapted from Mathers et al., 2012: 46. www.education.ox.ac.uk/wordpress/wp-content/uploads/2010/08/2.-Improving-quality-in-the-early-years.pdf (accessed 8 November 2017)

The Japanese philosophical principle of 'Kaizen', a Japanese word meaning continuous improvement, can be applied to the EYT/E by keeping thinking 'how can I improve my personal practice and support teams or individuals so that together we can make a difference?' (Reardon, 2013: 64). As a philosophy, the key to Kaizen for the EYT/E is in gaining involvement and a commitment to QI which means that everyone should be striving to do everything better every day regardless of their position. This links nicely to the EYFS (DfE, 2017a) vision of quality improvement that should be seen as a continuous cycle based on planning; implementing; reviewing and analysing. It must be viewed as a never-ending journey involving children, parents and professionals. The EYT/E role is to reflect on how to put in place systems for self-evaluation, which identify and agree improvement priorities and plans to implement and review any difference that the actions have made.

 Ideas for practice

How the SSTEW Scale Supports Quality Improvement (Early Childhood Matters – 4Children Conference, 10 March 2015)

The SSTEW scales build on the ECERS-R and ECERS-E/ITERS-R by focusing on the pedagogy within the setting and relating well to the EYT/E role in supporting learning and development and the high-quality interactions with and between children.

1. View this presentation featuring the SSTEW scales on this weblink: www.foundationyears.org.uk/files/2015/03/Eary-Childhood-Matters-a-presentation-by-Iram-and-Denise.pdf

    Presenters at the conference suggest that some staff/settings may not be ready for all of the subscales featured in SSTEW; particularly those relating to critical thinking, assessment for learning and supporting and extending language and communication.

2. How confident are you about your knowledge of child development and appropriate practice to be able to use them?

The EYT/E must be responsive to the changes in government direction and policy. In an endeavour to deliver quality ECE there is a lot to be learnt from the work of the quality gurus and their theories, by interpreting their findings and beliefs to suit our purposes. The work of American leadership gurus who featured in 1950s Japan, for example, Joseph Juran, W. Edwards Deming and Armand Feigenbum; the Japanese quality gurus who developed and extended the early American quality ideas and models, such as Kaoru Ishikawa, Genichi Taguchi and Shigeo Shingo; and the 1970–80s American Western gurus, notably Philip Crosby and Tom Peters, was all aimed at corporate business. The business of ECE is to provide quality early years provision. The quality gurus developed QA tools such as the Plan, Do, Check cycle, the Pareto Analysis, cause and effect diagrams, process control charts, management by walking about (MBWA), the McKinsey 7–S Framework, to name a few. Just because they were developed for industry does not mean to say that they cannot be adopted to use as early years quality improvement tools. For example, the concept of the Pareto Analysis, which is best described as the '80/20 rule', meaning that, if you are not careful, 80% of your time is spent on only 20% of what you are actually accountable for.

This chapter concludes by urging the EYT/E to develop the ability to recognise the important role that they play in supporting and leading high-quality provision in their school/setting. Their role is to understand that what they do and the way that they create, maintain and continuously improve on their teaching affects the quality of children's learning and development. It is their duty to give babies and young children the highest-quality ECE possible, to help them on their journey; achieve higher outcomes at school; and at the same time develop the social, emotional and cognitive abilities they need for life-long learning. The EYT/E must view QI as a never-ending journey and most certainly not as a destination; it must involve children, parents, professionals and the community at large.

 **Key points**

- Feel a sense of pride and ownership in the QI process.
- Engage and encourage others to commit to ongoing self-reflection and evaluation.
- Familiarise yourself with a wide range of QI tools to measure quality.
- Plan high-quality improvements on a continual basis.
- Identify and agree QI priorities for the delivery of high-quality EY teaching and learning.
- Create plans to implement QI priorities.
- Build in time-measured reviews to assess the quality of EY provision and practice as well as any impact made.
- Be mindful of inspection requirements and celebrate success.

FURTHER READING

Barber, J. (2017) *Quality of Teaching, Learning and Assessment in the EYFS*. London: Practical Pre-School.

This book explores ways of meeting Ofsted's expectations.

Campbell-Barr, V. and Leeson, C. (2016) *Quality and Leadership in the Early Years: Research, Theory and Practice*. London: Sage.

This book helps to unpick what is meant by the term 'quality' in the context of how to lead, in order to develop and achieve quality.

Reed, M. and Canning, N. (2012) *Implementing Quality Improvement and Change in the Early Years*. London: Sage.

This book examines the importance of reflective practice and the leadership attributes required in the workplace to effect change.

Slaughter, E. (2016) *Quality in the Early Years*. Maidenhead: Open University Press.

This book provides more detailed examples of providing 'quality early years practice' from the use of the environment, to policies, working with vulnerable children and babies to curriculum delivery and the use of research.

USEFUL WEB RESOURCES

The Foundation Years

www.foundationyears.org.uk

The Foundation Years QI section provides evidence to suggest that 'high-quality' EY practice has a lasting impact on children's outcomes, future learning and life chances.

Ofsted Early Years Inspection Handbook

www.gov.uk/government/publications/early-years-inspection-handbook-from-september-2015

Ofsted inspectors use this handbook (2015, revised 2017) when inspecting early years providers.

The National Children's Bureau – National Quality Improvement Network (NQIN)

www.ncb.org.uk/what-we-do/our-priorities/early-years/our-early-childhood-unit

This site explains how NQIN supports early years QI managers, policy-makers and extended services to improve outcomes for young children and their families.

Well-being and Involvement in Care Settings: A Process-oriented Self-evaluation Instrument

www.kindengezin.be/img/sics-ziko-manual.pdf

This site provides detailed information about 'Well-being and Involvement' environmental rating scales from Ferre Laevers' team at the Research Centre for Experimental Education, Leuven University.

Two-Year-Olds in England: an Exploratory Study

http://tactyc.org.uk/wp-content/uploads/2014/11/TACTYC_2_year_olds_Report_2014.pdf

This study from TACTYC published in 2014 explores dimensions of quality that are important for 2-year-old children's development.

HighScope

https://highscope.org/training

This site provides further information about the use of the HighScope curriculum and assessment tools.

The Effective Pre-School, Primary and Secondary Education Project (EPPSE)

www.ucl.ac.uk/ioe/research/featured-research/effective-pre-school-primary-secondary-
education-project

This link provides an overview of the UK's first major study to focus on the effectiveness of early years education.

Improving Quality in the Early Years

www.education.ox.ac.uk/wordpress/wp-content/uploads/2010/08/2.-Improving-quality-
in-the-early-years.pdf

This study by Sandra Mathers, Rosanna Singler and Arjette Karemaker (2012) consolidates some of the measures used to identify 'high quality' in the early years, to include Ofsted, Environmental Rating Scales and LA QI schemes.

 **Online resources**

Visit https://study.sagepub.com/education to find a selection of scholarly journal articles chosen to support each chapter.

6

PLANNING FOR EFFECTIVE TEACHING AND LEARNING IN THE EARLY YEARS (EY)

DENISE REARDON

Chapter overview

This chapter invites the reader to consider how their teaching has the potential to foster a love of learning at the start of the child's learning journey. This chapter explores the central role of the Early Years Teacher and Educator (EYT/E) in planning for effective teaching and learning in the early years. Key features to be explored in this chapter include balancing teaching and play with statutory government policies and frameworks; the cyclic nature of child observation; assessment and planning; the sharing of information and learning between parents/carers and the EYT/E; the practice of formative and summative assessment and the way that EYT/Es use their knowledge and understanding of play, learning and child development to assess the stage the child is functioning at and how this information is used to form a basis for planning purposeful teaching and learning activities. The chapter concludes by giving consideration to the child, family and school's readiness for the child's transition to the next phase in their learning journey – starting school.

PLAY AND EARLY LEARNING

The developmental and educational benefits of play in babies and young children's healthy intellectual, emotional and social development are universally acknowledged. The area of 'play' has been researched for well over a century by many eminent researchers, philosophers and social scientists from a range of professions and disciplines. Chapter 3, 'Early Years Movers and Shakers', explores many of those that have influenced today's practice. Learning through play in the early years provides opportunities for babies and young children to foster a love of learning, grow, develop and build strong relationships with others. The benefits of experiencing effective early learning are gathering a huge momentum across the UK and internationally and, as a consequence, there is much written and published about learning through play (see, for example, EPPE, Moyles, 2006; Broadhead et al., 2010; Whitebread et al., 2012). The United Nations (2013) promotes 'the right of the child to rest, leisure, play, recreational activities, cultural life and the arts'.

Key messages drawn from this for the EYT/E are to:

- allow children to play freely by themselves or with other children;
- listen to children's voices while they play;
- create manmade and natural environments that facilitate play;
- encourage physical activities, dexterity, balancing safety and discovery;
- expose children to creativity and cultural activities.

Whilst there is a vast array of research and publications available for the EYT/E and other professionals to read and digest, tensions exist between what is on offer and the 'pressures to "cover" the prescribed curriculum, meet government imposed standards etc.' (Whitebread et al., 2012: 3.1). Balancing the desire to give children the freedom to play spontaneously against government policies and frameworks is no easy task, it's all about defining the nature of play, its purposes and the pedagogical approach to be taken. Chapter 2 examines a principled pedagogical approach to Teaching and Learning in the Early Years.

 **Point for reflection**

How do you provide opportunities for children to play freely with regards to any statutory policies and frameworks that you work within?

The EYFS framework (DfE, 2017a) offers 'prime' areas that run through and support learning across a number of 'specific' areas of development. They are fundamental to stimulating children's interest in learning and building relationships. The 'specific' areas contain the essential skills and knowledge that grow out of the 'prime' areas, and provide important contexts for the child's learning and development. Interrelated to the 'prime' and 'specific' areas of learning and development there are Early Learning Goals (ELGs), which are used by EYT/Es to assess whether or not the child has met each aspect by the end of the Foundation Stage.

At the time of writing this chapter the Department for Education announced that 'it is looking at the feasibility of reducing the number of Early Learning Goals (ELGs) that are assessed, and limiting this to the three prime areas (Communication and Language, Physical Development, and Personal, Social and Emotional Development) and the specific areas of mathematics and literacy' (Nursery World, 2017). Chapter 12 addresses the nature of 'change' and the statutory duty imposed upon the EYT/E to keep abreast of any new government frameworks, policies and initiatives.

Table 6.1 provides an example of the way in which the prime and specific areas of development can be linked to ELGs.

In England, EYT/Es have a statutory duty under the Early Years Foundation Stage (DfE, 2017a) to deliver the three 'prime' areas and four 'specific' areas of learning and development featured in Table 6.1. The three 'prime' areas run through and support learning across the EYFS four 'specific' areas. They are fundamental to stimulating children's interest in learning and building relationships. The four 'specific' areas contain the essential skills and knowledge that grow out of the 'prime' areas, and provide important contexts for the child's learning and development. Interrelated to the 'prime' and 'specific' areas of learning and development are 17 Early Learning Goals (ELGs), also featured in Table 6.1. The ELGs are used by EYT/Es to assess whether or not the child has met each aspect by the end of the Foundation Stage.

PLANNING EARLY LEARNING

The EYT/E's pedagogical knowledge of early years practice combined with their knowledge of child development is used within their role to assess whether or not the learning and development needs of the children in their care are being met. Planning for successful early learning is extremely complex, it is a bit like the chicken and the egg idiom, a situation in which it is impossible to say which came first. Each stage of the 'Assessment and Planning Cycle' is dependent on the cyclic nature of the process, as illustrated in Figure 6.1 (p. 105). Fundamentally

Table 6.1 Linking prime and specific areas of development to Early Learning Goals (ELGs)

Prime and specific areas of learning and development	Early Learning Goals (ELGs) To be assessed at the end of the EYFS
Prime Areas	
Communication and Language Provide a rich language environment; to develop children's confidence and skills in expressing themselves; and to speak and listen in a range of situations	1. **Listening and Attention** – Listen attentively in a range of situations, for example, listen to stories, accurately anticipating key events, and respond to what they hear with relevant comments, questions or actions, pay attention to what others say and respond appropriately, while engaged in another activity 2. **Understanding** – Follow instructions involving several ideas or actions, answer 'how' and 'why' questions about their experiences and in response to stories or events 3. **Speaking** – Express themselves effectively, showing awareness of listeners' needs, use past, present and future forms accurately when talking about events that have happened or are to happen in the future, develop own narratives and explanations by connecting ideas or events
Physical Provide opportunities for children to be active and interactive, develop their coordination, control, and movement, understand the importance of physical activity, and making healthy choices in relation to food	4. **Moving and Handling** – Show good control and coordination in large and small movements, move confidently in a range of ways, safely negotiating space, handle equipment and tools effectively, including pencils for writing 5. **Health and Self-Care** – Know the importance for good health of physical exercise and a healthy diet, talk about ways to keep healthy and safe, manage own basic hygiene and personal needs successfully, including dressing and going to the toilet independently
Personal, Social and Emotional Help children to develop a positive sense of themselves, and others, form positive relationships and develop respect for others, develop social skills and learn how to manage their feelings, understand appropriate behaviour in groups and to have confidence in their own abilities	6. **Self-Confidence and Self-Awareness** – Confident to try new activities, say why they like some activities more than others, confident to speak in a familiar group, talk about their ideas, and choose the resources they need for their chosen activities, say when they do or don't need help 7. **Managing Feelings and Behaviour** – Talk about how they and others show feelings, talk about their own and others' behaviour, and its consequences, know that some behaviour is unacceptable, work as part of a group or class, and understand and follow rules, adjust their behaviour to different situations, and take changes of routine in their stride 8. **Making Relationships** – Play cooperatively, taking turns with others, take account of one another's ideas about how to organise their activity, show sensitivity to others' needs and feelings, and form positive relationships with adults and other children

Prime and specific areas of learning and development	Early Learning Goals (ELGs) To be assessed at the end of the EYFS
Specific Areas	
Literacy	9. **Reading** – Read and understand simple sentences, use phonic knowledge to decode regular words and read them aloud accurately, read some common irregular words, demonstrate an understanding when talking with others about what they have read
Link sounds and letters and to begin to read and write, given access to a wide range of reading materials (books, poems, and other written materials) to ignite their interest	10. **Writing** – Use phonic knowledge to write words in ways that match their spoken sounds, write some irregular common words and sentences which can be read by themselves and others with some words spelt correctly and others phonetically plausible
Mathematics	11. **Numbers** – Count reliably with numbers from one to 20, place them in order and say which number is one more or one less than a given number, use quantities and objects, add and subtract two single-digit numbers and count on or back to find the answer, solve problems, including doubling, halving and sharing
Provide opportunities to develop and improve skills in counting, understanding and using numbers, calculating simple addition and subtraction problems; and to describe shapes, spaces and measures	12. **Shape, Space and Measures** – Use everyday language to talk about size, weight, capacity, position, distance, time and money to compare quantities and objects and to solve problems, recognise, create and describe patterns, explore characteristics of everyday objects and shapes and use mathematical language to describe them
Understanding the World	13. **People and Communities** – Talk about past and present events in their own lives and in the lives of family members, know that other children don't always enjoy the same things, and are sensitive to this, know about similarities and differences between themselves and others, and among families, communities and traditions
Guiding children to make sense of their physical world and their community through opportunities to explore observe and find out about people, places, technology and the environment	14. **The World** – Know about similarities and differences in relation to places, objects, materials and living things, talk about the features of their own immediate environment and how environments might vary from one to another, make observations of animals and plants and explain why some things occur, and talk about changes
	15. **Technology** – Recognise that a range of technology is used in places such as homes and schools, select and use technology for particular purposes
Expressive Arts and Design	16. **Exploring and Using Media and Materials** – sing songs, make music and dance, and experiment with ways of changing them, safely use and explore a variety of materials, tools and techniques, experimenting with colour, design, texture, form and function
Enabling children to explore and play with a wide range of media and materials, as well as providing opportunities and encouragement for sharing their thoughts, ideas and feelings through a variety of activities in art, music, movement, dance, role-play, and design and technology	17. **Being Imaginative** – Use what they have learnt about media and materials in original ways, thinking about uses and purposes, represent own ideas, thoughts and feelings through design and technology, art, music, dance, role play and stories

Interconnect the 'prime' and 'specific' areas of learning and development with the following three 'Characteristics of Effective Learning':

- Playing and exploring
- Active learning
- Creating and thinking critically

Source: Adapted from the Statutory Framework for the Early Years Foundation Stage (DfE, 2017a)

any assessment and planning cycle followed by an EYT/E working in schools/settings should include the following dimensions:

1. Planning of well-researched, informed, inclusive and developmentally appropriate learning and play experiences.
2. Establishing a purposeful, accessible, enabling, well-resourced and safe learning environment.
3. Adopting an appropriate teaching/facilitating style.
4. Skilful observation of the children engaged in planned and unplanned early learning and play experiences with opportunities for extended child-initiated learning.
5. Engagement in reflective practice to make informed assessments and records of individual children's outcomes, and levels of attainment and progress.
6. Revisiting the planning stage to refine, consolidate or extend individual children's learning and development accordingly.

Photo 6.1 Purposeful play and learning – enjoying mark making with natural materials

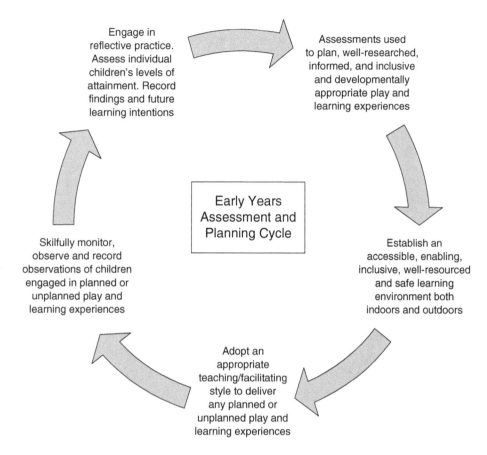

Figure 6.1 Assessment and Planning Cycle

FORMATIVE AND SUMMATIVE ASSESSMENT

Using both formative and summative assessment, based on observing children's play, learning and development is an integral part of the EYT/E role. Formative assessment involves undertaking observations of babies and young children on a daily or regular basis to identify what they have learnt and what needs to be done to move them on in their learning and development. Summative assessments take place twice during the time a child spends in the Foundation Stage. Traditionally, the first summative assessment takes place when a child is aged between 24 and 36 months. The second summative assessment is undertaken when a child is generally in the final term of the Reception class and is called the Early Years Foundation Stage Profile (EYFSP). At the time of writing this chapter the government has reported on its consultation of primary assessment in England, suggesting that the EYFSP will be retained and improved, to include a review of supporting guidance, in an attempt to cut teachers' and educators' workload (see DfE, 2017d for a link to access the consultation response).

Formative assessments are used by EYT/E to inform a child's summative assessment. The outcomes of the child's first summative assessment are recorded by the EYT/E and discussed with the parents/carers. This summative assessment is used to identify a child's strengths and their learning needs and is generally called a progress check.

 —— **Points for reflection** ————————————————————————

Review the progress check featured below and identify the child's strengths and areas for development.

The aims of the EYFS progress check are to:

- review a child's development progress in the EYFS three prime areas;
- ensure that parents have a clear picture of their child's development;
- enable practitioners and parents to understand the child's needs and plan activities to meet them;
- note areas where a child is progressing well and identify any areas where progress is less than expected;
- describe actions the setting intends to take to address any developmental concerns (including working with parent and other professionals where appropriate).

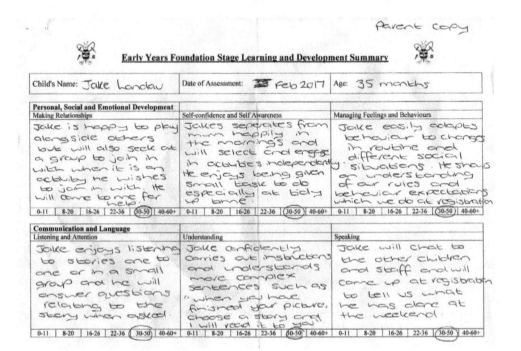

Parent copy

Early Years Foundation Stage Learning and Development Summary

Child's Name: Jake Landau   Date of Assessment: 23 Feb 2017   Age: 35 months

Personal, Social and Emotional Development

Making Relationships	Self-confidence and Self Awareness	Managing Feelings and Behaviours
Jake is happy to play alongside others but will also seek out a group to join in with when it is an activity he wishes to join in with. He will come to me for help.	Jakes seperates from mum happily in the mornings and will select and engage in activities independently. He enjoys being given small task to do especially at tidy up time.	Jake easily adapts behaviour to change in routine and different social situations. He shows an understanding of our rules and behaviour expectations which we do at registration
0-11	8-20	16-26	22-36	(30-50)	40-60+	0-11	8-20	16-26	22-36	(30-50)	40-60+	0-11	8-20	16-26	22-36	(30-50)	40-60+

Communication and Language

Listening and Attention	Understanding	Speaking
Jake enjoys listening to stories one to one or in a small group and he will answer questions relating to the story when asked.	Jake confidently carries out instructions and understands more complex sentences such as "when you have finished your picture, choose a story and I will read it to you"	Jake will chat to the other children and staff and will come up at registration to tell us what he has done at the weekend.
0-11	8-20	16-26	22-36	(30-50)	40-60+	0-11	8-20	16-26	22-36	(30-50)	40-60+	0-11	8-20	16-26	22-36	(30-50)	40-60+

Early Years Foundation Stage Learning and Development Summary

Physical Development		
Moving and Handling	Health and Self-care	
Jake moves his body in a range of ways such as crawling, jumping and slithering. He can catch a large ball when thrown to him.	Jake can identify his own coat at play time and will attempt to pull down the zip to take it off. Not yet toilet trained.	
0-11 8-20 16-26 22-36 (30-50) 40-60+	0-11 8-20 16-26 (22-36) 30-50 40-60+	

Keyperson's Comments
Jake has settled in really well at Busy Bees and comes in happily each morning. He is a happy little boy who shows curiosity and fascination with the toys that we have on offer. He is always willing to have a go at our craft/cooking activities and likes to show me what he has made. He shares the toys nicely and understands the need to take turns sometimes. He will come to me if he needs help or is upset. Jake is clearly enjoying his time with Busy Bees and it is a joy to watch him play.

 Early Years Foundation Stage Learning and Development Summary

Next Steps at Busy Bees		
support Jake with name tracing and number recognition.	support and encourage Jake with his toilet training when mum thinks he's ready.	observe and work with Jake on pronunciation of some words.

Parent/Carer's Comments
We are really pleased and very happy with the progress Jake has made since joining Busy Bees. It is great to see him forming friendships. Jake is very settled and always pleased to see his B.B. teachers and friends. We agree with all the comments made by Jakes key-person and will continue working with her on Jakes development.

Next Steps at Home		
20/3/17 we started really introducing toilet training with a few hours each day in big-boy pants.	encourage Jakes correct pronunciation of words he struggles with	introducing Jake to the phonics using the songs. The song of sounds and a poster on his bedroom wall.
		Kirsten Lindley 22/3/17.

Figure 6.2 Example of a progress check

Note: The EYFSP is currently under review and may be subject to significant change

The second EYFS summative assessment, the EYFSP, is undertaken by the EYT/E at the end of the child's time in the EYFS. The EYFSP is used to summarise the child's achievements against any ELGs. The EYT/E compiles a report and shares the results with the child's parents/carers informing them whether or not their child has met, exceeded or has not yet reached the expected levels of development and is deemed to be 'emerging'. If a child attends more than one setting/school the EYFSP must be completed by the school where the child spends most of their time. If a child moves to a new school during the academic year, the original school must send their assessment of the child's level of development against the early learning goals. The EYT/E will need to give a copy of the EYFSP to the school Year 1 teacher together with a short commentary on the child's skills and abilities in relation to the EYFS 'three key characteristics of effective learning' (see Figures 6.1 and 6.2). The EYFSP informs a dialogue between Reception and Year 1 teachers about each child's stage of development and learning needs and assists with the planning of activities in the National Curriculum, Key Stage 1.

 —— **Points for reflection**

Characteristics of effective learning

How do you plan and guide children's activities to allow:

- **Playing and exploring** - investigating and experiencing things, and 'having a go'?
- **Active learning** - enjoying, concentrating and persevering and being proud of achievements?
- **Creating and thinking critically** - discovering and developing own ideas, making links between ideas, and developing ways of doing things?

CHILD OBSERVATION AND ASSESSMENT

Child observation is widely acknowledged to be an essential and fundamental part of the EYT/E role as well as being an integral part of their school/setting's assessment and planning cycle. As part of the assessment process, parents and carers should always be encouraged to share their own observations of their child's progress. Child observation is a vital tool in understanding young children as learners and assessing the child's level of development in the EYFS; it is an integral part of the Assessment and Planning Cycle (Figure 6.1). Child observations provide a strong basis in which to engage in reflective practice. EYT/E observations involve skilfully watching babies and young children's movements, expressions, gestures, actions and behaviours, and listening to their babble, talk and interactions with other children and adults. Types of observational practice include making unstructured observations where everything that is happening is recorded; or systematic structured observations that are planned in advance where the person observing is acting as an objective observer. Very often, babies and young children can be observed by the EYT/E joining in with their play or by observing how they interact with others. Opportunities also arise during everyday conversations, for example during meal times, show and tell, story time, or while asking lines of open ended questions during their play. The EYT/E as observer should always adopt a friendly, sensitive and respectful manner towards the children and whatever activity they are engaged in. It is essential for the EYT/E to observe children in their play in a range of situations both indoors and outdoors, during planned and unplanned activities to inform their planning against the prime and specific areas of learning.

 Points for reflection

There are a wide range of observation methods and tools that can be used to assess the child's learning and development needs in the EYFS (DfE, 2017a), for example:

- Learning diaries
- Time sampling
- The target child
- Sociograms and histograms
- Narrative observation
- Event sampling
- Audiovisuals/digital media recordings to capture content specific information
- Learning stories as a narrative of the events that occurred
- Work samples, for example, drawings, painting, cutting, writing etc.

You may also be familiar with:

- The 'Mosaic Approach' (Clark and Moss, 2017), which is a way of listening and involving children (see Chapter 9)
- The Leuven scales to assess children's emotional well-being and involvement (Professor Ferre Laevers, 1994) (see Chapter 3)
- Accounting Early for Lifelong Learning (AcE) Programme (Pascal and Bertram, 2008) to assess children's social, emotional and dispositions to learning
- Bristol Every Child a Talker (BECAT) to identify children who need additional support with: listening, understanding, social and expressive language development.

1. Reflect on the child observational methods that you use in your own practice.
2. Research a new method to use and share the findings with your colleagues.

Familiarising oneself with a variety of different observation tools and methods will assist the EYT/E to identify the best possible approach to find out about babies and young children's interests, skills, abilities and needs and at the same time provide information towards the child's records. Undertaking observations, interpreting them and using them to plan for the child's future learning and development helps to provide a well-rounded and holistic picture of the child.

Non-statutory guides such as Early Years Outcomes (DfE, 2013b) and Development Matters (Early Education, 2012) can be used by the EYT/E to help them understand child development and use as part of the assessment and planning cycle (Figure 6.1). This type of guide supports the assessment of children's progress and help to identify the next steps in children's learning. They can be used to make best-fit judgements about whether a child is showing typical development for their age, may be at risk of delay or is developmentally ahead for their age.

PLANNING

Research informs EYT/E that right from birth, children are strong, resilient, competent, motivated and confident learners. They are able to explore, test their ideas, solve problems and try to make sense of their world through their senses. Planning meaningful play and learning activities means providing lots of first-hand experiences and experiential and active learning opportunities. Planning must also provide opportunities to promote children's independence and autonomy, encourage them to take risks and take charge of their own learning, initiate ideas and make decisions. Learning for babies and young children needs to take place in the social context with lots of talking and listening seen as pivotal in the learning process. Early Years Teachers and Educators must also plan learning to encourage babies and young children to communicate in a variety of ways and value their first/home language and cultural heritage (see Chapter 7). Learning cannot take place unless children's emotional needs are met (see Chapter 8) and they feel safe, secure and able to take risks.

To inform their planning, the EYT/E should work in partnership with parents/carers and seek their perceptions of their child and find out about any interests and strengths that their child may bring to the school/setting. Planning effective learning and teaching opportunities requires EYT/E to have a firm understanding and an awareness of babies' and young children's:

- Developmental milestones
- Patterns of behaviour
- Emotions, feelings, needs and interests
- Patterns and schemas of play

EYT/E planning should be personalised to the individual baby or child's interests and level of ability and at the same time offer challenging and achievable learning opportunities. They should engage in planning quality interactions that scaffold and prompt babies and young children's thinking, interests, strengths and lines of questions. Bodrova (2008) found that in scaffolding children's make-believe play it made a positive impact not only on the play itself but also on the child's development of early academic skills.

Idea for practice

Research the Vygotsky principle of 'scaffolding' on this weblink: https://youtu.be/9eSgt6r Stzgfor

Scaffolding for the EYT/E means skilfully observing opportunities to step in and help a baby or young child resolve a problem, carry out an activity, or achieve something that is beyond their level of capability. 'Scaffolding' babies and young children's learning means modelling the skill while they are trying something out, giving them clues and asking them appropriate questions, and then just as soon as they master the skill you withdraw your support and let them take over!

The English Study of Early Education and Development (SEED) reported good practice in relation to curriculum planning when practitioners:

- were grounded in the EYFS framework but tailored it to meet individual needs;
- capitalised on children's interests in order to achieve learning outcomes;
- were informed by on-going assessment;
- involved effective staff communication at all levels and regular evaluation through observation and staff discussion. (Callanan et al., 2017)

Planning learning opportunities and activities that encourage and support babies and young children to interact with one another, practise language, develop emotional well-being, ask questions, take and evaluate risks, develop resilience and have ownership for their learning are all part of the EYT/E role. Making sure that the environment is safe, calm, purposeful, challenging and supportive to all children's learning and development is also of paramount importance. EYT/E should plan a meaningful curriculum that provides the tools babies and young children need to succeed throughout their lives, regardless of culture, social class, gender, physical and cognitive capabilities and beliefs. Regular monitoring and evaluation of children's developmental milestones enables EYTE's to adjust their teaching in response to any areas of the child's learning and development that may be identified.

PLANNING SYSTEMS

Effective planning is essential if children are to make progress and learn through their play. Planning is approached by schools/settings in different ways and EYT/E should identify and follow whatever planning system is adopted by the school/setting that they are working in. The most familiar method used in schools/settings includes the use of short-term, weekly and long-term plans. Planning proformas also differ from school to school and setting to setting, however, the underlying principles are the same. Individual child observations, group observations, observations of children's interest and parent's contributions should be used to inform their planning. This information assists with the planning of activities and experiences that are based on the child's stage of development and learning needs. In England, long-term planning is often used to chart the learning opportunities for the whole year and ensure that each of the EYFS (DfE, 2017a) 'prime and specific' areas of learning and development are covered. Planning allows the EYT/E to:

- Consider the way that the indoor/outdoor learning environment is to be used and set up.
- Identify themes to be developed.
- Decide what equipment and resources are required.
- Use routines as a learning opportunity, plan festivals, outings, fund raising and other events.

Planning can be a challenge; it must be child-led and linked to the child's level of development and current interests. It must be flexible and easily adapted, not planned months in advance! It is advisable to evaluate and monitor all plans, both indoors and outdoors, to see if they are working and whether or not they need to be changed in response to the child/children's current needs and interests and make any adaptations to the indoor/outdoor environment as a result.

READINESS FOR SCHOOL

Early education policies and frameworks vary from country to country; whichever approach to early education is favoured will influence the way in which childcare professionals, teachers and parents prepare children for 'school readiness' in that country (PACEY, 2013: 3). However, a dichotomy exists between how governments and early years communities and parents perceive the purpose of early years education to be in preparing children to be ready for school. In England, the EYFS (DfE, 2017a) is based on the premise that it prepares children to be ready for school and life in general. The terminology 'school readiness' is seen by Whitebread and Bingham (2011), to be 'attractive to governments as it seemingly delivers children into primary school ready to conform to classroom procedures and even able to perform basic reading and writing skills'. This implies the purpose of early education is preparation for school rather than for 'life'.

Whilst Pascal and Bertram (2010) suggest that 'school readiness' is tantamount to 'life ready', the term 'school readiness' undervalues the role of early childhood education. PACEY (2013: 1), believe that the term 'school ready' relates to developing children's ability to:

- Have strong social skills
- Cope emotionally with being separated from their parents
- Become relatively independent in their own personal care
- Have a curiosity about the world and a desire to learn

Whilst politicians, academics, educationalists and parents agree to differ about a consistent definition of 'school readiness' (Graue, 2006; Maxwell and Clifford, 2004; Pianta et al., 2007), the Accounting Early for Lifelong Learning (AcE, 2010) project distinguishes 'school readiness' to be the way children learn and develop in the following four key areas:

1. Language development and communication skills
2. Attitudes and dispositions
3. Social competence and self-esteem
4. Emotional well-being

The consequences of this for the EYT/E is that preparing children to be ready for school is not just about teaching the academic skills such as numeracy and literacy but it is also about directing teaching activities to develop children's emotional wellbeing and language development (PACEY, 2013; Pascal and Bertram, 2010; UNICEF, 2012). Chapter 8, on promoting babies' and young children's personal, social and emotional well-being explores this topic in more detail. Chapter 7 explores the important aspects of developing children's language and communication skills.

UNICEF (2012) considers the term 'school readiness' to mean not only how ready the children are for school, but also how ready the school and parents are, for example:

- **Ready children**, focusing on children's learning and development
- **Ready schools**, focusing on the school environment along with practices that foster and support a smooth transition for children into primary school and advance and promote the learning of all children
- **Ready families**, focusing on parental and caregiver attitudes and involvement in their children's early learning and development and transition to school

The implications for EYT/E are that all three of these dimensions are equally important and work in tandem which each other. Transition between an early years setting and a school is a sensitive time for children and their families; it requires the EYT/E to become the envoy between the child, their family and the teacher working in the school. The importance of working collaboratively with teachers in schools and the child's parents/carers cannot be understated. Each player's role is crucial in their own right; however, collaboration and communication are key to improving children's school readiness (PACEY, 2013: 14). Chapter 12, 'Undertaking Wider Professional Responsibilities', explores ways of working collaboratively with parents and other professionals.

 Key points

- Child observation; assessment and planning are a cyclic process.
- There are a wide variety of different observation tools and methods to help you understand young children as learners and assess their level of development.
- Parents and carers should always be encouraged to share their own observations of their child's progress.
- Observe children in their play in a range of situations both indoors and outdoors, during planned and unplanned activities.
- Use planning to provide opportunities to promote children's independence and autonomy, to encourage them to take risks and take charge of their own learning, initiate ideas and make decisions.
- Learning for babies and young children needs to take place in the social context with lots of talking and listening.
- Learning cannot take place unless children's emotional needs are met and they feel safe, secure and able to take risks.
- Scaffolding children's learning means modelling the skill while the child is trying something out, giving them clues and asking them appropriate questions, and then, just as soon as they master the skill, withdrawing your support and letting them take over;
- School readiness must mean not only how ready the children are for school, but also how ready the school and parents are.

FURTHER READING

Abrahamson, l. (2015) *The Early Years Teacher's Book*. London: Sage.

The author addresses EY practice, study skills and meeting EYT status requirements.

Hallet, E. (2016) *Early Years Practice – For Educators and Teachers*. London: Sage.

This book links theory to practice and considers the role of the reflective practitioner.

Broadhead, P., Howard, J. and Wood, E. (2010) *Play and Learning in the Early Years – From Research to Practice*. London: Sage.

This book explores ways to provide high-quality play experiences as an essential part of good early years education.

Palaiologou, I. (2016) *The Early Years Foundation Stage: Theory and Practice*, 3rd edn. London: Sage.

This book offers a close examination of early learning through the use of different lenses, namely political, social and pedagogical lenses, thus helping the reader to develop different perspectives.

USEFUL WEB RESOURCES

Statutory Framework for the Early Years Foundation Stage: Setting the Standards for Learning, Development and Care for Children from Birth to Five

www.foundationyears.org.uk/files/2017/03/EYFS_STATUTORY_FRAMEWORK_2017.pdf

This framework is mandatory for all early years providers in England (from 3 April 2017): maintained schools; non-maintained schools; independent schools; all providers on the Early Years Register; and all providers registered with an early years childminder agency.

The United Nations World Fit for Children (WFFC) mission statement of 2002

www.unicef.org/specialsession/docs_new/documents/wffc-en.pdf

This is an excellent example of more current concepts of school readiness, namely, a good start in life, in a nurturing and safe environment that enables children to survive and be physically healthy, mentally alert, emotionally secure, socially competent and able to learn. The WFFC goals highlight the importance of a caring, safe and stimulating environment for the holistic development of young children.

Bristol Early Years Research

www.bristolearlyyearsresearch.org.uk

This website promotes opportunities for rich professional learning and innovation through reflective practice and school/setting-based research and inquiry. It is a platform for sharing and inspiring early years practice within Bristol and beyond.

 **Online resources**

Visit https://study.sagepub.com/education to find a selection of scholarly journal articles chosen to support each chapter.

7

COMMUNICATION, LANGUAGE AND LITERACY IN THE EARLY YEARS

DENISE REARDON

Chapter overview

This chapter seeks to contextualise the Early Years Teacher and Educator (EYT/E) role in developing children's ability to communicate, use language and develop a love of literacy. The chapter includes ideas to connect theory to early years practice within the confines of any national or local policies, guidelines and frameworks that the EYT/E operates within. A theoretical argument about the EYT/E's knowledge of teaching early speech, listening, reading and mark-making/writing is presented. Ways to develop children's disposition to sustained shared thinking (SST), talking with other children and adults, making sense and communicating their thoughts to others is also considered. Creating language- and literacy-rich environments featuring rhythm, sound, song, books, storytelling, playful reading and writing with ideas about what they should include are also incorporated in the chapter. Due to the complex nature of developing babies and young children's communication, language and literacy, this chapter does not intend to be a complete resource in itself, but to give basic signposts to useful sources of information and guidance.

EARLY COMMUNICATION AND LANGUAGE

Early Communication and Language (CL) is crucial for young children to master: 'it is the essential key for learning, communication and building relationships with others as well as for enabling children to make sense of the world around them' (Brock and Rankin, 2008: 1). The EYT/E is not alone in developing babies' and young children's CL; the child's parent/carers, families, friends and even government policy and statutes play a key role. Early CL and literacy are not just curriculum areas in their own right, each area is vital for all learning and development and must be encouraged across the whole of the curriculum. There is a need for the EYT/E to balance their everyday pedagogical practice and support to parents in order to enrich babies' and young children's acquisition of CL, increase their vocabulary and help them to develop into capable thinkers, readers, writers and language users.

 Ideas for practice

Making provision for early communication, language and literacy involves the EYT/E providing babies and young children with the opportunities to experience a language-rich environment in which to develop their confidence and skills in expressing themselves and speak and listen to others in a range of situations. Examples of good practice drawn from real-life experiences of teaching early CL are featured in the Study of Early Education and Development (SEED) good practice report (Callanan et al., 2017). They include:

- Creating a 'language rich' environment through the use of songs, nursery rhymes and stories
- Providing time for adult–child and peer-to-peer interaction
- Extending children's language and enriching their vocabulary
- Engaging in high-quality adult–child interactions is viewed as essential for speech and language development
- Listening to the child and the importance of having one-to-one time with them
- Using assessment effectively to identify any developmental delays in speech and language and putting in place additional support
- Encouraging home learning and the quality of parent–child interactions through providing activities for children to do at home with their parents and encouraging reading at home.

[1]   What do you do to support children's CL?
[2]   How does what you do translate to the curriculum framework you are working within?
[3]   How can you make your CL teaching even better?

Over the past decade there has been much research and government interest in the areas of early communication, language and literacy, as identified in Table 7.1.

Table 7.1 Early CLL research, reviews and reports

Date	Document
2006	The Rose Review promotion of phonics, particularly 'synthetic phonics', as a necessary foundation for the teaching of early reading
2007	I CAN Early Talk Programme
2008	Bercow Review of Services for Children and Young People (0-19) with Speech, Communication and Language Needs
2008	Letters and Sounds: Principles and Practice of High-Quality Phonics (Primary National Strategy)
2008 & 2009	Every Child a Talker (ECAT) (DCSF)
2010	Phonics: Choosing a Programme and Teaching Phonics (DfE)
2015	Reading: The Next Steps, Supporting Higher Standards in Schools (DfE)
2015	Early Words Together (National Literacy Trust)
2015	Sustained Shared Thinking and Emotional Well-being (SSTEW) (Institute of Education - Iram Siraj, Denise Kingston, Edward Melhuish)
2018	I CAN, in partnership with the Royal College of Speech and Language Therapists, will undertake an independent review of the state of provision for children's Speech, Communication and Language Needs (SLCN), to be entitled 'Bercow: Ten Years On'

 Points for reflection

Many of the research-informed documents featured in Table 7.1 are designed to support those working in the early years to understand ways to create a developmentally appropriate CL environment by encouraging:

- children to enjoy experimenting with language;
- practitioners to improve their skills and knowledge;
- parents' understanding and involvement in children's language development.

Consider what you need to do to improve:

[1] Your own skills and knowledge.
[2] Parents' understanding and involvement in their child/children's language development.

LEARNING LANGUAGE

Babies' and young children's language acquisition generally follow a similar pattern, with children starting to develop communication skills from birth. However, it is important for the EYT/E to understand that babies and young children develop listening, thinking, speech, communication and language skills at different rates. Some develop quickly, while others may take longer. Some children may need additional support and the earlier this is detected the better it is for the child. CL are essential tools for life; we cannot function without them, and neither can a child! If the EYT/E believes that a child's language is cause for concern, they must discuss this with the child's parents and/or carers and agree how to support the child. 'Children with language impairments (LI) are at risk of behavioural problems, of emotional and psychosocial difficulties …' (DCSF, 2008a). In 2018 it will be 10 years since the government published the Bercow Report (DCSF, 2008a), a review of services for children and young people with CL needs. The past 10 years have seen major changes, with an overhaul of the education system and widespread reforms to the SEND system. The EYT/E is working in a challenging landscape, in terms of services and politically. In the context of any changes it is imperative that the EYT/E keeps up to date with the current policy and issue of children's CL needs.

A common early intervention approach for pre-school children with poor CL is Parent–Child Interaction Therapy (PCIT)' (Klatte and Roulstone, 2016).

The EYT/E must consider whether a child may have a hearing loss or even deafness. An ear infection can affect the child's ability to engage in CL activities. Children may be identified as having a special educational need (SEN) or a disability that requires specialist support from a speech and language therapist or any other relevant service. Chapter 11 discusses ways to work in partnership with parents to support their child's needs. In England, the EYT/E must assess children's CL skills in English. If a child does not have a strong grasp of the English language, the EYT/E must explore the child's skills in the home language with the child's parents and/or carers, 'to establish whether there is cause for concern about language delay' (EYFS 1.7, DfE, 2017a). The EYT/E, in making personalised provision to meet children's individual CL needs, can ask the parent and/or carer to provide them with examples of the basic signs or language that the child uses at home. Case Study 2.1 in Chapter 2 features a Trainee EYT teaching a CL activity to a child with English as a second language.

Areas that might affect communication

- **Bilingualism** – listening to and using more than one language at the same time can impact on a child's language development.
- **Stammering** – some children get stuck on words when they are talking; they may repeat words or sounds or prolong sounds. This can affect their confidence in communicating.

- **Voice** – Some children have difficulty with the quality of their voice, for example it can sound hoarse or husky. This affects different children in different ways and may affect confidence in communicating.
- **Hearing/auditory processing difficulties** – some children may need to be referred to specialist health or speech/language services. This can affect their ability to hear and confidence in communicating. Auditory processing is often difficult for children with autism.
- **Selective mutism** – is a complex childhood anxiety disorder characterised by a child's inability to speak and communicate effectively in select social settings, such as pre-school/school. These children are able to speak and communicate in settings where they are comfortable, secure and relaxed.
- **English as a second language** – children whose home language is not English need to be given opportunities to develop and use their home language in play and learning, supporting their language development at home, and at the same time have sufficient opportunities to learn and reach a good standard in English language.

Source: Adapted from The EYFS (DfE, 2017a) and Children's Speech & Language Therapy, Coventry and Warwickshire Partnership Trust (www.coventrychildrensslt. co.uk (accessed 29 October 2017)

 Points for reflection

Early language acquisition

There are a number of theories about how young children acquire language; however, 'no one perspective tells the whole story' (Brock and Rankin, 2008: 3).

- Which of these perspectives do you identify as being the most important?

Theories of early language acquisition

Theorist	Perspective	Theory
Professor B. Skinner	Behaviourist	The association of an object with the word and reinforcement provided by the adult when the child tries to say the word
Professor N. Chomsky	Nativist	We are born with a Language Acquisition Device (LAD) and that language is seen as part of a larger mental system
Jean Piaget	Cognitive	The idea that a child's intellect grows as they interact with and act upon their environment. As a child develops, they acquire language as a symbol system to help to code and communicate perceptions and understanding

(Continued)

Theorist	Perspective	Theory
Jerome Brunner	Interactionist	The roots of language lie in the early attempts of infants and carers to interact and communicate with each other
Lev Vygotsky	Socio-culturism	Children learn CL strategies through interacting with their environment and significant others
Current neuroscientists	Neuroscience	The presence of patterned and coloured visual stimuli, sounds and objects to touch and manipulate is ample stimulation for the developing CL sensory cortices of the human brain

Source: Adapted from Blakemore and Frith (2005: 26) and Brock and Rankin (2008: Appendix 1)

The 'One Hundred Languages of Children' poem (see Chapter 3) talks about the child using art, music, dance, building blocks, writing, talking, singing as ways to communicate what they see and feel and to help them build knowledge and understand the world around them. Cognitive and developmental psychologists featured in the Reflection activity above also recognise the importance of providing opportunities for children to engage with a range of objects and 'significant others' in purposeful, stimulating environments. Chapter 9 explores ways of developing a creative approach to teaching and learning in the early years.

Photo 7.1 Children purposefully following a cookery recipe

EARLY THINKING SKILLS

Looking at the world through the eyes of a baby or a young child and engaging in their thought processes can be achieved by engaging in 'sustained shared thinking' (SST). The concept of 'sustained shared thinking' can be defined as 'An episode in which two or more individuals "work together" in an intellectual way to solve a problem, clarify a concept, evaluate activities, extend a narrative etc. Both parties must contribute to the thinking and it must develop and extend' (Siraj-Blatchford et al., 2002). Evidence from both REPEY REPPE and EPPE suggests that involvement in sustained shared thinking, or what Bruner (1983, 1999) called 'joint involvement episodes', may be especially valuable in terms of early years CL development (Pugh and Duffy, 2006: 172). The Sustained Shared Thinking and Emotional Well-being (SSTEW) rating scales (Siraj et al., 2015) can be used by the EYT/E to support children's (aged between 2 and 5 years) SST and early communication development. Chapter 5 discusses the way that the SSTEW rating scales can be used to strengthen other environment scales (including ECERS-E, ECERS-R or ITERS-R) with a focus on the way that they can be used by the EYT/E to 'get a picture of what high-quality ECE and care can look like' (Siraj et al., 2015).

 Ideas for practice

Identify a target child or a group of children engaged in a play activity indoors or outdoors.

- Ask them to elaborate on what they are doing – for example, '*I really want to know more about ...*'
- Listen and re-cap – for example, '*So you think that ...*'
- Offer your own experience – for example '*I like to ...*'
- Clarify ideas – for example, '*Ok, so you think that ...*'

Engaging in SST allows the EYT/E to tune in to the baby or child's interests by engaging in the thought processes connected to the activity they are engrossed in, whether it is block play, small world play, painting, model-making, socio-dramatic play, mark-making or purely free play.

How babies think

Babies' and young children's cognitive abilities far surpass those that psychologists long attributed to them. They can, for instance, imagine another person's experiences and grasp cause and effect:

- Children learn about the world much as scientists do – in effect, conducting experiments, analysing statistics and forming theories to account for their observations.
- The long helplessness of babies may be an evolutionary trade-off, a necessary consequence of having brains wired for prodigious feats of learning and creativity.

Source: Adapted from Gopnik (2009)

Similar to Gopnik (2009), Dowling (2013: 15) supports the notion that children have their own thoughts, and suggests that 'we can provide conditions which entice their ideas and help grow their minds'. In providing the right conditions, Delafield-Butt and Trevarthen (2015) believe that 'Human exchanges of purposes and feelings are mediated by motor signals of a complexity not possessed by any other primates – of the head, the eyes, the face, the vocal system, the hands, and the whole body, all active in well-ordered sequences from birth, and all conspicuously shaped to make signals that another human being will appreciate'. It is therefore important for the EYT/E to consider the use of body language and the relationship between rhythmic movements, fine motor skills and language development in their teaching.

Babies and young children need purposeful activities that allow them to discover the world through moving and engaging in their senses. The learning brain and the body work together; babies and young children 'will initially find out about the world around them through physical experiences and express their thoughts and feelings through movement, sound and gesture' (Dowling, 2013: 31).

EARLY LISTENING

It is important to consider listening separately from speaking as the physical skills involved are different. Listening is part of the communication process, for example listening, thinking and responding.

To support children to listen and pay attention, encourage them to:

- Listen to stories, music, rhymes, and sounds in the natural world
- Anticipate key events in their daily and weekly routines
- Respond to what they hear
- Make relevant comments
- Ask questions
- Make actions
- Pay attention to what others say
- Respond to other children and adults
- Engage in SST

These are all high-level skills and very often children are accused of not listening rather than the EYT/E understanding the child's lack of ability to do so. The English EYFS (DfE, 2017a) early learning goal for Listening and Attention asks children to 'listen', 'anticipate', 'respond', 'make comments', 'pay attention' and engage in SST. Each one of these aspects make a different demand on the child; each aspect requires the child to master a different type of ability. In his publication *Your Image of the Child: Where Teaching Begins*, Loris Malaguzzi (1993) believes that we teach children to listen by being good listeners ourselves. The EYT/E must therefore reflect on the way that they listen to babies and young children and act as good role-models.

 —— **Ideas for practice** ———————————————

- Plan a fine or gross motor activity, for example, building blocks, finger-painting, dough, water/sand play, or small world play. Your activity will help to form new neural connections that are necessary for planning and controlling movement.
- Observe the way that a child or a group of children communicate during the activity, for example, the way they use their head, their eyes, their face, their voice, their hands, and their rhythmic body movements.

Dowling's (2013: 21) advice to the EYT/E is to:

- Have regard for children's thinking.
- Thinking involves the whole child and is strengthened through close relationships and real motivating experiences.
- Young children's thinking is best developed through weaving support into their everyday activities.
- When young children think they assimilate and accommodate innovative ideas and make connections to come up with a new notion in learning.

Early years children engage in different types of listening, all for different purposes: for example, appreciative listening – listening to rhyme, rhythm, pitch and pattern in poetry and music; discriminative listening – making fine aural discriminations in word play and phonic sounds; and reactive listening – paying attention to instructions and acting upon them. The EYT/E also needs to be aware of the cognitive demands made on children, for example during story time babies and young children are encouraged to listen receptively or fairly passively; when being asked to do something else their thinking switches to being responsive and physically active as they process the information they have been given in order to engage in the activity; their thinking becomes critical and constructive when they are asked to reorganise something or re-state what they understand. Each one of these cognitive processes makes a different demand on the child.

Photo 7.2   An Early Years Teacher listening to the 'voice of the child' to make an assessment using a tablet

Listening is both a dynamic and a collaborative part of the communication process (see Figure 7.1). As a speaker, babies and young children need to be aware of the listener, and vice versa. Being able to communicate is not just about talking; it is being able to listen as well.

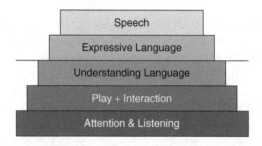

Figure 7.1   Building blocks of language development (*Source*: Adapted from 2017 Children's Speech & Language Therapy, Coventry and Warwickshire Partnership)

 **Points for reflection**

What do you do to develop babies and a young child's attention and listening skills?

Babies and young children need to be given the opportunity to physically hear as well as to listen and pay attention to whoever is talking to them. They need to be supported to develop their attention and listening skills before their language can start to develop. Children's attention begins to develop from the time they are born and allows them to observe and listen to what others are saying or doing.

1. What do you do in your teaching to support children to pay attention, hear and listen?
2. Do you have concerns about any of the children in your care, if so what measures have you put in place to support their needs?
3. How do you support children with English as an additional (second) language to listen and understand?

EARLY TALKING

Similar in nature to developing babies' and young children's thinking and listening skills, developing their ability to become a competent talker is equally as complex. The EYT/E will of course act as a role-model for children to learn to talk and learn through talking; however, this does not imply that the baby or child will simply imitate what the EYT/E says to them. Learning language is not as simple as transmitting words to a baby or child and them directly imitating you. Babies and young children use talk:

*   In their role-play to seek out familiar/appropriate language.
*   To express their wants and needs.
*   To take control of situations and protect themselves from hurting themselves, harassment or bullying.
*   To build and maintain relationships through cooperation and using language reciprocally.
*   To explain what they are doing by linking talk to actions.
*   To accompany their actions as a running commentary.
*   To convey information about imaginary or perceived encounters.
*   To find out about things and ask questions.
*   To comment on what they notice going on around them.

'Babies orient toward speech automatically and almost all babies, as long as they are bought up in an environment where language is spoken, learn to speak naturally and effortlessly' (Blakemore and Frith, 2005: 27).

Points for reflection

Speaking requires the EYT/E to teach early years children to:

- Express what is going on in their imagination
- Say what they are thinking
- Express ways to put across their ideas
- Speak about what has been going on in their lives
- Talk about what interests them
- Express their likes and dislikes
- Speak about what have they seen
- Show awareness of the listeners' needs
- Use past, present and future tenses accurately
- Talk about events that have happened or are about to happen in the future.

 Ideas for practice

1. Choose one aspect of the Speaking ELG.
2. Have a discussion with a target child.
3. Assess their stage of development.
4. Plan for future learning.

EARLY READING, WRITING AND PHONICS

Children in England by the end of the Foundation Stage are expected to 'Read and understand simple sentences, use phonic knowledge to decode regular words and read them aloud accurately, read some common irregular words, demonstrate an understanding when talking with others about what they have read … [in addition to using] phonic knowledge to write words in ways which match their spoken sounds, write some irregular common words and sentences which can be read by themselves and others with some words spelt correctly and others phonetically plausible' DfE (2017a). This push to familiarise children with 'synthetic phonics' as a tool for reading is not always favoured by teachers and academics.

There is particular concern about the inclusion of 'pseudo-words' otherwise known as 'alien words' in the phonics check (Standards and Testing Agency,

2016, updated 2017) which is undertaken by children at the end of Year 1 in primary school. The purpose of the phonics check is to assess whether children have learnt phonic decoding to an appropriate standard or if they need more support to improve their decoding skills. The check consists of 20 real words and 20 alien (pseudo) words that a child reads aloud individually to the teacher. A survey of schools conducted by Sheffield Hallam University on behalf of the United Kingdom Literacy Association suggests that 'the non-words confuse children who have been taught (in the words of one teacher) "to try to make sense of what they read". Arguing that "there is more to reading than just phonics"' (Hodgson, et al., 2013: 2). The EYT/E must, therefore, use their professional judgement to determine the most appropriate formats for phonic teaching in their school/setting. The argument about phonics disadvantaging reading comprehension has recently been tested by research at University of Royal Holloway London, which suggests that learning to read by sounding out words helps reading aloud and comprehension (Science Daily, 2017). However, children cannot learn phonics before they are competent conversationalists or even before they are completely verbal! The EYT/E can help children to 'tune in' to sounds (way) before they can be expected to work with (sounds) phonemes in words and use letters. Babies and young children need to develop the ability to distinguish between sounds, and become familiar with rhyme, rhythm and alliteration and the relationship between spoken and written sounds. 'Material resources are not absolutely necessary to support language acquisition and developments ... interactions with people are fundamental to development' (Goouch and Lambirth, 2017: 18).

Figure 7.2   A school in East Sussex displays examples of the 'Standards and Testing Agency (2016) Alien (pseudo) words' in the hallway above the children's coat pegs so that each time they go to their coat peg they see the alien words and comment

It is important for the EYT/E to understand that learning to read and write requires a complex set of skills of which phonic awareness is only one. 'Letter sounds should be introduced carefully – letters don't make sounds, people make them, and yet they point to a letter shape and ask a child "what sound does it make?"' (Reardon, 2013: 99). Children are often taught to use the words pho-neme, grapheme, digraph, trigraph, etc. This is so that they don't use the word 'sound'. Of course, the parents will say 'he is learning his sounds'! Also, parents and some teachers are inclined to 'over-voice', it is important to try to enunciate pure sounds correctly, especially for lower case letters, and not to add sounds like 'uh' or 'er' to the end, for example 'auh', 'ber', 'cer' instead of purely *a b c*!

Role-modelling to babies and young children must be fun, so be wary of working with visual letter shapes, as potentially it can stop children listening – 'for example, words like Charlotte, Christopher and cheese all begin with the letter C, but all begin with a different phonic sound, which can cause confusion and lead children to "switch off" to that aspect of learning' (Reardon, 2013: 13). Goouch and Lambirth (2017: 18) believe playing with rhyme, for example 'Incy Wincy Spider', encourages 'participatory language play ... leaving sufficient space for joining in with vocalisa-tions and later with rhyming pairs .... encouraging imitative behaviour, modelling, engaging joyfully – and having time for the many repetitions that will be called for '.

Early reading is all about fostering babies' and young children's understand-ing and enjoyment of stories, books and rhymes – they need to understand that print conveys meaning, both fiction and fact, and learn how to read a range of familiar words and simple sentences. They need to be encouraged to develop an understanding about the purpose of reading and reading conventions, for exam-ple the way to hold a book, turn pages, the direction of the print and the patterns and shapes in words. To become a competent writer the child needs to discover the relationship between the spoken and written word, as well as the relationship between reading and writing and physical activity.

It is the EYT/E role to promote a shared understanding about the ways that chil-dren develop and learn pre-reading and pre-writing skills. Traditional methods of sitting children down for long periods of time, giving them worksheets to complete, and encouraging children to learn letters of the alphabet and numbers by rote are no longer perceived as good practice. Babies and very young children are not physically capable of sitting still for sustained periods of time and are not developmentally ready to write or read. With regards to undertaking activities that require children to be seated, a rule of thumb has always been one minute for each year of a child's life plus one minute, so for a 2-year-old, this is only three minutes. 'The most advanced form of movement is the ability to sit still' (Goddard Blythe, 2000: 19).

A PLAYFUL LANGUAGE-RICH ENVIRONMENT

Research in the field of developmental psychology has shown us that there are links between language learning, behaviour, social skills and children's self-esteem. 'A fun-damental characteristic in brain development is that environmental experiences are as important as genetic programmes' (Blakemore and Frith, 2005: 32). Such evidence gives the EYT/E the impetus to provide a rich and stimulating language environment.

When babies are about one-year old they start to move from sounds to words. In a process called *fast-mapping*, babies begin to map words to objects on the basis of words they hear other people use. From about 18 months to two years, when most infants have developed a core of around 20–50 single words, the speed at which they learn new words accelerates. By the time children are five, most children have a vocabulary of 2,000 words or more, and this pace of learning new words continues in the primary years of school. (Blakemore and Frith, 2005: 43)

Children need to be given 'the opportunities and time to express their thoughts and feelings in an 'unrushed atmosphere' (Bruce and Spratt, 2011: 3). The EYT/E's settings/schools must be bursting with opportunities for baby babble, talking, listening, singing, rhyming and storytelling. 'These are the building blocks of literacy and make the difference to how quickly and easily they acquire language' (Brock and Rankin, 2008: 7).

This chapter concludes by proposing the following characteristics for playful communication-friendly environments (both planned and spontaneous, indoors and outdoors):

PLAYFUL COMMUNICATION-FRIENDLY ENVIRONMENTS

Must include CLL activities that are:

- Inclusive and reflect equality of opportunity
- Relevant to the varying developmental needs of each child
- Designed, where appropriate, in consultation with parents/carers (including bilingual), speech therapists and practitioners to meet the needs of every child

With opportunities for children to:

- Play and explore with communication, language and literacy (CLL)
- Physically and actively participate in CLL activities
- Be imaginative and creative with sounds, letters and words

The EYT/E must let children immerse themselves in language during:

- All curriculum activities
- Physical movement, music, action songs, rhymes, poems
- Practical activities, such as cooking, gardening and forest environments
- Creative activities such as art, music, dance, role-play and stories

(Continued)

- Imaginative play, small world play and role-play
- Literacy activities such as story time, looking at/reading fiction and nonfiction books
- Mathematical and scientific enquiry

Let children talk, talk, talk in order to:

- Try out language
- Engage in episodes of sustained shared thinking
- Express their thoughts, ideas and feelings
- Use home languages other than English to communicate with others
- Try out language other than English, including sign language
- Problem solve in other curriculum areas, for example – expressive arts, mathematics, science and technology

Let children listen:

- To adults and their peers
- To children who have English as an additional language
- During formal and informal situations, including show and tell time, meal and snack time, story time, and during everyday play activities
- While engaged in music, word, and sound games

Let children become readers by:

- Seeing reading as meaning
- Displaying clear and legible print in English and other languages (as appropriate) at child height, on displays, signs, labels, and in role-play areas
- Reading the signs and notices on displays, names on pegs, interests tables, labels on resources and equipment
- Reading environmental language, for example, outdoors – naming streets, traffic signs, shop names etc.
- Providing access to a regularly changed selection of books including bilingual books and different types of writings in a comfortable space
- Engaging in the media and ICT
- Encouraging parents to take them to a public library, having a librarian visit, attending or holding a Book Fair
- Encouraging them to handle books, turn pages, and talk about pictures, texts and express preferences
- Letting them choose a book to take home and share with their family
- Reading to them in formal and informal situations
- Providing opportunities for visual and oral discrimination of letters and sounds, sequencing events and stories, early recognition of significant words, through games, rhymes and play activities

Let children become writers by providing opportunities to:

- Develop children's fine motor skills, for example, feeding themselves from an early age and using cutlery when ready, lacing beads, threading counters, playing with blocks, construction and manipulative activities
- Engage in mark making, become an emergent writer, create pictures and patterns in a variety of media, while encouraging them to adopt a suitable posture and an effective pencil grip
- Observe adults modelling writing for a variety of purposes, including lists, letters, messages and child observations
- Make cards, books, notices, etc. with a variety of media
- Observe adults acting as a scribe and reading back comments on drawings, stories etc.
- Developing their knowledge about letter shapes and sounds.

 Key points

- Early CLL is not just a curriculum area in its own right, it is vital for all learning and development and must be encouraged across all curriculum areas.
- Babies and young children develop CLL skills at different rates. Some develop quickly, while others may take longer.
- Children learn about the world much as scientists do by conducting experiments, analysing statistics and forming theories to account for their observations.
- It is important to consider the use of body language and the relationship between rhythmic movements, fine motor skills and language development.
- Develop children's ability to distinguish between sounds, and become familiar with rhyme, rhythm and alliteration and the relationship between spoken and written sounds.
- Give children time to express their thoughts and feelings in an 'unrushed atmosphere'.

FURTHER READING

Blakemore, S.J. and Frith, U. (2005) *The Learning Brain*. Oxford: Blackwell.

This book reviews what we really know about how and when the brain learns, and considers the implications of this knowledge for educational policy and practice.

Brock, A. and Rankin, C. (2008) *Communication, Language and Literacy from Birth to Five*. London: Sage.

These books help the reader develop their knowledge, skills and practice in encouraging and promoting communication, language and literacy for babies and young children.

Bruce, T. and Spratt, J. (2011) *Essentials of Literacy from 0–7*, 2nd edn. London: Sage.

Goouch, K. and Lambirth, A. (2017) *Teaching Early Reading and Phonics*, 2nd edn. London: Sage.

This book presents an argument in favour of children developing an understanding and joy of reading amidst the current climate of synthetic phonics instruction.

Reggio Children (2011) *The Hundred Languages of Children, The Reggio Emilia Experience in Transformation*, 3rd edn. Reggio Emilia: Reggio Children.

This book documents the comprehensive and innovative approach used to utilise the 'hundred languages of children' to support their well-being and foster their intellectual development.

Whitehead, M.R. (2004) *Language and Literacy in the Early Years*, 3rd edn. London: Sage.

This book provides comprehensive coverage of issues in language, literacy and learning, focusing on the age range from birth to 8 years.

Roulstone, C. and Sharynne, M. (2011) *Listening to Children and Young People with Speech, Language and Communication Needs*. Guildford: J&R Press.

This book considers the voices of children and young people with speech, language and communication needs and offers a range of creative techniques and solutions for listening to them, all drawn from the insights of researchers, speech and language therapists, social workers, psychologists, teachers, advocates and parents.

USEFUL WEB RESOURCES

Early Words Together – The National Literacy Trust

www.literacytrust.org.uk/early_words_together

Early Words Together is a parental engagement and language development programme. Practitioners receive training and resources to help parents support their children's language development and school readiness. The programme is designed to benefit children aged 2–5.

The Ontogenesis of Narrative: From Moving to Meaning

http://strathprints.strath.ac.uk/54366

In this paper Jonathan T. Delafield-Butt and Colwyn Trevarthen (2015) explore the way that from birth infants imitate others' actions in shared tasks, learn conventional cultural practices, and adapt their own inventions, then name topics of interest.

Phonics Instruction and Early Reading: Professional Views from the Classroom

https://ukla.org/downloads/NATE_Phonics_and_early_reading_report.pdf

This paper from the National Association for the Teaching of English explores reading as a complex set of skills of which phonic awareness is one important element.

Key Stage 1: Phonics screening check administration guidance

www.gov.uk/government/publications/sta-assessment-update-25-april-2017/25-april-2017-schools

Guidance and information on the phonic screening check (April 2017).

Online resources

Visit https://study.sagepub.com/education to find a selection of scholarly journal articles chosen to support each chapter.

8

PROMOTING BABIES' AND YOUNG CHILDREN'S PHYSICAL AND EMOTIONAL WELL-BEING

DILYS WILSON

Chapter overview

This chapter will explore the concept of well-being and consider the factors involved in creating a physically and emotionally enabling early years (EY) environment for babies and young children. It will explore what being in an EY setting feels like for babies and young children and how the EY Teacher and Educator (EYT/E) can develop positive relationships with them and their families. Relationships are at the centre of EY practice and the chapter will consider how important these relationships are in mediating and managing the expectations for all involved in group care and education settings. For children, settling into an EY setting, moving rooms within the setting or starting school are significant transitions where they may struggle to feel secure and make sense of the daily rituals and routines which are very different from home. The chapter will examine how the Key Person approach can support children's learning and development by ensuring that their physical and emotional well-being is carefully thought about. Behaviour is considered within the context of the child's emotional world and the chapter will explore an approach to understanding behaviour as a means of communicating the feelings, experiences and relationships that children find confusing or overwhelming. The well-being of the EYT/E is also explored as an essential aspect of EY practice.

INTRODUCTION

Well-being as a concept is infused with different meanings depending on the perspectives of the professional discipline or policy focus and therefore remains dynamic and difficult to define. Within the context of the EY setting, promoting babies' and young children's well-being includes their subjective experiences of belonging, enjoying the play and learning opportunities, building strong friendships, feeling safe and cared for. In other words, the ethos that EYT/Es create in the EY setting to support children's well-being is guided by the needs of the child at the centre and supported by the policies and procedures that are agreed and put in place. Although well-being as a concept is much broader than the physical and emotional aspects discussed here, young children's capacity to engage in their play and learning is directly linked to their physical and emotional development and well-being.

RELATIONSHIPS WITH PARENTS

Building open relationships with parents is a good place to start to begin to understand a child's well-being. The EY setting is only one influence on the child and family within many and it is important to understand the complex system of relationships that each child experiences within the family culture, community and wider society. Bronfenbrenner's ecological environment model provides a structure to illustrate the many influences impacting on each child's physical and social and emotional well-being (Knowles and Holmstrom, 2012). The child's first influences are from the family within the 'microsystem' but families are also influenced by the community in which they live, the 'mesosystem'. The model extends further to consider the wider aspects of society including national and global areas of influence that impact indirectly on the child within the family, within the community. This also recognises that building bridges with communities and across professional boundaries can be extremely important for supporting children's well-being.

 —— **Points for reflection** ——————————————————

The parents and practitioners involved in the London Metropolitan University/National Children's Bureau Project 'Talking about Young Children's Wellbeing' (2009-2011) used the following metaphors to represent aspects of well-being:

- An inner glow: representing internal subjective well-being based on the child's experiences of emotional well-being and secure attachment.

- A set of Russian dolls: representing external factors that impact on the child's well-being. Like Bronfenbrenner's ecological environment model, the child is represented by the smallest doll in the middle and is affected by the well-being of the adults caring for them, influenced by wider social and economic circumstances and policy.

DEFINING CHILDREN'S WELL-BEING

Models such as Bronfenbrenner's help us to focus on seeing an often complex set of circumstances in a clearer and more organised way. Roberts' model of well-being (2010: 45) also offers a way of making sense of the factors influencing children's well-being by exploring the building blocks that are necessary for a sense of well-being to emerge and develop from birth. Her model illustrates the interaction between physical well-being and communication through relationships as the foundation on which other states of emotional well-being can flourish. The EYT/E working within the English context will recognise the links between this and the EYFS (DfE, 2017a) prime areas for learning and development, Communication and Language (see Chapter 7), Physical Development, and Personal, Social and Emotional Development, which 'are particularly crucial for igniting children's curiosity and enthusiasm for learning, and for building their capacity to learn, form relationships and thrive' (DfE, 2017a: 7).

Roberts (2010) uses 'belonging-and-boundaries' as the next construct in her well-being model. Here she emphasises the need that children have for trusting relationships with others and an environment where they can play and explore. She argues that promoting well-being for babies and young children involves their need to feel valued in their physical and emotional environments and to have safe and respectful limits for their behaviour. The Report on Early Intervention (Allen, 2011) and the subsequent evaluation of intervention programmes by the Early Intervention Foundation (see eif.org.uk) echo this. Providing support for parents/carers to understand the benefits of attuned interactions and relationships with their babies and young children also helps them to develop strategies to manage behaviour in a more developmentally responsive way (Asmussen et al., 2016). If children experience positive early relationships and experiences in their families and in their EY settings where there are clear boundaries in place to support their behaviour, children will begin to regulate their own feelings, expression and actions. Returning to Roberts' model of well-being, she uses the term 'agency' to describe the sense of validation that children achieve from recognising and experiencing the effect of their own communications and actions. As they become increasingly competent in using their own initiative and self-efficacy, this in turn has a positive impact on their subjective well-being.

—— **Ideas for practice**

The main purpose for having a well-being model is to make it possible to think about the best situations and experiences for nurturing resilient well-being. This is reminiscent of the three components of agency: being in the world ('sense of self'), exploring and understanding the world ('learning') and acting on the world ('influencing'). (Roberts, 2010: 50)

1. Reflect on a child who you think demonstrates 'agency' in their relationships and through their play.
2. Write a list of bullet points identifying what you have observed to show this with reference to:

*   The child's 'being in the world' or 'sense of self'.
*   The way they 'explore and understand the world' and 'learn'.
*   How they 'act on the world' or 'influence' it.

Photo 8.1   Children enjoying engaging in creative play with paint

There are several tools available for the EYT/E to use in their EY setting to support their observation and assessment of children's well-being, as also discussed in Chapters 3, 5 and 6. The Leuven Well-being and Involvement Scale developed by Ferre Laevers and his team (1994) focuses on the individual child's level of physical and emotional well-being. Children who have a high level of emotional well-being are more likely to have a high level of involvement in their play. Using the scale regularly can help to identify children who may not be emotionally secure enough to enjoy engaging in the activities and experiences available to them. Alternatively, it can also be used as an audit tool to review the appropriateness of the provision.

The Sustained Shared Thinking and Emotional Well-being (SSTEW) Scale (Siraj et al., 2015) can also help the EYT/E to observe and assess how emotionally enabling and stimulating the EY environment is and how effective the practitioners are in promoting children's emotional literacy and thinking and learning. The scale is divided into five areas of practice and set out in the following sub-scales:

Sub-scale 1: Building trust, confidence and independence

Sub-scale 2: Social and emotional well-being

Sub-scale 3: Supporting and extending language and communication

Sub-scale 4: Supporting learning and critical thinking

Sub-scale 5: Assessing learning and language

 Ideas for practice

The SSTEW Scale is intended for assessing provision for children aged 2–5 years. The following descriptions from Sub-scale 2: Social and emotional well-being indicate excellent practice (Siraj et al., 2015: 20):

7.1: Staff provide opportunities for children to talk about feelings and needs – often using the children's own experiences. They may use stories or props, e.g. 'puppet misses his family, how shall we make him feel better?'

7.2: Children are asked to show or say what they can understand from the non-verbal expressions of others in the group, from story books, photos, DVDs etc.

7.3: Staff support children in communicating with, and recognising and responding to the feelings of others, including where children may have difficulty expressing their needs or wants.

(Continued)

7.4: Staff look beyond the children to explain their feelings, making changes within the environment/routine etc. when necessary.

1. Make a list of the strategies you use in your setting to support children's emotional literacy.
2. How well do they work for you?
3. What could you do to improve these strategies?

THE KEY PERSON RELATIONSHIP

From exploring the concept of well-being, it seems clear that babies and young children thrive when they experience caring and consistent relationships, firstly within their families and then with a widening circle of adults who actively support their learning and development and their social relationships with other children. Settling-in policies and procedures provide the EYT/E with a way of supporting children's transitions from home to nursery but it is the role of the key person that determines the settling-in process and sets the tone for the partnership with the family. Within the English context, the Key Person role is part of the EYFS Statutory Framework (DfE, 2017a) and it is based on the understanding that babies and young children starting in an EY setting will become more secure if they can develop close relationships with their key person. The EYFS Key Person Principles into Practice Card (Table 8.1), which is now stored in the government's national archives (see DCSF, 2008d), provides a good explanation about why the Key Person role is so important for babies and young children and is still relevant to the EYT/E in practice today.

SECURE ATTACHMENT RELATIONSHIPS

Babies need adults to care for them as they are unable to care for themselves and it is through their early experiences of relationships and the extent to which the adults caring for them are able to do so sensitively that they gradually begin to build up an expectation of how they will be responded to. These experiences influence their growing sense of self and how they learn and behave in their interactions with others, including how they express their needs and feelings in their families and EY settings. Attachment theory (Bowlby, 1988) provides us with a way of making sense of the importance of these relationships. The attachment process begins at birth with reflexive infant behaviours such as sucking or grasping that trigger immediate responses from their caregivers. Babies internalise these early experiences and develop what Bowlby called an 'internal working model' as a kind of blue print for their expectations of relationships through having their needs and communications responded to. Not all babies and young children arrive in an EY setting with an experience of secure attachment and sensitive caregiving. It is important for the EYT/E to understand the experience of each child and to recognise that there are many factors that influence

Table 8.1 Key Person EYFS Principles into Practice Card

Secure attachment	Shared care	Independence
• A key person helps the baby or child to become familiar with the setting and to feel confident and safe within it • A key person develops a genuine bond with children and offers a settled close relationship • When children feel happy and secure in this way they are confident to explore and to try out new things • Even when children are older and can hold special people in mind for longer, there is still a need for them to have a key person to depend on in the setting, such as their teacher or teaching assistant	• A key person meets the needs of each child in their care and responds sensitively to their feelings, ideas and behaviour • A key person talks to parents to make sure that the child is being cared for appropriately for each family • A close emotional relationship with a key person in the setting does not undermine children's ties with their own parents • Careful records of the child's development and progress are created and shared by parents, the child, the key person and other professionals as necessary	• Babies and children become independent by being able to depend upon the adults for reassurance and comfort • Children's independence is most obvious when they feel confident and self-assured, such as when they are in their own home with family, or with friends and familiar carers such as a key person • Babies and children are likely to be much less independent when they are in new situations, such as a new group or when they feel unwell or anxious

Effective practice	Challenges and dilemmas	Reflecting on practice
• Ensure that rotas are based on when a key person is available for each child • Provide a second key person for children so that when the main key person is away there is a familiar and trusted person who knows the child well • Plan time for each key person to work with parents so that they really know and understand the children in their key group • As children move groups or settings, help them to become familiar with their new key person	• Reassuring others that children will not become too dependent on a key person or find it difficult to adjust to being a member of a group • Meeting children's needs for a key person while being concerned for staff who may feel over-attached to a child • Reassuring parents who may be concerned that children may be more attached to staff than to them • Supporting children's transitions within and beyond a setting, particularly as children reach four or five years of age	• Imagine what your setting seems like to a parent and their child when they first arrive. It may seem busy, friendly, noisy, lively, exciting and fun to you • How might it seem to an anxious parent and their child of 18 months who has just experienced a violent family break up? • How might it seem to a five-year-old who has been living in one room with a parent who is depressed and makes little conversation?

Source: http://webarchive.nationalarchives.gov.uk/20130401151715/https://www.education.gov.uk/publications/eOrderingDownload/DCSF-00012-2007.pdf (accessed April 2017)

physical and emotional well-being. Children have different temperaments and dispositions as well as the experiences they bring from their own family relationships with parents, siblings and extended family members. This has a significant influence on how they develop relationships with the adults and children in their EY setting and the behaviour that they display.

Even if children have had difficult previous experiences, developing a secure attachment relationship with their key person in the EY setting can help them enormously. Jools Page (2011) has drawn attention to the attachment needs that babies and young children have when they start at an EY setting. She uses the term 'professional love' to help EYT/Es think about their role in providing emotional support for babies and young children and she argues that babies should have an authentic experience of feeling loved by their key people. This includes the hugs and the physical and emotional contact that babies need and expect from close relationships. It is important for the EYT/E to be aware of the complex mix of feelings involved for all parties and to recognise their own personal bias.

 Ideas for practice

The Professional Love in EY Settings (PLEYS) project (2015, see weblink below) led by Jools Page at Sheffield University used a range of research methods including questionnaires, interviews, focus groups and social media to find out about early years practitioners' views and practices on 'love, intimacy and care in early years settings'.

One of the questions asked was what response would you make to a child saying, 'I love you'? Nearly half of all practitioners (47%) claimed that they would respond to a child by saying 'I love you' back. Further responses typically fell into one of six categories:

1. Limited reciprocation, 'I like you' or similar (20%).
2. No reciprocal acknowledgement; praising or thankful 'that's nice' or 'lovely!' (15%).
3. Diversion phrasing involving love, e.g. 'I love spending time with you too!' (2%).
4. Explaining or exploring other relationships, loves …. 'Who else do you love?' (2%).
5. Non-verbal response only, e.g. smiles or hug (1%).
6. Saying that they are part of a collective loving setting, e.g. 'You are loved', 'I love all the children in this nursery' (2%).

Source: http://professionallove.group.shef.ac.uk (accessed April 2017)

There are six responses to 'I love you', it could be commented that less than 50% of the responses meet the real needs of the child.

Reflect on what might have influenced the practitioners who took part in the PLEYS project to respond the way they did?

How would you respond to a child saying 'I love you'?

ROUTINES AND TRANSITIONS

The relationships that have been discussed show how physical and emotional well-being interact closely with each other. Manning-Morton and Thorp (2003) highlight why it is so important to implement sensitive care routines in EY settings. Just as the baby learns from close contact with a key person who can hold them in mind and help them to make sense of feelings that they may not yet have words to express, sensitive touch and physical holding are just as important. Babies and toddlers in particular are dependent on the EYT/E for comfort, which may involve being held or rocked or gently stroked. Elfer et al. (2011) provide accounts from EY practitioners about their reticence to engage in physical contact with children because of their concerns over safeguarding. Although it is important for the EYT/E to ensure that they respond to the baby or child's need or request for a cuddle rather than their own, they should also recognise that physical contact and closeness is important for children's physical and emotional well-being. Nappy changing, for example, is a routine that involves physical contact and intimate care but the procedures can be organised in an accountable way for it to become a routine that involves thoughtful care and a shared learning experience for those involved. Inviting the baby or toddler to take part in each stage of a familiar and predictable nappy changing process helps them gradually to exercise their agency and independence by becoming more actively involved.

Other daily routines such as snack and mealtime or preparing for rest or sleep time provide a clear structure for babies and young children. Visual timetables can help them to recognise the sequence of the day and provide a sense of security, especially for younger children who are still developing a concept of time. Manning-Morton and Thorp (2015: 47) stress that children under 3 years of age need to have 'a balance between having familiar predictable times of day and the flexibility to change times according to children's particular needs and growth patterns'. When children are tired or hungry they are more likely to be upset or to need reassurance from their key person so mealtimes and sleep routines need to be carefully thought about to ensure that the children feel comfortable eating together in a group or going to sleep in an unfamiliar place.

 **Case study 8.1**

Transition to school

As a childminder, I often observe that some young children and their families, become anxious around the beginning of the summer term, prior to starting school in September. Sophie who started attending my setting when she was only 9 months old, will have just turned 4 when she is due to start school after the summer holidays. As her key person, I have got to know

(Continued)

Sophie well and I know that she takes time to warm up to new scenarios and needs time to adapt to transitions. Her parents and I have worked very closely through the different transitions she has had to go through, e.g. separation anxiety when starting at my setting, sleeping in her own room/own bed, potty-training, starting nursery part-time. Sophie has had some contact with the school when picking up her brother at the end of a school day, and maybe a couple of visits to the school office with her parents. Knowing her history of adapting to new situations, I didn't think that these sporadic visits would be enough to familiarise her with the school. I also doubted that these few visits would be sufficient to help her to understand that she would be leaving my setting and attending the school full-time from September onwards. During my EY ITT training I was on placement in a Reception class and thinking of my experience with Sophie I offered to develop a 'readiness for school' pack to help parents prepare their children for the transition to school and for the school to prepare for the new children. The idea was very well received by the school and the Reception class teacher shared ideas and information which helped to shape and finish the pack.

Introduction to the 'Readiness for School Pack'

Let's get ready!

We very much look forward to welcoming our new children and their families into our school community in September. We hope that you will find the practical information in this **Readiness for School Pack** helpful and interesting as you help us prepare your child to become part of our school community.

Transition to School

Starting school is a major transition for children and their families. It is a period of change that can be both challenging and exciting.

Your child will have already been through a number of different transitions. For example: moving home, going to pre-school or nursery or the birth of a new sibling. Their day also involves natural transitions, such as moving from play time to meal times, drop off and pick up times if they have older siblings at school, visiting relatives or friends and, of course, settling themselves down to sleep at night.

We, as a school, aim to support both you and your child to make this transition as smooth as possible. It is important to understand that this transition experience starts well before, and extends far beyond, your child's first day of school. Children are often excited but sometimes daunted by the experience of starting school. It is therefore vital to involve them in the transition process and listen to their perspective.

UNDERSTANDING CHILDREN'S BEHAVIOUR

As babies and young children develop and begin to assert their independence through increased mobility and verbal expression, their behaviour will change as they begin to encounter new situations that require responses and actions of which they have no previous experience. Accommodating this new developmental territory without a map often makes it a risky venture. Until they learn how to manage their feelings and develop self-regulatory skills, young children's behaviour can often be experienced by parents, practitioners and other children as volatile and challenging. Roberts (2010) argues that babies and young children need to be supported in their behaviour by the boundaries in place in the EY setting through the establishment of trusting relationships where children feel secure. Children also need help to understand the boundaries and develop strategies to manage conflict so that they start to learn to know what to do when they feel overwhelmed. To achieve an environment where children feel that they belong, the EY team will need to agree what their ethos is by acknowledging their own values and beliefs in consultation with families so that they can share expectations and boundaries for behaviour. Some children have more experience of being understood and helped with the way they express their feelings in their home environments than others, but even so, the culture of an EY setting is very different from home and children need help in understanding the expectations and routines in this new environment.

 Point for reflection

Manning-Morton and Thorp (2015: 81) provide the following examples of EY practices that 2-year-olds might find confusing:

Participating in finger painting is encouraged but smearing food over the table results in a practitioner's disapproval. Experimenting with squirting bottles in the water play is celebrated but spraying the toilet with wee is heavily discouraged.

How would you help these 2-year-olds to understand the boundaries for their behaviour?

Babies and young children are skilled communicators from birth and will have absorbed their family cultures and ways of relating to others. Musgrave (2017) highlights how more serious underpinning factors such as chronic or complex medical conditions or the impact of on-going stressful situations in their families will have a direct impact on children's behaviour and the way they manage and express their feelings. From their experience of the settling-in process and their observations of babies and young children, the EYT/E will be aware of the different social and emotional skills children exhibit. Observations, parent/carer review meetings, blogs, newsletters, home visits and getting-to-know-you forms all help to enhance communication and provide opportunities to share information with families. Reflecting together on a child's behaviour can shed light on possible contributory factors such as changed family circumstances or health concerns, and lead to more attuned responses and targeted support strategies.

Other ways of thinking about children's behaviour include trying to understand what their current interests and preoccupations are and how that impacts on their play and relationships with other children. Arnold (2010) has observed the schemas, or repeated patterns of play, that children engage in and considered what can be understood about children's emotional states from the way they play and access the physical and emotional EY environment. EY settings are very different from the environment children experience at home and research suggests that even securely attached children experience higher levels of the stress hormone cortisol when they arrive at nursery (Groeneveld et al., 2010). Understanding that children react to potentially stressful situations in different ways and have distinctive ways of expressing their emotions and managing the feelings that they experience is an important starting point.

 —— **Points for reflection** ————————————————

Arnold (2010: 149) reflects on how one of the children that she observed 'seemed to be comforted by carrying out a *connecting* action shortly after a painful separation. His urge to *connect* or fix objects was very strong and enduring over time, as though he was working on something very important to him.'

- Consider how this child might behave if he wasn't able to fulfil his 'urge' to manage his feelings through his play.
- Have you observed any schemas or repeated patterns of play that children engage in that might suggest that they are exploring their emotional experiences?

THE WELL-BEING OF THE EY STAFF TEAM

Another factor of importance when thinking about the physical and emotional well-being of the children is to ensure that the EYT/Es and other practitioners working alongside them feel valued and sufficiently supported in roles that often involve emotionally charged situations. Supervision is an EYFS requirement (DfE, 2017a) and if organised thoughtfully it can provide a structure to help practitioners to process their day-to-day relationships and experiences with colleagues, their key children and families. Supervision practice is discussed further in Chapter 12 but the case study below illustrates how group supervision can be organised to promote well-being and support practitioners' personal and professional development.

Case study 8.2

Group supervision

At First Class Day Nursery we have introduced group supervision into our large and busy setting. The nursery caters for over 270 families each week and employs 38 full- and part-time staff. Although each staff member has regular individual supervision, in order for the process to be truly effective we decided to introduce group supervision to meet the welfare and professional development needs of the staff more effectively. The aims of the group supervision process were to provide the staff team with a safe place to explore the various issues and challenges arising in their work and to support them to develop and grow both as individuals and in their practice. Prior to introducing group supervision, we asked the staff team for their views and opinions about it. Senior staff then modelled the process at a whole team meeting and once again everyone was asked for their feedback.

The staff team valued the opportunities to explore their work and to learn from the work of others but there were also concerns about finding the opportunities to meet in a quiet space and at a convenient time. We addressed these practical challenges by encouraging

Photo 8.2 Practitioners working alongside each other to support children's learning

(Continued)

practitioners to meet in the staff room in small groups of four for 50 minutes each fortnight and this solution suited everyone. To ensure that all practitioners felt fully at ease and well supported during supervision it was essential that the supervisor appointed to each group was an experienced practitioner and did not hold line management responsibility for any of the group members. Each group of four staff consisted of a mixture of experienced and newly qualified practitioners who were working with children of different ages. This model of supervision provided opportunities for staff to learn from the work of others and to share their own experiences. Supervisors were encouraged to see the group process as entirely collaborative although with the understanding that they were responsible for holding the boundaries of time and to maintain the focus of the work.

Practitioners are encouraged to spend 5 minutes preparing for supervision and to arrive with a brief written outline of the material they wish to discuss. This also helps to maintain a working agenda. The first 5 minutes of the session are spent checking in and ensuring that there are no safeguarding issues which would need to take precedence. The practitioners presenting each week are allocated 20 minutes each and they focus on one issue arising from their work. These might be challenges encountered or even successes to be celebrated. All members of the group are invited to contribute to the issues being explored and to share the exploration knowing that the space is confidential. Constructive feedback is encouraged and staff are supported to find their own way forward. Ideas for reading and research are also shared and training opportunities identified. The final 5 minutes of each session is spent completing an action plan with SMART targets to be addressed which is then signed by the supervisor who will support the staff member to achieve this. Feedback from this process, which has been fully embedded for some time now, has been entirely positive. Staff report greater feelings of well-being and staff retention is high.

 Ideas for practice

SMART Targets

1. What challenges are you currently facing in your teaching /professional practice?
2. Use the table below to identify your own SMART targets to set yourself an action plan.

Specific	What do you want to achieve?
Measurable	How will you know if the target has been achieved?
Agreed	Have you discussed what you want to achieve with your colleagues?
Realistic	Is your plan achievable?
Time-bound	What is the time frame for achieving the target?

 **Key points**

- The child is at the centre of the wider web of family and community relationships.
- Open and positive key person relationships support children and their families.
- Secure attachment is important for children's well-being.
- Well-managed routines and transitions help children to cope better with change in the future.
- Children communicate something about their feelings and experiences through their behaviour.
- A happy and well-supported EY staff team has a positive impact on the well-being of the children.

FURTHER READING

Arnold, C. (2010) *Understanding Schemas and Emotion in Early Childhood*. London: Sage.

This book builds on the extensive research on the schemas children use to support their cognitive development by exploring how children's thinking also includes making sense of their feelings and emotional experiences.

Manning-Morton, J. and Thorp, M. (2015) *Two-Year-Olds in EY Settings*. Maidenhead: Open University Press.

The strength of this book is how it captures the experience of 2-year-olds by focusing on their unique developmental characteristics as they embark on their learning journey from home to the EY setting.

Musgrave, J. (2017) *Supporting Children's Health and Wellbeing*. London: Sage.

The aspects of health in relation to well-being are discussed and explored in detail throughout this book. It offers an important perspective on the issues relating to children's health and possible impact on young children's development and well-being.

Roberts, R. (2010) *Wellbeing from Birth*. London: Sage.

A model of well-being provides the structure within which to explore a range of themes arising from research and leading to practice. The examples of children's relationships and behaviours bring the concepts and theory to life.

Siraj, I., Kingston, D. and Melhuish, E. (2015) *Assessing Quality in Early Childhood Education and Care: The Sustained Shared Thinking and Emotional Wellbeing (SSTEW) Scale*. London: IoE Press/Stoke-on-Trent: Trentham Books.

This environment rating scale provides an excellent tool for exploring the effectiveness of EY provision in providing a secure and stimulating environment.

USEFUL WEB RESOURCES

The Early Intervention Foundation

www.eif.org.uk/publication/foundations-for-life-what-works-to-support-parent-child-
    interaction-in-the-early-years

Information on the Early Intervention Foundation website provides an overview of the work done by this independent charity. This includes a downloadable report evaluating a range of programmes providing support for EY parent–child interactions.

Well-being and Involvement in Care Settings: A Process-oriented Self-evaluation Instrument for Care Settings

www.kindengezin.be/img/sics-ziko-manual.pdf

Here you can find a manual providing the background to the Leuven Scales of well-being and involvement from Ferre Laevers' team at the Research Centre for Experimental Education, including guidance on how to use the scales, evaluate the findings and plan what to do next.

Professional Love in EY Settings (PLEYS) project (2015)

http://professionallove.group.shef.ac.uk

The Professional Love in Early Childhood Education and Care website explains the research project and offers access to professional development materials, including the Attachment Toolkit.

 **Online resources**

Visit https://study.sagepub.com/education to find a selection of scholarly journal articles chosen to support each chapter.

9

DEVELOPING A CREATIVE APPROACH TO TEACHING AND LEARNING IN THE EARLY YEARS

DENISE REARDON AND DYMPNA REED

Chapter overview

This chapter invites the Early Years Teacher and Educator (EYT/E) to reflect on ways to embrace and role-model a creative approach to teaching and learning in the early years.

Ideologies and principles of teaching creatively are explored throughout this chapter to show how creativity in the early years is intuitive, intrinsic and holistic, it equips children with a whole new way to see, explore and understand the world. Attention is drawn to neuroscience findings that advocate creative experiences and opportunities in the early years are both critical and essential for brain growth and development. Ways of developing children's dispositions to creativity are featured strongly in this chapter, for example, learning how to make creative connections, solve problems, learn from 'mistakes', develop the traits of perseverance and resilience, draw on imagination, investigate new possibilities and boundless ways of seeing the world. The chapter offers the EYT/E the opportunity to critically examine a range of research-informed ways to enrich their teaching and develop early years children creatively.

INTRODUCTION

A creative developmental approach to teaching

A creative developmental approach to teaching in the early years requires the EYT/E to adopt a teaching style that encourages EY children to develop creative dispositions to their learning, develop new skills, help them make connections between one area of learning and another with the intention of developing their confidence and extending their knowledge and understanding. Sharpe (2004: 1) believes that every child in the early years can be 'considered to have creative potential and to be capable of creative expression'. Whilst the English ECE context is led by the statutory requirements of the EYFS, it is important to understand that children in the early years learn creatively from their own ideas and the world around them long before they start a school/setting. More often than not they hold on to their own ideas, with their view of the world being regularly different to the views held by their teachers, parents and carers. The EYT/E can obtain a great deal of insight into a child's world by 'tuning in' (Trevarthen, 1995) to the way that they represent the world in their everyday activities.

 Points for reflection

Professor Lilian Katz (2011), believes that our role in the early years is to support and guide children's learning and offers the following 'words of caution':

Knowledge and Understanding

'If children are coerced into behaving that they know they understand something, but they really don't then we undermine their confidence in their own intellectual powers, their own questions, ideas and thoughts, and they soon give up.' (Dweck, 1991 [cited in Katz, 2011: 121])

Skills or Skilfulness

'Skills are different from knowledge and tend to require practice, and for young children should be acquired in the context of purposefulness.'

Dispositions

'Dispositions are habits of mind with intentions and motives (attitudes), for example,

- Reading skills vs the disposition to be a reader
- Listening skills vs the disposition to be a listener

The main point here is that it is not much use to have the skills if the process of acquiring them is so painful that the learner never wants to use them.'

Feelings

'... many capacities for feelings are inborn. But many important feelings are learned from experience and simply cannot be learned from instruction, exhortation or indoctrination. Feelings of self-esteem are strengthened with experience of overcoming difficulties, coping with low moments, observing and noting one's progress.'

Identify a 'purposeful' skill that you have helped a child to develop; what was the child's reaction to learning this new skill, how did it make them feel? Developing a skill in the early years does not have to be anything outstanding, e.g. mastering the creative fine motor skills to make scissors cut; a baby learning to feed him/herself with a spoon; the social skill of having the confidence to stand up and join in an action rhyme or a verbal skill of knowing when and when not to raise your voice.

WIRING EY BRAINS THROUGH CREATIVE EXPERIENCES

The EYT/E must understand that aside from the child's genetic predispositions, their brain growth is based on the creative experiences and opportunities that is afforded to them. Research undertaken by neuroscientists tells us that high-quality social and cultural experiences are more critical in the early years for the development of healthy brains and well-rounded personalities than at any other time during the rest of childhood and adulthood. These critical experiences include providing imaginative, creative and cultural opportunities to help children make meaning and deepen their understanding (David et al., 2003). Fundamentally the EYT/E must provide rich, stimulating and creative experiences so that the children in their care use the neurons and synapses in their brain to process information about the world around them. Denying high-quality, creative experiences in the early years 'for whatever reason (entitlement, economics, cultural, societal), the synapses that are predisposed to imagination, auditory, linguistic, physical or creative thinking skills will be pruned, making it difficult to reconnect those synapses further down the line' (Early Arts, 2017).

In England, the EYT/E must provide creative experiences that allow brain growth within the statutory requirements of the EYFS. 'The complexity of the brain lies not only in the genes, but also in the interaction with the outside world, which shapes the brain accordingly' (Britto, 2014).

Fundamentally, Beckley (in Curtis et al., 2014: 29) believes that problems may arise if children's brains are not exposed to the three EYFS prime areas of learning and development, which are Communication and Language, Physical

Development, and Personal, Social and Emotional Development, and that it is not so important to expose children's brains to the four EYFS specific areas of learning and development, namely Literacy, Mathematics, Understanding the World and Expressive Arts and Design, as they are not so age-dependent and can be developed later. However, a word of caution here, many authorities believe that the prime and specific areas sit comfortably side by side each other, and one or more of the areas can be used to support the other. There are endless creative ways to make the EYFS come alive, for example through the sheer exuberance of the indoors/outdoors, through storytelling, music, poetry, rhythm, art, block play, model making, role-play, small-world play, puppets etc., etc., etc.!

Professor Lilian Katz (2011) offers her principles for teaching (Table 9.1) which are based on her life-long study, personal experience and that of other ECE teachers who have shared their insights with her. Despite each principle being grounded in North American practice and research, they are considered transferable to not only the English ECE context but also to ECE contexts in other countries across the globe.

Table 9.1 Professor Lilian Katz's Principles for Teaching

Principle 1: A developmental approach means that what we teach and how we teach changes with the age of the learners, and the experience that comes with age

Principle 2: Just because children can do something, i.e. normative - does not mean they should do it

Principle 3: If we want children to have self-esteem, we must esteem them

Principle 4: The younger the children, the more important it is to strengthen their disposition to look more closely at events and phenomena in their own environment that are worth learning more about

Principle 5: Unless children have early and frequent experiences of what it feels like to understand something in depth, they cannot acquire the disposition to seek in-depth knowledge and understanding - to engage in lifelong learning

Principle 6: We must keep in mind the distinction between the academic and intellectual goals of education at every level

Principle 7: Introduction to formal academic instruction too early, and too intensely, may result in children learning the academic details, but at the expense of the dispositions to use them

Principle 8: Children come to school with different frequencies of exposure to academic types of activities, e.g. counting, reading, signs, listening to stories, being read to, learning songs, holding pencils, trying to write their names, etc.

Principle 9: The younger the children the larger the role of adults helping them to achieve social competence

Principle 10: The younger the children, the more they learn through interactive experiences, active vs passive, interactive vs receptive experiences, or from the transformation of information

Principle 11: Young children must have opportunities to work on a topic over an extended period of time

Principle 12: Children should be working part of the time at investigating phenomena and events around them that are worthy of their attention and understanding

Source: Katz (2011)

— **Ideas for practice** —

By encouraging creativity and imagination, we are promoting children's ability to explore and comprehend their world and increasing their opportunities to make new connections and reach new understandings. (Duffy, 2006)

1. Look at the Mathematics areas for development in learning (ELGs) within the EYFS and research ways to teach them creatively, for example through:

    a. Number rhymes and games that have a mathematical content to help children learn how to count, add and subtract, sort, order, recognise and create patterns, using mathematical language to describe what they are doing.
    b. Art, craft, junk modelling activities that help children explore shapes, space and measures.
    c. Role-play areas that allow children to develop 'Maths talk' in everyday situations, for example shopping, dentist, hospital, homes, vets etc.
    d. The use of indoors and outdoors to help children physically explore shapes, spaces and measures in both man-made and natural environment.
    e. Displays of numbers, shapes, sizes, patterns, symmetrical patterns.
    f. Displays of books, poetry and rhymes featuring mathematical concepts, e.g. counting, matching, sorting, different sizes and shapes etc.

2. Identify ways that mathematical learning and development features in the curriculum framework that you teach in.

CREATIVITY AND PHYSICAL DEVELOPMENT

It is impossible to say which area of learning is more important than the other. Goddard Blythe (2011: 145) signals research to suggest that physical development in the early years acts as a linchpin holding all the areas of learning together. Based on this premise, one of the very first areas of development a baby masters is the physical control of his or her body movements in order to focus, feed and snuggle up to his mother. Goddard Blythe believes 'throughout life, movement acts as the primary medium through which information derived from the senses is integrated, and knowledge of the world is expressed' (2011: 131). It is well researched that babies learn through their senses and in doing so they move to touch, to feel and to investigate the world around them. Children in the early years possess an innate ability to engage in gross and fine motor activities, for example, rolling, rocking, stretching, crawling, walking, climbing, running, jumping, moving to music, feeding, picking up small items, pressing buttons and making marks; all precursors to the development of handwriting. The EYT/E must creatively engineer spaces and resources to enable babies and young children to move and gain control in all sorts of ways.

 Ideas for practice

1. Take the time to observe:

    - A baby mastering the physical control of his/her body
    - A toddler grasping pencil control
    - A young child balancing on climbing apparatus

2. Identify any aspects of Physical Development featured in the curriculum framework that you work within.

 Case study 9.1

EY Teacher attending a conference in London with Lilian Katz speaking

She was impressive. She was talking about rewards and her disapproval of offering badges, points, incidental awards to children as it gave them the notion that they did things to please adults whereas there should be a deeper understanding that we learn and achieve to please ourselves – just like babies do. In those days (1990s) stickers had just come into vogue and it was all the rage to send children home daily with a chest full of them and to have weekly points systems. She agreed with awards for significant achievements but day-to-day learning had to be done for the love of learning itself!

Teaching a creative developmental approach raises many questions such as 'should' or 'how can' the EYT/E teach EY children to 'create and think critically' 'develop their own ideas' and 'make links between ideas and develop strategies for doing things'. Lilian Katz's Principle 1 (Table 9.1) warns about teachers across the globe 'suffering from the "Push Down" phenomenon that is doing earlier and earlier to children what we should probably do later' (2011: 120). It is extremely important for the EYT/E to understand what is developmentally appropriate for EY learning. Goddard Blythe (2011: 138) offers neuroscience findings to suggest that up to the age of 7 a child's brain processes:

- limited verbal language but understands non-verbal aspects of language;
- receives information primarily in a visual way;
- is expert in solving puzzles (visuo-spatial);
- is good at visual perceptions – drawing.

Which results in 'right side of the brain learning', e.g.:

- learning and sequencing information through movement, song, rhyme and dance, with a natural ability to copy musical melodies and rhythm, e.g. learning the alphabet and multiplication tables;
- a belief that anything is possible and entertains fantasy.

Like many other eminent authorities, Goddard Blythe (2011: 138) believes the early years are a time when children should be learning through play, 'exploring the physical environment, building sand castles and dens, playing games, learning traditional dances, rhymes and stories, learning patterns through movements'.

Case study 9.2

EYT observation of a child playing on a sandy beach

Photo 9.1   Alice creating sculptures from natural materials on the beach

Alice at 4 years old takes every opportunity to be creative. She has a strong need to create and to produce satisfying results, which she can take pride in and admire. She uses whatever materials are at hand - on the beach it is stones, shells, seaweed, sand, pebbles etc.

(Continued)

She writes her name in the sand to show ownership. In the woods it is twigs, conkers, soil, acorns, leaves etc. When helping to make a cake or biscuits she uses a multitude of decorations usually created in sugar paste and food colouring to represent her previous creations on the beach or in the woods – a pink shell, a red squirrel, yellow primroses and so on. Frequently she draws her designs and then executes. Alice lives on the Isle of Wight near many lovely beaches. She finds a clear space and then searches the beach for appropriate materials. She enjoys making both symmetrical and non-symmetrical patterns. Occasionally she will include man-made found materials. She has an affinity for circular shapes and that is part of earlier schematic learning related to rotation and connection. These are repeated behaviours and urges that forge brain development. The photo with stones (Photo 9.1) shows her ability to grade and sort mathematically whilst maintaining the circular pattern. Alice has a good understanding of the natural world and is not dismayed when the tide comes up and washes over her beach sculptures.

 Point for reflection

Teaching children to communicate and use language

Critically examine, question and reflect on your approach to teaching early years children to communicate and use language.

In the early years children acquire dispositions to learn from people, experiences and the world around them. Learning cannot take place if we don't feel good about ourselves or the people around us and neither can EY children. Chapter 8 examines ways that the EYT/E can support EY children's well-being, feelings and emotions. Lilian Katz believes 'What children should learn and should do must be decided on the basis of what best serves their development in the long term (dynamic) – to the extent that we know it!' (2011: 121).

 Ideas for practice

1.   Read Chapter 8 to:

a.   Critically examine how creative and meaningful your approach is to teaching children's personal, social and emotional (PSE) development.

b.   Explore ways to make links with PSE across the EYFS.

TEACHING CREATIVELY THROUGH THE ENVIRONMENT

Teaching creatively through the environment is fun, it allows children to look more closely at events, explore natural phenomena, investigate, experiment and bolster their self-confidence. Lilian Katz believes that 'As children get older, we must help them make better sense of others' experiences and environments, those far away in both time and place' (2011: 124).

There are boundless opportunities for EY children to engage in the environment, make their own decisions and take ownership of their learning. By going outdoors, EY children can experience first-hand the impact of changing seasons and 'take care of nature, from growing food to designing wildlife habitats. The creation of natural environments in school grounds means that everyone gets to enjoy and to value nature as well as take responsibility for it' (Learning through Landscapes, n.d.)

The Scandinavian Forest School (FS) is another approach that has been integrated into many schools/setting here in the UK. Forest School rests 'on the belief that the natural woodland environment provides so much that is different to the indoor environment' (Miller and Pound, 2011: 140). The FS approach is child-centred, 'where children can explore their surroundings, their skills and abilities, including engaging in imaginative play' (Sharp and Murphy, in Curtis et al., 2014: 27).

 Ideas for practice

The Mosaic Approach (MA) (Clark and Moss, 2017, 3rd edn) offers the EYT/E a way to listen, consult and seek the views of children. (Information about the MA can be found on the National Children's Bureau (NCB) website, see weblink below.)

1. Use the Mosaic Approach to support teaching children's understanding of the world around them and beyond.
2. Identify the links with any curriculum framework that you work within.

PROCESS VERSUS PRODUCT

One of the most important rules for guiding EY activities is that the process is always far more important than the product. 'Process' according to the 'Alliance for Early Childhood' (Hardy, n.d.) means allowing children to explore materials freely, without the pressure to copy someone else's ideas or stay within the lines! Process is the joy of experimenting with paints, watching colours mix, feeling textures, gluing various sizes, shapes, and colours of paper together to create a collage. Process is freedom to experiment and enjoy the feeling of creating without being concerned with the outcome or the product. Process in the early years is creating something that is uniquely the child's and not a copy of someone else's.

Ideas for practice

Research the creative approach developed by the Reggio Emilia atelier, the *atelierista*, the school and its teachers. Information can be found on this weblink: www.reggiochildren.it/activities/atelier/?lang=en (accessed 29 October 2017).

1. Organise an 'atelier' in your school/setting with a diverse range of creative media for children to play freely with.
2. Support the child as an equal learning partner.
3. Tune in to the diverse ways the child approaches the activity and communicates.
4. Allow time and space for children to:

   - express their creativity and develop their skills
   - facilitate their own learning
   - experience a sense of freedom and independence
   - explore and pursue their interests in a confident manner
   - express themselves in all types of different languages
   - experience and interact with the natural environment

5. After the activity record the children's connections, responses, ideas and interests against any curriculum framework that you work within.

Whilst it is acknowledged that EY children come to a setting/school with different levels of ability, England is a multicultural, multiracial society with many EY children bringing experience of an extensive history of culture, art, and music, drama and dance traditions. EY children can learn from their peers how to respect and understand similarities and differences in race, religion and cultural diversity through the arts. It is important for EY children to develop sensitivity, understanding and tolerance of other cultures (Yared and Taha, 2014).

 Ideas for practice

Write Dance (WD) (Oussoren, 2017) is a creative approach to developing EY writing skills. Information can be found on this weblink: https://uk.sagepub.com/en-gb/eur/write-dance-in-the-early-years/book234102 (accessed 6 August 2017).

1. Research the use of WD to inform your teaching.

Case study 9.3

Under Fives Explore the Gallery

By Abigail Hunt, a visual artist and freelance arts educator, in collaboration with the EY and Families Team at Tate Britain in London.

The children explore the gallery spaces physically, using their whole bodies as well as their eyes. Although touching artworks is not allowed, there are ways to touch the space and explore differently. Together they touched the stone and marble pillars and talked about how similar this might feel to a large sculpture. They lay on the floor and looked 'up up up up' at installations of lights and the high-up patterns in the vaulted ceilings. They noticed the temperature changes of the metal grates in the floors where

Photos 9.2, 9.3 & 9.4   Early years children engaging with visual resources and artworks

@ Abigail Hunt, Object/Image/Word Family Studio and Swatch resource both created by Abigail Hunt and Tate Early Years and Families Programme

(Continued)

the heating comes into the galleries. Children independently mimicked and made shapes and forms with their bodies that echoed the shapes in the sculptures – both figurative and abstract. Other children then followed this idea and tried this too. Some found links from themselves to things in the artworks – noticing colours in the clothing they were wearing, sculptures of groups of people that reflected their own families and paintings of things they were familiar with like brushing teeth, swimming and jump-ing. Children responded amazingly to the opportunity to lead adults around a space. Their choices of where to go and what to look at were considered and thoughtful, and their reflections – be they spoken or physically shown (dependent on age and levels of language) were insightful, offering fascinating insights into the depths of their imagi-nations. One major aim was to really allow space and time for things to happen and for young children to make their own choices. Making possibilities and suggestions of usable resources available to them, but allowing for them to take or leave these as they wish is key.

 Point for reflection

Abigail Hunt (Tate Britain) does not largely work in direct response to the setting/school curriculum and often works on independent projects within schools and galleries where the curriculum links are often pointed out later in the project rather than being identified at the beginning.

- Identify any areas of learning and development that occurred in Abigail's case study above.

CONCLUSION

Teaching a creative developmental approach in the early years helps to wire chil-dren's brains. Creative approaches like the 'Under Fives Explore the Gallery', the 'Mosaic Approach', 'Write Dance', 'Learning Through Landscapes', 'Forest School' and 'Reggio Emilia' (see Chapter 3) at their core provide an assumption that chil-dren in the early years form their own ideas, opinions and inspiration and are gifted with unique ways through which they can express their ideas creatively. The 'I-can-think-this-out-for-myself' and 'let's-work-this-out-together' approach provides opportunities for children to share ideas and to learn to work effectively with each other. Your role is to encourage this!

This chapter ratifies a creative developmental approach to teaching, in as much as providing the necessary resources, environments and conditions to allow chil-dren to flourish and the necessary time to enjoy the learning process. A creative developmental approach to teaching in the early years means that the EYT/E must tune into the child, think outside the box, be well informed, change with the age of the child, and the creative experiences that come with each age.

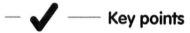

Key points

- Brain growth in the early years is based on connecting neurons and synapses - use them or lose them.
- Tune in to the way EY children express themselves.
- Consider physical development and movement as a linchpin that holds all areas of learning and development together.
- Purposeful skills are different from knowledge and tend to require time, space and practice.
- Let the creative dispositions you want the children to acquire be seen by them in use by you.
- Let EY children make genuine decisions and choices, not phoney ones.
- Avoid the use of templates and stepping in, let children explore a variety of media and experiment.
- The most important rule for guiding creativity is that the process is always far more important than the product.

FURTHER READING

Briggs, M. and Davis, S. (2008) *Creative Teaching: Mathematics in the Early Years and Primary Classroom.* Abingdon: Routledge.

Briggs, M. and Davis, S. (2014) 2nd ed. *Creative Teaching: Mathematics in the Primary Classroom.* Abingdon: Routledge.

This book encourages you to envisage and develop learning environments where children can take risks, enjoy and experiment with mathematical thinking, and discover and pursue their interests and talents in an imaginative yet purposeful way.

Bruce, T. (2011) *Cultivating Creativity – For Babies and Young Children.* Abingdon: Hodder Education.

The author of this book shows how early years teachers and practitioners can promote creativity in children. It explores the journey children take in developing their creativity, and helps teachers and practitioners to nurture creativity.

Curtis, W., Ward, S., Sharp, J. and Hankin, L. (2014) *Education Studies – an Issues Based Approach*, 3rd edn. London: Sage.

This book covers a range of current educational issues, while providing some background information, which allows the reader to gain an insight into policies and practice.

Duffy, B. (2006) *Supporting Creativity and Imagination in the Early Years* (Supporting Early Learning). Maidenhead: McGraw-Hill/Open University Press.

This book discusses the importance of creativity in society and uses real life examples of young children's rich imaginations and creativity and ways of planning experiences to support this.

Gandini, L. et al. (2004) *In the Spirit of the Studio: Learning from the Atelier of Reggio Emilia*

This book looks at the rich combinations and creative possibilities among the different (symbolic) and many languages of EY children.

House, R. (2011) *Too Much Too Soon: An Erosion of Childhood*. Stroud: Hawthorn Press.

This book advocates alternative ways for slowing childhood down, making better policy-making decisions and encouraging learning when children are developmentally ready.

Oussoren, R. (2017) *Write Dance*, 3rd edn. London: Sage.

This book introduces an exciting and innovative way to use music and movement to introduce handwriting to children. 'Write Dance' movements are designed to help children feel happy and comfortable with their bodies, improve their motor skills and provide a strong foundation for writing.

Sharpe, C. (2004) 'Developing young children's creativity: what can we learn from research?' NFER. Available at www.nfer.ac.uk/publications/55502/55502.pdf

In this article the author considers evidence from research and theory as it applies to developing young children's creativity.

Wright, S. (2010) *Understanding Creativity in Early Childhood*. London: Sage.

This book investigates the important roles of imagination and narrative play in the early years and beyond. The chapters explore why children create, the creative processes and what their creations mean.

USEFUL WEB RESOURCES

Under Fives Explore the Gallery – Tate Britain

www.tate.org.uk/whats-on/tate-britain/workshop/under-fives-explore-gallery

This site introduces the notion of experimenting with a range of materials while discovering exciting routes and journeys through the galleries as a playful way to discover connections between EY children's everyday lives and the art and architecture of Tate Britain.

Learning through Landscapes

www.ltl.org.uk/childhood/nature.php

This site is for anyone who shares a passion for creating stimulating outdoor learning and play experiences for children and young people.

The Mosaic Approach, featured on the NCB website

www.ncb.org.uk/listening-and-participation-resources

The Mosaic Approach offers a creative framework for listening to young children's perspectives through talking, walking, making and reviewing together.

'Children's Art: It's the Process, Not the Product that Counts'

www.theallianceforec.org/library.php?c=1&news=36

This article by Kathy Hardy, MEd on the Alliance for Early Childhood website looks at the way children have a natural tendency to create and the way that art provides the opportunity to represent, symbolise experiences and make sense of the world around them.

'The Role of Multicultural Art in a Culturally Diversified Society'

This thesis, available online, investigates teachers' awareness, attitudes and practices of multicultural issues in art education.

https://gupea.ub.gu.se/bitstream/2077/38262/1/gupea_2077_38262_1.pdf

 **Online resources**

Visit https://study.sagepub.com/education to find a selection of scholarly journal articles chosen to support each chapter.

10

SAFEGUARDING AND PROMOTING THE WELFARE OF ALL BABIES AND YOUNG CHILDREN

DYMPNA REED AND JENNIFER SMITH

Chapter overview

Early Years Teachers and Educators (EYT/E) have a statutory duty to safeguard and promote the welfare of babies and young children. This chapter focuses on both the statutory and practical aspects of safeguarding and how the EYT/E should respond to safeguarding children within the confines of any legal requirements, national policies, guidelines, and statutory and non-statutory frameworks that are in place. A key feature of this chapter includes examining the roles and responsibilities of EYT/Es working with babies and young children in schools/settings. The chapter features realistic causes for concern written as brief case studies/scenarios, covering the safeguarding of babies and young children. Explanation of working with other professionals and the roles of other key agencies such as social services, the Local Safeguarding Board and the Designated Safeguarding Lead are explored. The chapter examines the role of safeguarding from prevention and early help through to statutory intervention and serious case review. It considers the associated risks to young children from radicalisation and online technologies, as well as hearing the 'voice' of the child. This chapter therefore invites you to critically examine the serious nature of promoting the safeguarding and welfare of babies and young children in practice. This chapter does not intend to be a complete resource, but to give basic signposts to other sources of information and guidance regarding a very important issue. The government and Ofsted frequently update safeguarding information and regulation and this can be accessed on their websites. It is essential to keep informed and to update documentation and training as required.

STATUTORY SAFEGUARDING DUTY

As a consequence of several deeply tragic incidents involving babies and young children, the ramifications for safeguarding practice across schools and the early years sector is paramount. This chapter therefore seeks to explore the significant role played by the EYT/E in keeping babies and young children safe from harm and neglect and in leading and guiding other staff members in prevention and care.

Under the duties and requirements for early years providers and their staff, it refers to section 40 of the Childcare Act 2006 and gives information about Serious Case Reviews and Child Death Reviews and the responsibilities of the Local Safeguarding Children Board (LSCB). In September 2016, the government produced the updated document *Keeping Children Safe in Education* with a requirement that 'all staff must ensure they have read Part 1 and Annex A' (DfE, 2016). This applies to all schools, colleges and maintained nurseries. Ofsted produced updated guidance in August 2016, 'Inspecting safeguarding in early years education and skills', which informs pre-school practitioners and schools and colleges about the inspection process regarding child protection.

The media contains frequent examples of young children being abused or neglected but unfortunately many of these children are not always attending at early years settings. It is important that if a child has very irregular attendance that extra care is taken to monitor and record any suspicions. Furthermore, from July 2015, following the Counter-Terrorism and Security Act 2015, the British government placed a responsibility on all schools and registered early years childcare providers to have 'due regard to the need to prevent people from being drawn into terrorism'. The Prevent Duty (DfE, 2015; HM Government, 2015b) is a legal requirement and has become part of the safeguarding responsibilities of schools and early years settings. EYT/Es have a role to play, in so far as they must consider what they can do to protect children from becoming radicalised; this topic is explored later in this chapter. As a consequence of these vital aspects of safeguarding, the ramifications for practice across the early years sector have impacted significantly on the role played by the EYT/E.

In your role as an EYT/E, you will need to show that you have a good working knowledge of up-to-date legislation, policies and procedures related to safeguarding and the welfare of children. This area is hugely significant, and you will need to show how you establish and maintain a safe and secure environment for babies, toddlers or young children and lead other staff members by cascading your good practice. It is also essential to keep up to date with current legislation and documentation as there are frequent updates and developments.

The principles in all current documentation can be stated as:

1. The needs of the child always come first.
2. Practitioners must be prepared for early intervention.
3. Safeguarding and welfare is the responsibility of everyone.

'Safeguarding and promoting the welfare of children in England is everyone's responsibility. Everyone who comes into contact with children, their families and carers has a role to play in safeguarding children' (DfE, 2016). Box 10.1 sets out what EYT/Es working in schools/settings in England need to know and what they need to do.

BOX 10.1

EYT/E Statutory Safeguarding Duties

Early Years Teachers and Educators have a statutory duty under the Early Years Foundation Stage (DfE, 2017a), the Special Educational Needs and Disability (SEND) Code of Practice (DfE, 2014a; DfE/DH, 2015) and the Prevent Duty (DfE, 2015; HM Government, 2015b) to:

- Promote the welfare of children and provide a safe learning environment.
- Know and act upon the legal requirements and guidance on health and safety, safe-guarding and promoting the welfare of the child.
- Know and understand the school/setting child protection policies and procedures.
- Identify children who may benefit from early help and prevent concerns from escalating.
- Follow the school/setting referral procedures.
- Know who the 'Designated Safeguarding Lead' (DSL) is and understand their role to provide support to staff members to carry out their duties as well as liaise closely with other services.

This means:

- Protecting all children in their care from maltreatment.
- Preventing impairment of children's health and development.
- Ensuring children grow-up in circumstances consistent with the provision of safe and effective care.
- Taking action to enable all children to have the best possible outcomes.

Source: Adapted from: EYFS (DfE, 2017a) and Working Together to Safeguard Children (DfE, 2015, updated 2017)

KEY SAFEGUARDING POLICIES

The EYT/E must be aware of their responsibilities and any school/setting policies and procedures that are in place. There are three key policies that need to be in place in the school/setting which must be read and understood, they include:

- The Child Protection policy
- The Behaviour/Code of Conduct policy outlining expectations of staff members
- The role of the Designated Safeguarding Lead

These documents must form part of the staff induction programme. EYT/E should receive an Induction Pack with copies of Concern Forms and be made aware of the school/setting policies and where to locate them. It is good practice to sign a central document to say policies have been read, understood and that the Early Years Teacher or Educator agrees to uphold the content of them. It is also important to regularly revisit these policies as an 'aide-memoire' and to take note of any changes and updates. Safeguarding policies must be reviewed annually ensuring all policies conform to statutory requirements. Good practice requires EYT/E to attend regular training in safeguarding at least every two years with regular updates so that they have the skills and knowledge to safeguard children effectively.

Early years schools and settings must ensure that their safeguarding policies and procedures are made available to staff, volunteers and parents/carers. They must include information about:

- A member of staff acting inappropriately
- A whistle-blower reporting a safeguarding concern
- The use of mobile phones and cameras
- The safe transit and transfer of documents from one setting to another or to a case conference, with a signed consent form from the manager or head teacher
- A missing child and failure to collect a child at the agreed time
- Staff administering medicines
- Ill or infectious children and infection control
- Emergency evacuation
- Health and safety/risk assessment
- Photographs and digital images
- Equality of opportunities
- SEND
- The Key Person
- Recruitment including vetting, induction, supervision and appraisal
- Behaviour management
- Social networking and e-Safety
- Substance misuse, drugs, alcohol and medication (to include no smoking)
- Healthy eating/feeding
- Sun safety
- Parental communication

Additionally, EYT/Es must also be up-to-date with LSCB guidance and procedures which are frequently updated by the Local Area Designated Officer (LADO). As it is a principal objective for EYT/Es to ensure that all babies, toddlers and young children in their care are kept safe and protected from harm and neglect, they will need to regularly monitor their own and others' practice to ensure that they continuously comply with the procedures set out in the EYFS Statutory Framework (DfE, 2017a). In their own personal practice and in their support of others, EYT/Es must be alert to any issues for concern in the child's life at home or elsewhere.

In the statutory guidance *Keeping Children Safe in Education* (DfE, 2016) we are reminded that staff in schools and maintained nurseries must be aware of the 'Early Help' process so that children are protected before situations escalate.

CATEGORIES OF ABUSE OF CHILDREN BY ADULTS

The following categories of abuse are identified by the National Society for the Prevention of Cruelty to Children (NSPCC, 2009).

Physical abuse

- Hitting, shaking, throwing, poisoning, burning/scalding, drowning, suffocating/strangling etc.
- Induced illness, feigning symptoms, Munchausen's (fabricated illness by proxy).

Sexual abuse

- Forcing or enticing a child to participate in a sexual act or activities, even if child is not aware.
- Physical contact including penetrative or non-penetrative acts.
- Non-contact activities, e.g. looking at pornographic materials, watching sexual activities, grooming activities.
- Issues where boundaries are blurred, e.g. intimate adult care: tickling, cuddling, bathing, nappy changing, etc.

Neglect

- Persistent failure to meet basic physical and psychological needs.
- Serious impairment of child's health due to inadequate food, clothing, shelter.
- Lack of protection from physical harm and danger.
- Preventing access to medical care or treatment and not managing conditions such as epilepsy or diabetes.

Emotional abuse

- Persistent **emotional** ill-treatment such as telling them they are unloved, unwanted, worthless, inadequate etc., resulting in fear and feeling in danger and being in a hyper-watchful state.
- The exploitation or corruption of children.
- Child witnessing the abuse of others.
- Emotional abuse is involved in all other forms of abuse.

Children can sometimes be abused by other children, this is known as peer-on-peer abuse and it is often a form of bullying, verbal abuse or small acts of violence. This can be very disturbing for the victim and destructive for the perpetrator. The EYT/E needs to be alert to preventing this and dealing with it. Using the theme of 'Positive Relationships' from the EYFS (DfE, 2017a) is very supportive under these circumstances.

THE DESIGNATED SAFEGUARDING LEAD (DSL)

The governing body or management committees in your school/setting should appoint, with an explicit job description, an appropriate senior member of staff from the leadership team to the role of Designated Safeguarding Lead (DSL). The DSL takes the lead responsibility for Safeguarding and Child Protection in the school/ setting. They will be trained to a high standard to bring the necessary knowledge and skills to their role. They must receive updated training at least every two years, including any Prevent Duty (DfE, 2015; HM Government, 2015b) awareness and training. Dates of training received must be recorded in an easily accessible Training Log and staff absences from training noted. The DSL will ensure that safeguarding policies and procedures are annually reviewed and updated. They contribute (along with other staff) to inter-agency working in line with any statutory guidance. The DSL's name and photograph should be displayed. It is essential to have a deputy DSL who is available for advice if the DSL is not on the premises.

If the EYT/E has a safeguarding concern during the school/settings hours it must be reported immediately to the DSL or Deputy. It is of utmost importance that the DSL or Deputy is available on the premises during school/setting hours and that the EYT/E is allocated time to discuss the safeguarding issues with the DSL and other parties/agencies. They also have an obligation to promote an ethos and a culture of listening to children and taking account of their feelings concerning any measures that have been put in place to protect them. Chapter 11 critically examines the concept of 'listening to the voice of the child' within the context of the United Nations Convention on the Rights of the Child (UNCRC) (United Nations, 1989), the Equality Act 2010 and the Children and Families Act 2014. Remember that babies and very young children are not able to speak for themselves and staff in schools and settings are their 'voice' in a time when they may need protection and care.

 —— **Points for reflection** ————————————————————

Governing bodies and management committees must ensure that those working with children receive training, updates and guidance regularly.

- Did you undergo SEND and Prevent Duty training as part of your induction programme?
- What safeguarding updates have you attended within the last two years?

- How do you receive regular updates, for example, via e-mail/e-bulletins, staff meetings?
- How confident are you that you are provided with relevant skills and knowledge to safeguard children effectively?

SAFER RECRUITMENT

In order to safeguard babies and young children, schools and settings must ensure the suitability of any adult that has contact with babies and young children. When employing people to work with young children, it is essential for schools/settings to create a culture of safer recruitment. Recruitment procedures need to help deter, reject and identify people who might abuse children. The advertisement should have a statement that says all positions are subject to an enhanced Disclosure and Barring check (DBS, 2012, updated 2017). At least one member of an interview panel must hold a Safer Recruitment training certificate. Governing bodies, management committees and employers must act reasonably in making decisions about the suitability of prospective colleagues based on the following checks and evidence:

- Criminal record checks
- Barred list checks
- Prohibition from teaching checks
- References
- Interview information
- Verification of candidates' identity
- Physical and mental fitness for the role
- Verification of person's right to work in the UK
- Verification of appropriate qualifications

For most appointments in a school/setting Ofsted and the Disclosure and Barring Service (2014, updated 2017) require that an enhanced DBS check is required. An enhanced DBS provides the same information as a standard check plus any information that a chief police officer believes to be relevant and considers ought to be disclosed. Once the checks are complete the DBS provides a printed DBS certificate to the applicant. This certificate, together with a 'Proof of Identity and Right to Work in UK' (Home Office, 2017) must be shown to the potential employer before taking up the post (Education and Skills Act 2008). This information about staff must be held in the 'Single Central Record' (SCR) which is available in a secure form in all settings that work with children. Often this is the first document to be checked by Ofsted at inspection. In June 2016 the government clarified the position with regard to 'disqualification by association' (Disqualifications under the Childcare Act 2006, Regulation 9). In sections 19–26 this is explained and it states schools and settings need to gather sufficient and accurate information about whether any member of staff in a relevant childcare setting is disqualified by association with someone with a known record of child abuse.

ALLEGATIONS OF ABUSE

Keeping Children Safe in Education (DfE, 2016) points out allegations that might indicate that a person would pose a risk of harm if they continue to work in regular or close contact with children, these include:

- behaved in a way that has harmed a child, or may have harmed a child;
- possibly committed a criminal offence against or related to a child;
- behaved towards a child or children in a way that indicates he or she would pose a risk of harm to children.

Definitions of abuse:

- **substantiated** – sufficient evidence to prove the allegation;
- **malicious** – insufficient evidence to disprove the allegation and there has been a deliberate act to deceive;
- **false** – there is insufficient evidence to disprove the allegation;
- **unsubstantiated/unfounded** – insufficient evidence to either prove or disprove the allegation. The term does not imply guilt or innocence.

Employers must have a duty of care to their employees to ensure their actions protect the child and the subject of the allegation.

RESTRAINT/POSITIVE HANDLING

Occasionally in any education setting it may be vital to employ restraint, also known as 'positive handling'. This must only be carried out after appropriate training, with justification and with the least force possible (DfE, 2013c). This intervention can potentially give rise to allegations against staff. The decision to use restraint must be recorded and incidents regularly monitored and reviewed to show correct policies and procedures were followed. Where an allegation is made, the LADO must be consulted and an internal investigation must take place. Agreed outcomes must be identified and noted.

The EYT/E has a significant role to ensure that children are taught about safeguarding, *according to their level of understanding*. This needs to be part of the teaching including e-safety and covering relevant issues through Personal, Social and Emotional (PSE) development. Chapter 8 critically explores ways of promoting children's PSE development in more detail. It has been noted over the years investigating particular cases that children with SEND are particularly vulnerable to child abuse in its many forms.

 **Case study 10.1**

Complex SEN and Child Protection

Consider this case study and reflect on the needs of this child and how best to support him.

Child B is a 4-year-old child with autism. His language is developing well and he can speak in sentences of appropriate complexity when he chooses to but this happens very infrequently. He presents as a placid child, compliant with all requests. With his peers, he is similarly passive and does not complain if toys are taken from him. Child B has never cried at school and shows very little variation in mood, being neither happy nor sad. Concerns have been registered since he started in Reception for low-level neglect. He is generally well presented in school uniform with tidy hair, however Child B's feet are generally dirty and there is a recurrent head lice problem. He shows no awareness of strangers and will take the hand of any adult who may be visiting the unit. Communication with home is unusual in that the home/school book is recorded in daily but no meetings have taken place since the initial transition to school meeting was attended, and the initial home visit has still not been achieved despite several attempts to do so. Attendance is poor with often no reason provided for absence. There are several indicators that require professionals to be very alert. The pupil's level of SEN means that his ability to communicate about things that worry him is very limited.

Support to develop a child's communication in instances like Child B featured in the case study is a priority as a means of supporting their ability to develop the skills to keep themselves safe. EYT/Es under the school/setting PSHE programme have a duty of care to support and encourage children's learning to be safe including being safe online; they must encourage children to tackle learning to be safe in small, achievable and personalised steps.

A welfare log is a crucial document to monitor and track all incidents of low-level concern, for example observations of unusual behaviour, welfare concerns or poor attendance. Evidence that accumulates over time can be used by the DSL to demonstrate patterns and provide a factual and accurate picture that can be presented if necessary to gain access to services and support for a child and their family. In the case of Child B, in the case study above, the EYT/E together with the DSL would use evidence from the welfare log to persist and carry out a home visit.

INFORMATION SHARING

All organisations should have arrangements in place which set out clearly the processes and the principles for sharing information internally. In addition, these arrangements should cover sharing information with other organisations and practitioners, including third party providers to which local authorities have chosen to delegate children's social care functions, and the Local Safeguarding Children Board (LSCB). One approach to aid effective information sharing is the use of Multi-Agency Safeguarding Hubs, where teams may be co-located physically or locally. (HM Government, 2015)

The DfE provides information about how concerns should be reported and the appropriate channels to follow, for example, the Prevent Duty and concerns about possible Female Genital Mutilation requires the EYT/E to go directly to the police as all abuse is an illegal activity. Children's lives may be saved by the EYT/E being willing to speak up and to be persistent in the defence of the child. First Aid records, attendance records, the bullying log and the restraint log should all be cross-referenced against Child Protection files. If a child makes a disclosure to a known and trusted adult in a school/setting the adult must NEVER promise 'to keep it a secret if you tell me'. In fact, the adult needs to be very clear with the child that they need to share the information in order to help and protect. It is essential to share as quickly as possible with the DSL and to record the facts on the Concerns Form.

INSPECTING SAFEGUARDING

The EYT/E must be familiar with what Ofsted inspects and reports on. A general overview of the Ofsted inspection requirements is explored in Chapter 5. A key feature of Ofsted inspections is to determine whether the arrangements in place for safeguarding children in the schools/settings are effective. Ofsted evaluates how well providers fulfil their statutory responsibilities and how well staff exercise their professional judgement in keeping children safe.

 Points for reflection

'Cause for concern' scenarios

Which of these scenarios do you consider to be a cause for concern, either **immediate or long-term**?

	Immediate concern	Long-term concern
Rosie (18 months) is brought to nursery each morning wearing the same nappy she has slept in all night.		
Tilly (21 months) scratches her limbs until the skin is oozing. Despite requests for soothing cream none is sent into the setting.		
Jonnie (nearly 4) likes milk in a bottle and to suck a dummy during the day. He talks with the dummy in his mouth.		
Tom (3.2) is aggressive and controlling with the other boys in the group and always expects others to do what he wants to do.		
Nkosi (2.8) is timid and shy and plays with the dolls in the role-play area when no other child is present.		
The twins Peter and David (3.5) talk only to one another in their own language and do not answer if an adult speaks to them.		
Shanjita (3.10) has recently moved into a new flat and says it is very cold there as Mummy has no money left for the radiator.		
Violet (4.3) drew a picture of her looking after her baby brother while Mum and Dad went down the road to the pub.		
Frankie (2.10) likes wearing the dresses and hats in the box. He has a pink hair slide and cried when Mum wouldn't buy him pink shoes.		
Vu (5.3) said he could kneel up but not sit down as his bottom hurt. He explained that he had been naughty and daddy was very cross.		
Lily (4.2) has difficulty with any form of physical exercise as she is already in the very overweight category for her age.		
Jack (3.6) is dressed in old clothes and canvas shoes even in winter. He often has nits and his parents consider this to be normal at nursery.		
Bilan (4.7) has parents from Somalia. The mother has informed the nursery that she is taking the child to visit her grandmother for 6 weeks.		

- If placed in any of these situations with whom primarily would you discuss your concerns?
- How would you record your concerns?
- How might you support the individual child/children?
- How would you handle the situation, e.g. what words might you use to speak to any of the parents/carers?
- Which external agencies might you approach for help?
- What outcomes might you hope for to obtain resolution?

KEEPING CHILDREN SAFE

There are many levels and critical aspects associated with the delivery of the EYFS (DfE, 2017a) Safeguarding and Welfare Requirements. No one aspect is more important than the other, although some are far more life-threatening in terms of harm and neglect to the child than others. Following the Counter-Terrorism and Security Act 2015, the UK government placed a responsibility on all schools and registered early years childcare providers to have 'due regard to the need to prevent people from being drawn into terrorism'. This is now part of the safeguarding responsibilities of schools/settings under the Prevent Duty (DfE, 2015; HM Government, 2015b). On another level, EYT/E are concerned with ensuring that staff–child ratios (DfE, 2017a) are adequate to ensure safety, and that the needs of the children are met (see Appendix 2). On yet another level, there is a need to ensure that the school/setting's premises and equipment, both indoors and outdoors, are safe, secure and positioned appropriately for babies' and young children's development, learning and play (DfE, 2017a). Of equal importance, on another level, lies the accountability for the safe storage of medicines and the medical needs of sick children (DfE, 2017a). Each of these significant safeguarding and welfare aspects will be examined in more detail below.

The Prevent Duty

The Prevent Duty that became law in England during 2015 places a duty on all school/settings to have due regard to preventing people being drawn into terrorism. In order to protect children, EYT/Es must be alert to any expression of extremist views posed by a child (PACEY, 2017). Protecting young children from the risk of radicalisation is regarded as part of the EYT/E's role under their wider safeguarding duties, and is similar in nature to protecting children from other forms of harm and neglect. Specific background factors may contribute to a young child's exposure, for example family, friends or online or a specific need for which an extremist or terrorist group may appear to provide an answer. Sadly, the Internet and the use of social media, in particular, has become a major factor in the radicalisation of many children.

The fundamental British Values are implicitly embedded in the EYFS (DfE, 2017a) and do not have to be taught separately but staff members need to be aware of their importance.

What is radicalism?

Radicalism refers to people who support terrorism and forms of extremism.

What is extremism?

Extremism is vocal or active opposition to fundamental British values, including democracy, the rule of law, individual liberty and mutual respect and tolerance of different faiths and beliefs.

Source: Adapted from the Iona School & Nursery Prevent Duty Policy (2015)

As with managing all aspects of safeguarding, the EYT/E must be alert to any changes in children's behaviour as this could indicate that they may be in need of help or protection. Informed professional judgement is essential to identify children who might be at risk. Any concerns about an individual child must be followed up using the school/setting safeguarding procedures, including discussing with the DSL, who will, where deemed necessary, take the appropriate action. The DfE has a dedicated telephone helpline (020 7340 7264) to enable staff and governors to raise concerns relating to extremism.

Staff–child ratios

Staff ratios are very specific and are dependent primarily on the ages of the babies and children in the setting and on the qualifications of the staff. There are different ratios when a practitioner with qualified teacher status (QTS), Early Years Teacher Status (EYTS) or Early Years Educator is working with children.

Appendix 2 at the end of the book provides an overview of the EYFS (DfE, 2017a) staff–child ratios that are current at the time of writing this chapter.

The physical environment

The EYT/E must ensure that the school/setting's premises and equipment, both indoors and outdoors, are safe, secure and positioned appropriately (DfE, 2017a). Babies and young children need adults to be vigilant and help them develop and learn safely through their play. All this should lie within the setting/school Health and Safety policy and requires undertaking frequent risk assessments and daily checks, especially in public outdoor areas that might run the risk of animal faeces, discarded sharps, broken glass etc. Babies, and young children are often curious and need supportive, enabling adults to foster an understanding about the dangers posed to them; they need to grow and learn, knowing how to keep themselves safe.

Children love to take risks, even one-year-olds are very capable of climbing onto furniture, pressing electrical switches or swiping images on an i-pad or phone. Computers, electrical equipment and plug sockets need to be safely concealed and positioned, and health and safety risks need to be explained appropriately to children as they move about and interact with their environment. Risk assessments must be conducted and reviewed – this means risk-assessing just about everything – some on a daily basis, some on particular occasions and some when new equipment is purchased. Risk assessments should identify aspects of the environment that need to be checked on a regular basis, when and by whom and how the risk will be removed or minimised (DfE, 2017a). Trips and slips can occur if children are not aware of the dangers of steps, water spillages and leaving toys and equipment lying around. Helping children to become more aware of the consequences of their own actions and for taking care of others is also included in the EYFS (DfE, 2017a).

Doors and gates need to be locked and monitored to prevent strangers wandering in or to stop children wandering out! A system of identifying visitors and recording who enters the setting is essential. In many settings, staff often wear uniforms with their names embroidered on a T-shirt or they wear a lanyard. Visitors should sign in and wear a visitor's badge. In some cases, it may be necessary to ask for identification or a current DBS certificate. Parents should ensure that people other than themselves who collect the child are known to the staff and a letter is included in the child's records.

 Point for reflection

Children are being denied the chance to develop 'resilience and grit' because of schools' over-zealous health and safety policies, the [Ofsted] chief inspector of schools says. (Christopher Hope, Chief Political Correspondent of *The Telegraph*, 5 August 2017, www.telegraph.co.uk/news/2017/08/05/children-denied-chance-develop-resilience-strict-health-safety; (accessed 29 October 2017).

• How does your school/setting Health and Safety policy give children the chance to develop 'resilience and grit'?

 Ideas for practice

How do you ensure the safety and suitability of the school/setting environment and equipment?

• Reporting and dealing with accidents, hazards and faulty equipment.
• Ensuring the safety of children, staff and others in the case of a fire or any other emergency.
• Understanding the emergency evacuation procedure and rehearsing it.
• Knowing who checks the fire alarms, smoke detectors, and fire extinguishers, to make sure that they are in working order, and how often they are checked.
• Making sure the fire exits are clearly identifiable and free of obstruction, and easily opened from the inside.
• Checking that children for whom a Court Order is in place are known to staff and not released to anyone with a no-contact order.

Accidents, injuries and storage of medicines

The EYT/E must follow the school/setting procedures to notify Ofsted of any serious accident, illness or injury to, or death of, any child while in their care, and of the associated action taken. Notification must be made as soon as is reasonably practicable, but in any event within 14 days of the incident occurring (DfE, 2017a). At the time of this publication, newly qualified EYT/Es in England must hold either a full or emergency Paediatric First Aid (PFA) certificate within 3 months of starting work if they are to be included in the ratios (DfE, 2017a).

There are Local Authority regulations concerning the administration of medicines, so please refer to your LA's website. Medicines must not usually be administered to a child unless they have been prescribed by a doctor, dentist, nurse or pharmacist and where written permission for that particular medicine has been obtained from the child's parent and/or carer. EYT/E must ensure that a written record is kept each time a medicine is administered to a child.

 Points for reflection

- What is your role in the case of an accident or an injury in your school/setting?
- Where are the first aid boxes located?
- What procedures are there to keep written records of accidents, injuries and first aid treatments?
- Who informs parents and/or carers about any accident or injury sustained by the child?
- What is in the school/setting policy for administering medicines?
- What is the policy for administering medicines to children?

Outings

The EYT/E must adhere to any school/setting policy about outings and the safe transportation of children. This includes any legislation about the use of car restraints and booster seats (see Department for Transport, 2017). Written parental permission for children to take part in outings is required and written risk assessments must be undertaken to identify any hazards that may arise from the outing.

This chapter concludes by urging the EYT/E to always be mindful of their role in protecting and safeguarding the babies and children in their care.

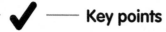 **Key points**

- Safeguarding and welfare is the responsibility of all adults, not just the managers and leaders; early intervention is key to protecting the child.
- If you have a concern you have a duty to follow it through using the procedures in your school or setting. This should include a dated log of information-sharing and events, signed by the DSL.
- Each individual should have knowledge and understanding of all policies and procedures, including updated documents from the LA and the government.
- You cannot promise the child confidentiality.
- Risk assessments should be rigorously carried out and health and safety checks completed.

FURTHER READING

Linden, J. and Webb, J. (2016) *Safeguarding and Child Protection: Linking Theory and Practice*: London: Hodder Education.

This book promotes best outcomes for children and helps to determine that the actions and interventions of practitioners ensure the welfare and well-being of vulnerable children.

Reid, J. and Burton, S. (2014) *Safeguarding and Protecting Children in the Early Years*. Abingdon: Routledge.

This book provides a critical analysis of policy construction, together with implications for good practice.

Barrington, F. (2015) *Known to Social Services*. Malta: Faraxa Publishing.

This book follows the experiences of a social worker into a housing estate, meeting serious issues to be resolved such as domestic violence, child abuse, paedophiles and ex-convicts.

USEFUL WEB RESOURCES

Prevent Duty: Departmental Advice for Schools and Childcare Providers

www.foundationyears.org.uk/files/2015/06/prevent-duty-departmental-advice.pdf

Guidance from the DfE on the Counter-Terrorism and Security Act 2015 which contains a duty on specified authorities to have due regard to the need to prevent people from being drawn into terrorism.

Statutory Framework for the Early Years Foundation Stage: Setting the Standards for Learning, Development and Care for Children from Birth to Five

www.foundationyears.org.uk/files/2017/03/EYFS_STATUTORY_FRAMEWORK_2017.pdf

This website clearly sets out the mandatory standards that from April 2017 schools and childcare providers must meet for the learning, development and care of children under 5.

Safeguarding children: latest documents

www.gov.uk/topic/schools-colleges-childrens-services/safeguarding-children/latest

This Gov.UK site provides essential information about safeguarding children.

Statutory guidance: *Working Together to Safeguard Children*

www.gov.uk/government/publications/working-together-to-safeguard-children--2

This is a statutory guide to inter-agency working to safeguard and promote the welfare of children. It is frequently updated.

Keeping Children Safe in Education

www.gov.uk/government/publications/keeping-children-safe-in-education--2

This is a statutory guide for schools and colleges on safeguarding children and safer recruitment. A consultation took place in 2016 and this is the update.

Protecting Children from Radicalisation: The Prevent Duty

www.gov.uk/government/publications/protecting-children-from-radicalisation-the-prevent-duty

This is guidance (April 2015) for schools and colleges and childcare providers on preventing children and young people from being drawn into terrorism.

Information Sharing: Advice for practitioners providing safeguarding services to children, young people, parents and carers

www.gov.uk/government/publications/safeguarding-practitioners-information-sharing-advice

This advice (issued in March 2015) helps practitioners and their managers to decide when and how to share personal information legally and professionally.

The National Society for the Prevention of Cruelty to Children (NSPCC)

nspcc.org.uk

This site has multiple resources, training opportunities and materials to inform practitioners and to support children and young people.

Safeguarding in Schools

www.safeguardinginschools.co.uk

This site provides an online free weekly briefing.

The Children's Commissioner, *Safeguarding Policy Handbook*, 2013, updated 2017

www.tes.com/teaching-resource/safeguarding-policy-handbook-6352049

This Handbook explains the ethical approach and requirements for safeguarding and supporting children and young people involved in all work undertaken by and for the Children's Commissioner's Office.

 **Online resources**

Visit https://study.sagepub.com/education to find a selection of scholarly journal articles chosen to support each chapter.

11

RESPONDING TO THE STRENGTHS AND NEEDS OF ALL BABIES AND YOUNG CHILDREN

DENISE REARDON

Chapter overview

This chapter invites the Early Years Teacher and Educator to reflect on the ways that they practise and role-model an inclusive approach in all aspects of their teaching and learning in the
early years. The first part of the chapter sets out to review the EYT/E's legal duty to promote
children's rights, inclusion and anti-discriminatory practice within the Early Years Foundation
Stage Statutory Framework (DfE, 2017a), the United Nations Convention on the Rights of the
Child (UNCRC) (United Nations, 1989), which came into force in the UK in 1992, the Equality
Act 2010 and the Children and Families Act 2014. The chapter then goes on to examine ways
that the EYT/E can support SEN and disabled children's learning and development. The chapter
concludes by reviewing the importance of record keeping in order for the EYT to support better
outcomes for children with SEN and disabilities. Each section of this chapter provides an overview on a particular aspect of the United Kingdom (UK) inclusion, SEN and disability reforms
that are in place at the time of publication and the way that they potentially impact on the
EYT/E's professional role. Each section also features the statutory requirements of the English
EYFS Statutory Framework as well as the National Guidance on the Special Educational Needs
and Disability (SEND) system for children and young people aged 0-25, from 1 September 2015.

THE EARLY YEARS TEACHER AND EDUCATOR ROLE IN PROMOTING CHILDREN'S RIGHTS, INCLUSION AND ANTI-DISCRIMINATORY PRACTICE

Early Years Teachers and Educators (EYT/E) in England working within the EYFS framework (DfE, 2017a) have a duty of care with regards to the law, regulations and statutory guidelines relating to disabled children, those with Special Educational Needs (SEN) and any child displaying a recognised medical condition. The UNCRC is reflected in UK legislation, in particular, for disabled children and children with SEN, and ratified into the Equality Act 2010 and the Children and Families Act 2014. EYT/Es therefore must be very aware of the legislation that governs their role and their ability to promote children's rights, inclusion and anti-discriminatory practice. EYT/Es working in schools within the United Kingdom (UK) may be familiar with the UNICEF-accredited programme 'Rights Respecting Schools Award' (RRSA) which can also be explored with young children across early years settings, the Foundation Stage and Key Stage 1. The RRSA recognises achievement in putting the UNCRC at the heart of a school, academy, free school or setting's planning, policies, practice and ethos. The EYT/E's role is to sign up to such policies, guidance and frameworks and put them into practice. It is vitally important for the EYT/E to create an inclusive stimulating environment that encourages an ethos where children feel safe, secure, valued, respected, nurtured and allowed to flourish.

 —— **Points for reflection** ————————————————

The United Nations Convention on the Rights of the Child (UNCRC) (United Nations, 1989) advocates that every child has rights, whatever their ethnicity, gender, religion, language, abilities or any other status. They are:

1. The right to affection, love and understanding.
2. The right to adequate nutrition (food) and medical care.
3. The right to protection from all forms of neglect, cruelty and exploitation.
4. The right to free education and to full opportunity for play and recreation.
5. The right to a name and a nationality.
6. The right to special care if you have a disability.
7. The right to be amongst the first to receive help in times of disaster.
8. The right to learn to be a useful member of society and to develop individual abilities.

9. The right to be brought up in a spirit of peace and universal kindness.
10. The right to enjoy their childhood regardless of race, colour sex, religion, national or social origin.

- How do you promote children's rights?

THE INCLUSIVE EARLY YEARS TEACHER

To promote babies', toddlers' and young children's rights, inclusion and anti-discriminatory practice, you must teach in a way that treats all children fairly, irrespective of their race, ethnicity, culture, religion, gender, sexual orientation, family background, learning difficulties and/or disabilities. In doing this, you may wish to consider ways that you (may) have influenced, shaped, contributed to, or implemented policy and procedures to promote equality of opportunity for the children in your care, including any support for children with special educational needs or disabilities.

This may sound like something that comes naturally, but meeting these needs is highly complex and requires you to be constantly watchful and receptive. There are clear examples to support EYT/Es in meeting children's individual needs outlined in the EYFS Statutory Framework (DfE, 2017a).

 **Points for reflection**

Reflecting on children's rights, inclusion and anti-discriminatory practice

1. In England the EYFS is based on a set of guiding principles and seeks to provide: equality of opportunity and anti-discriminatory practices, ensuring that every child is included and supported – *How do you make this happen in your school, academy, free school or early years setting?*
2. There is a requirement that your school, academy, free school or early years setting will have a Special Educational Needs Co-ordinator (SENCO) with schools also having an Individual Needs Assistant (INA) in situ for children with an Education, Health and Care Plan (EHCP) – *Who is the nominated SENCO and /or INA in your place of work?*
3. The EYFS inclusive approach is designed to be responsive to babies and young children's individual needs – *Think of an example or examples to show how you have responded to a baby or young child's individual needs.*

(Continued)

4. Your school, academy, free school or early years setting must have arrangements in place to identify and support children with SEN or disabilities and make information available to parents about how the setting supports their child – *What measures are in place at your school, academy, free school or early years setting?*

Source: adapted from the Statutory Framework for the EYFS (DfE, 2017a)

EQUALITY OF OPPORTUNITY

The Early Years Teacher's and Educator's role is to promote equality of opportunity and be vigilant against anyone that seeks to upset, harass or victimise any disabled baby or child. The school, setting or EY network that you work in must make reasonable adjustments to ensure that disabled children are not at a substantial disadvantage compared with their peers. This includes adjustments to any provision, criterion or practice, making physical alterations, and providing auxiliary aids and services (DfE, 2014b). This duty is anticipatory; it is your role to look ahead and anticipate what any disabled child in your care might need and what adjustments might need to be made to prevent them being disadvantaged.

 Ideas for practice

- 'The EYFS seeks to provide ... equality of opportunity and anti-discriminatory practice, ensuring that every child is included and supported' (DfE, 2017a: 5).
- 'Providers must follow their legal responsibilities under the Equality Act 2010' (para. 3.58).
- 'Providers must have arrangements in place to support children with SEN or disabilities' (para. 3.67).

Here are some examples that you may wish to consider to help ensure that your teaching and learning style promotes equal opportunities:

- Be positive about differences between children and other people and support children's acceptance of difference.
- Celebrate and value cultural, religious and community events and experiences.
- Provide books and resources which represent children's diverse backgrounds and which avoid negative stereotypes.
- Provide positive images of all children, including those with disabilities.
- Support children's understanding of difference and empathy.
- Encourage positive attitudes and challenge negative attitudes with the use of props such as puppets and dolls to tell stories about diverse experiences, ensuring that negative stereotyping is avoided.

- Encourage children to talk about their own home and community life, and to find out about other children's experiences.
- Strengthen the positive impressions children have of their own cultures and faiths, and those in their community, by sharing and celebrating a range of practices and special events.
- Visit different parts of the local community.
- Provide role-play areas with a variety of resources reflecting diversity.
- Share stories that reflect the diversity of children's experiences.
- Ensure that children learning English as an additional language have opportunities to express themselves in their home language some of the time.

Source: adapted from wigan.gov.uk Equal Opportunities Policy and Procedure (2014)

As discussed previously, part of your role is to contribute to an ethos that reflects positive values, attitudes and dispositions to differences and diversity so that every child feels secure and not at a disadvantage because of their ethnicity, culture or religion, home language, family background, special educational needs, disability, gender or ability under the Equality Act 2010 (Government Equalities Office and Equality and Human Rights Commission, 2010). The Act incorporates the Disability Discrimination Act 1995, stating that children with disabilities must not be treated less favourably than children without a disability. EYT/Es need to identify ways to make 'reasonable adjustments' for SEN and disabled children to participate in their teaching and learning. This may mean identifying and accessing suitable equipment or adapting the physical environment. The way that you approach this is crucial; children and colleagues need to see how you respect diversity and differences in others.

In my previous roles as an Early Years Advisory Teacher and university lecturer, I sometimes found people working in early years settings situated in predominately white-populated areas struggling with the concept of inclusion and diversity. They expressed concerns that as they were based in what they perceived as a 'predominantly white' area they did not have to worry too much. It was my role to inform them of the legislation and encourage them to reflect on the importance of providing opportunities for their children to learn about other cultures, religions and differences. All children will most certainly experience environments that are diverse as they travel through life, so it is very important that positive attitudes are fostered right from an early age. Early Years Teachers and Educators have a fundamental role in helping children understand that people are not all the same and that they need to respect the rights of individuals who look, act and move in different ways to them or hold different cultural and/or religious beliefs.

Fiona Robertson, the Head of Education at East Lothian Council, believes it is not acceptable to say that 'We treat all children the same so we meet the requirements ... children are not the same; even identical twins are different in some way. ...

[The EYT/E] must treat children as unique individuals and offer them equal opportunities to participate rather than treating them all in the same way' (Robertson, 2017: 26).

In summary, inclusion for EYT/E means accepting children's differences and providing them with physical access to the school, academy, free school or early years setting. Your role requires you to adopt an inclusive teaching style, work in partnership with parents and/or carers to modify resources and activities in order to meet a child's individual needs and let them take part in all learning experiences.

 Point for reflection

A sense of belonging is a very important aspect of a child's well-being and development. Creating inclusive learning opportunities that are available to all children means that you will help them to value who they are, build their confidence and self-esteem and an understanding and empathy towards themselves and others.

• How do you create a sense of belonging?

 Ideas for practice

Here are some examples that you may wish to consider to ensure that you are inclusive in your teaching and learning:

• Listen to and value all children's voices.
• Observe children and assess whether the learning environment encourages access to all children. Are there potential barriers, e.g. steps, kerbs, objects lying around preventing children with physical impairments moving around?
• Provide teaching and learning opportunities and resources that appeal to the senses, including sight, hearing and touch, exploration of colour pattern, texture and sound through the different senses, to meet the needs of visually impaired children.
• Ensure your knowledge about different ethnic groups, religions and cultural groups is kept up-to-date.
• Actively avoid gender stereotyping and challenge any expression of prejudice or discrimination by children or adults.
• Provide activities that encourage children to develop cognitive skills like cause and effect, co-ordination, dexterity and agility.
• Ensure that children have a choice between busier, more active areas and quieter spaces.
• Use symbols and visual/sensory timelines to provide information and instructions.

SPECIAL EDUCATIONAL NEEDS AND DISABILITY

Early Years Teachers and Educators have a duty of care to keep themselves up-to-date with any Special Educational Needs and Disability (SEND) policy changes and reforms. At the time of writing this chapter, the UK government is requiring Clinical Commissioning Groups (CCGs) and Local Authorities (LA) to work together to integrate services across the 0–25 age range. This means that Early Years Teachers and Educators need to develop the skills and competencies to work collaboratively with parents and carers and other professionals in order to offer help for the child at 'the earliest possible point'. They will need to develop age-appropriate strategies to seek the views of SEND children, and fully involve parents and carers in decisions about what support they want to put in place to support their child. Reforms set out in the Children and Families Act 2014, and the new SEND Code of Practice: 0–25 years (DfE, 2014a; DfE/DH, 2015) means working in partnership with parents and carers; this topic is explored in more detail in Chapters 8 and 9 with further exploration of the EYT/E wider professional role to work with other colleagues in Chapter 12.

In the UK, the SEND reforms complement the EYFS. Box 11.1 looks at what the EYT/E needs to know and what they need to do.

The Children and Families Act 2014 in relation to SEND focuses on outcomes and improving progress for children and young people with SEND, for example, through the processes detailed in Box 11.1.

BOX 11.1

A summary of the SEND Code of Practice (ibid. 2014a)

Integration

- Education, health and social care services are required to cooperate at a local level to meet children and young people's needs.
- LAs and health commissioning groups will be required to commission services jointly for children and young people with SEND. This will help ensure that services are joined up around a common set of outcomes and those parents and young people are clear what support is available locally.

Assessment and planning

- The majority of children with SEN or disabilities will continue to have their needs met within mainstream early years settings.

(Continued)

- SEN Support: a graduated approach to identify and meet SEN, within early years provision following the principles and commitments of the EYFS Statutory Framework in involving parents in identifying needs, deciding outcomes, planning provision and seeking expertise at whatever point it is needed.

Health services

- Inform the parent and the LA if a child under compulsory school age is identified as having SEN or disability (e.g. through the neo-natal screening programmes or the Healthy Child Programme two-year-old check).
- Early years providers will work together with parents/carers to agree ambitious outcomes for identified children and set clear progress targets, and be clear in their planning about how resources are going to support and reach the targets.
- Parents will be fully involved in discussions about their child's progress and reviews of the provision needed to achieve the agreed outcomes.
- Education Health and Care (EHC) Plans are intended for those with more complex needs.
- The EHC assessment and planning process is much more joined up, outcome focused and delivered in partnership with parent carers. It will be delivered and agreed within a maximum of 20 weeks.
- A LA should conduct an EHC needs assessment for children under compulsory school age when the special educational provision required to meet the child's needs cannot reasonably be provided from the resources normally available to the early education provider or school, or when it is likely the child will need an EHC Plan in school.
- Where young children do need an EHC Plan, the LA must seek advice from the early years setting in making decisions about undertaking an EHC needs assessment and preparing an EHC Plan.
- LAs should consider whether the child's current early years provider can support the child's SEND or whether they need to offer additional support through a plan.
- Families of children with an EHC Plan must be offered a personal budget.
- Children with SEND and with a 'statement' will be transferred to an EHCP following a review of a 'statutory assessment' by the LA who seek information from key professionals in order to produce an EHCP and identify the correct placement and support for the child.
- All children develop at their own pace. Where a child has a complicated and long-term need which covers education, health and care, an EHC Plan may be appropriate. However, there are other issues, such as speech and language delay or behavioural problems, which are not necessarily caused by a special educational need or disability.

Source: adapted from The Key for School Leaders, SEND Code of Practice: a summary https://schoolleaders.thekeysupport.com/pupils-and-parents/sen/managing/the-sen-code-of-practice-a-summary/?marker=live-search-q-send-result-1

From an EYT/E's point of view, your role in supporting children with SEND is to:

- Have arrangements in place to identify and support children with SEND.
- Include children with SEN in all the opportunities available to other children so they can achieve well.
- Monitor and support children to ensure that they develop and learn as appropriate.
- Identify any developmental issues.
- Keep well informed and knowledgeable so that you can publicise services to parents and carers and signpost any support that is available locally for their child.
- Work with parents to address any identified problems, and, if appropriate, encourage the parent to refer their child for an EHC assessment.
- Maintain a record of children under your care, which must be available to parents and must include how the setting supports children with SEND.
- Work collaboratively with the LA in reviewing the provision that is available locally and developing the local offer.

TYPES OF SETTINGS EYT/ES WORK IN AND THE IMPLICATIONS FOR SEND

Maintained early years provision

If you work in a maintained setting, you must identify the qualified teacher designated as the SENCO whose role is to ensure that everyone working in the setting understands their responsibilities to children with SEND. They will support you to make sure parents are closely involved and that their insights inform any special educational provision made for their child. The SENCO may also need your help to inform parents about making special educational provision for a child or preparing reports on:

- the implementation of the SEN policy;
- the arrangements for the admission of disabled children;
- the steps being taken to prevent disabled children being treated less favourably than others;
- the facilities provided to enable access to the school for disabled children and their accessibility plan showing how they plan to improve access over time.

All of the above complement your existing duties under the EYFS Statutory Framework (DfE, 2017a) and the Equality Act 2010.

Childminders and those in group provision on domestic premises

Early Years Teachers and Educators very often work as childminders. The nature of the role means that you may work in isolation, however, you are encouraged to identify a person to act as SENCO. If you are registered with a childminder agency or are part of a network, you may be sharing that role between yourselves.

Private, voluntary and independent (PVI) settings

In England, only maintained settings are required to provide children with EHC plans. However, it is best practice for all PVI settings to have a SENCO, whether specific to the setting or as a group of settings. If a PVI setting has the infrastructure to be able to support a child with complex needs, they can do so. If you work in a 'good or outstanding' early years setting, this is well-established practice (Foundation Years, 2014).

THE SEND GRADUATED APPROACH

The SEND Code of Practice graduated approach featured in Box 11.2 is based on an 'assess, plan, do, review' approach to support children with SEND. This resonates strongly with the Early Years Foundation Stage (DfE, 2017a), which all Ofsted registered settings must follow.

BOX 11.2

The Graduated Approach to SEND

The graduated approach is based on a cycle of action that can be revisited with increasing detail, increasing frequency and with the increased involvement of parents. It is usually led by the Early Years Teacher or Key Person, supported by the setting's SENCO. Throughout the graduated approach, the EYT or the child's Key Person remains responsible for working with the child on a daily basis and implementing agreed interventions. At each stage of the cycle the EYT/E or the Key Person and SENCO informed by the child's views, as age appropriate, consult with the parents whether the child is making expected progress, and whether or not:

- Special educational provision and SEN support continues to be required;
- To revisit the cycle in more detail or with increased frequency;
- More specialist assessment may be called for;
- Staff require more specialist advice or the child requires more specialist support;
- More specialist expertise is needed to inform reasonable adjustments and access arrangements for a disabled child;
- The child requires an EHC needs assessment.

Source: Council for Disabled Children, https://councilfordisabledchildren.org.uk (accessed February 2017)

The graduated approach cycle of action[1]

Assess

- The Early Years Teacher, Educator or Key Person works with the setting SENCO and the child's parents to bring together all the information and analyses of the child's needs.
- Special educational needs are generally thought of in four broad areas of need and support:

  o Communication and interaction
  o Cognition and learning
  o Social, emotional and mental health
  o Sensory and/or physical needs

- These broad areas of need are not definitive; the Code of Practice recognises that individual children often have needs that cut across all of these areas and that children's needs may change over time.
- Where there is a need for more specialist expertise to identify the nature of the child's needs, or to determine the most effective approach, specialist teachers, educational psychologists or health, social services or other agencies may need to be involved.

Plan

Where the broad approach to SEN support has been agreed, the Early Years Teacher, Educator or Key Person and the SENCO should agree, in consultation with the parent:

- The outcomes they are seeking for the child
- The interventions and support to be put in place
- The expected impact on progress, development, behaviour
- Date for review

Plans should:

- Take into account the views of the child
- Select the interventions and support to meet the outcomes identified
- Base interventions and support on reliable evidence of effectiveness
- Be delivered by practitioners with relevant skills and knowledge
- Identify and address any related staff development needs

---

[1]This text is adapted from the SEND Code of Practice, para 5.40–5.43 and the Council for Disabled Children: https://councilfordisabledchildren.org.uk (accessed February 2017).

Do

The Early Years Teacher, Educator or the Key Person:

- Remains responsible for working with the child on a daily basis
- Implements the agreed interventions or programmes

The SENCO supports the Early Years Teacher or Key Person in:

- Assessing the child's response to action taken
- Problem solving
- Advising on effective implementation

Review

On the agreed date, the Early Years Teacher, Educator or Key Person and the SENCO working with the child's parents, and taking into account the child's views, should:

- Review the effectiveness of the support
- Review the impact of the support on the child's progress
- Evaluate the impact and quality of support

In the light of the child's progress, they agree:

- Any changes to the outcomes
- Any changes to the support
- Next steps

Points of information[2]

- **Definition of SEN**: a child has a special educational need if they have a learning difficulty or disability that calls for special educational provision.
- **A learning difficulty** is a significantly greater difficulty in learning than the majority of children of the same age.
- **A disability** is a (disability) condition that prevents or hinders a child from taking advantage of the facilities generally available.
- **Special educational provision** is provision that is additional to or different from that which is normally available in mainstream settings.
- **For a child under the age of 2**, special educational provision means provision of any kind.

---

[2]From the Children and Families Act 2014 (Part 3).

- **A child under school age** has SEND if he or she is likely to have SEND when they reach school age, or would do so if special educational provision were not made for them.

— 🔍 —— **Case study 11.1** ————————————————————

An EYT's record of Child X, a 4-year-old boy with moderate learning difficulties and a diagnosis of ASD

Child X is interested and engaged in all learning, loves to work with adults and is developing good verbal skills. He has moved from using symbols to indicate needs such as toilet to exchanging them for motivating toys. He is now increasingly using his rapidly expanding vocabulary to gain attention and acquire resources.

He experiences frequent episodes of anger and frustration that often require him to be guided to a time-out room where, with the support of timers and reference to a personalised themed 'working for' chart, he can calm and return successfully to his classroom. The strategies used to support him to self-regulate and express his feelings appropriately form his behaviour plan. This plan is written by the team working with him and is informed by his speech and language programme and his IEP profile which identifies strengths, motivators and barriers to progress. The strength of the plan lies in the joined up working of a range of professionals and collaboration with his family.

The multi-agency pupil progress meetings held three times a year by the school are the central system for tracking and monitoring all aspects of pupil progress and welfare. Each pupil is assessed against their own strengths and needs and progress is measured against what can be expected of the individual and what success looks like for them. Analysis of strengths and success for the child identify barriers, areas of concern or requiring development. Evidence from welfare reports including e-safety, behaviour records, achievement of personal development targets and reward certificates create a detailed and accurate picture of need enabling appropriate resourcing and action to be identified.

From this point a pathway of action can be created and shared with all adults and professionals involved. The focus for support is, in this case, on developing the child's emotional literacy; enabling him, through the modelling of language and action, to recognise the feelings he has and what to do to get back to a safe and happy place. Motivators that are personal and meaningful provide an incentive to keep trying when it gets hard.

RECORD-KEEPING

Early Years Teachers and Educators need to maintain records of the children under their care as required under the EYFS. These records must be available to parents and they must include the details of the support their child is receiving (DfE/DH, 2015: para 5.50).

Key requirements for records are:

- The progress check at 2 years old, which requires settings to review progress and provide parents with a short, written summary of their child's development.
- If a parent or carer requests an EHC assessment, a range of evidence will need to be gathered.

It is good to know that the EYFS (2017a: 2.2) advocates that 'Paperwork should be limited to that which is absolutely necessary to promote children's successful learning and development. Parents and/or carers should be kept up-to-date with their child's progress and development.' Paperwork has the potential to swamp or overwhelm any decision-making process that is key to improving outcomes for children with SEN. The schools chapter of the SEND Code of Practice (DfE/DH, 2015) recommends that a short note is made of the discussions held with parents and shared with them. This is good practice for EYT/Es too. After you have had a discussion with parents or carers you should write up:

- The outcomes they are seeking for the child
- The interventions and support to be put in place
- The expected impact on progress, development, behaviour
- Date for review

If you are involved in putting an EHC needs assessment into place, the LA requires evidence of:

- The child's developmental milestones and rate of progress
- The nature, extent and context of the child's SEN
- The action taken by the early years provider
- Evidence that, where progress has been made, it has only been achieved by support that is more than that which is normally provided
- The child's physical, emotional, social development and health needs

 Points for reflection

The school, academy, free schools or early years setting that you work in should have a standard approach to record-keeping with a standard format to capture essential information. Based on this assumption, consider how the approach you use enables you to:

- Focus on outcomes and any potential impact
- Focus on the participative assess, plan, do, review cycle without excessive paperwork
- Capture the essential evidence

- Meet the setting's needs for information
- Meet parents' needs for information
- Meet other professionals and the Local Authority's requirement for information
- Capture parents' views
- Capture children's views

Source: Adapted from 4Children and the Council for Disabled Children: https://council-fordisabledchildren.org.uk (accessed February 2017)

Good communication between parents and providers is seen as crucial in the Study of Early Education and Development (SEED) (Griggs and Bussard, 2017: 7), especially with reference to coordinating the strategies to be put in place for the child with SEN or a disability. The EYT/E, by proxy, then must be able to communicate with parents and carers and give feedback. Finding time to communicate with parents in itself can be problematic; SEED emphasised that discussions between parents and the identified person 'typically took place during the drop-off and pick-up periods, although most settings also had parents' evenings where progress could be discussed more formally' (Griggs and Bussard, 2017: 8).

 Case study 11.2

From the Study of Early Education and Development (SEED, 2017)

The most common way in which parents and settings communicated with one another, was informal information sharing during drop-off and pick-up time. This typically involved short discussions about what activities the child had been doing, minor changes in the child's health or events in the child's life. Settings felt that this kind of informal information sharing worked well and helped foster positive and receptive relationships with parents. However, although these discussions were informal, settings were also aware that care had to be taken in terms of how they communicated with parents and what they communicated to them, as one setting explained:

'It's taken me about 30 years to work this out – that if you tell parents something they make up the rest ... If you say, "Oh, your child struggles to line up for lunchtime," they then think they're struggling throughout the whole day in nursery ... they make up the rest of the information ... It's got to be very, very specific, so they can't get the wrong end of the stick.' (voluntary setting, South East, Ofsted rated Good).

(Continued)

Effective communication with parents was supported by:

- Being non-judgemental and building trust
- Getting to know parents individually and tailoring the mode of communication to their preferences
- Ensuring effective communication between staff so that all staff felt able to answer parent queries

Parent feedback – One way setting staff tried to facilitate more consistent communication with parents was to provide them with parent books which allowed both parents and staff to write information about the child and their progress. Parents were encouraged by staff to write any changes or developments in order to keep the setting up to date. In some cases, settings then used the information provided by parents to re-enforce behavioural strategies within the setting and to help integrate children socially.

Source: SEED: Meeting the needs of children with special educational needs and disabilities in the early years (Griggs and Bussard, 2017)

 Key points

- It is wise to familiarise yourself with the various current items of legislation to support the education and care of children with SEND.
- Most SEND children can, with support, have their needs met in a mainstream setting by staff providing inclusive learning opportunities and employing anti-discriminatory practice.
- EYT/Es must work collaboratively with the parents/carers to identify, at the earliest possible point, the needs of the child. Early identification is key to answering those needs.
- An EHC assessment must be undertaken when that need is greater and the wishes of the parents must be taken fully into account.
- Good record-keeping helps build up evidence of the need for an EHCP.
- An EHC plan may require schools and settings to employ an Individual Needs Assistant in mainstream or award a place in a named special school.
- All schools and settings must have a designated SENCO.
- Reviews of the needs of the child must be undertaken annually by the SENCO in conjunction with the parents and the LA.

FURTHER READING

Nutbrown, C., Clough, P. and Atherton, F. (2013) *Inclusion in the Early Years.* London: Sage.

This insightful text shows how the attitudes of adults in early years settings can influence practice, arguing for a broad definition of inclusion.

Peer, L. and Reid, G. (2016) *Special Educational Needs – A Guide for Inclusive Practice.* London: Sage.

This book provides a wealth of information and guidance for students and professionals on how to achieve effective, inclusive practice.

Hodkinson, A. (2015) *Key Issues in Special Educational Needs and Inclusion.* London: Sage.

Covering the 0–25 age range, this book helps the EYT/E to contextualise SEND in relation to historical, ideological and political developments. A variety of case studies, reflections and activities help students question practice.

USEFUL WEB RESOURCES

Essential reading and more detailed information can be found at the following websites:

Council for Disabled Children
www.councilfordisabledchildren.org.uk

Special Educational Needs and Disability Code of Practice: 0–25 years
www.gov.uk/government/publications/send-code-of-practice-0-to-25

This is statutory guidance issued in 2015 for organisations who work with and support children and young people with special educational needs and disabilities.

UK government information, resources and support for SEND
www.foundationyears.org.uk/files/2014/07/The-SEND-reforms-1-pager.pdf
www.gov.uk/government/publications/send-guide-for-early-years-settings

Multiple resources on Special Educational Needs and Disability and the legislation and support that can be obtained are available at:
www.gov.uk

Barnardos

www.barnardos.org.uk/factsheet_15_-_sen_support_-_early_years.pdf

This charitable society has helped vulnerable and underprivileged children for 150 years by its fostering and adoption programme, support for young carers, and prevention of child poverty. They undertake research and produce publications that may be useful.

Respecting Rights in Schools

www.unicef.org.uk/rights-respecting-schools/the-rrsa/introducing-the-crc

This is an initiative by UNICEF working with schools in the UK to create safe and inspiring places to learn, where children are respected, their talents are nurtured and they are able to thrive. The Rights Respecting Schools Award recognises a school's achievement in putting the UNCHR objectives into practice.

The Early Years Foundation Stage which seeks to provide equality of opportunity and anti-discriminatory practice, ensuring that every child is included and supported.

www.foundationyears.org.uk/files/2017/03/EYFS_STATUTORY_FRAMEWORK_2017.pdf

 **Online resources**

Visit https://study.sagepub.com/education to find a selection of scholarly journal articles chosen to support each chapter.

12

UNDERTAKING WIDER PROFESSIONAL RESPONSIBILITIES

JULIE VAGGERS

Chapter overview

This chapter considers some key areas for professional development for the Early Years Teacher and Educator (EYT/E) who might be reflecting on their wider professional responsibilities. It considers the complexities of team working and gives a brief overview of change management theory. It reflects upon the barriers to working collaboratively and how to overcome them and explores ways of building strong professional relationships for effective practice. The chapter also examines the concept of good authority where each member of the team takes responsibility for the vision of the setting and how to develop a trusting dialogue with parents, staff and professional partners where each member of the team seeks to understand as well as to be understood.

DEFINING WIDER PROFESSIONAL RESPONSIBILITIES

The Department for Education defines fulfilling wider professional responsibilities as follows:

- Make a positive contribution to the wider life and ethos of the school
- Develop effective professional relationships with colleagues, knowing how and when to draw on advice and specialist support
- Deploy support staff effectively
- Take responsibility for improving teaching through appropriate professional development, responding to advice and feedback from colleagues
- Communicate effectively with parents with regards to pupils' achievements and well-being

For the Early Years Teacher and Educator this is an opportunity to look up from their daily work with children and consider the wider horizon. It requires the EYT/E to reflect on their contribution to the setting and their impact on children's progress. They should also consider the quality of their relationships with colleagues and parents. A useful starting point to consider is whether as an EYT/E your purpose, vision and values are aligned to those of the setting.

 Points for reflection

- What is the purpose of your setting? What does it exist to do and why are you there?
- What is the vision for the future? Is this where you want to be?
- What does the setting value about children and families? Do these values match your own beliefs?

If the EYT/E is strongly aligned with their setting it is likely that this passion and shared commitment is easily seen in their wider contribution to the life of the setting. To meet this standard an EYT/E cannot be a reluctant leader. It is important to demonstrate effective leadership, even if you do not have a clearly designated leadership role. This can be done by:

- Building a reflective team with a shared ethos
- Supporting colleagues through change
- Shaping an inclusive and integrated culture
- Having a strong sense of good authority

A REFLECTIVE TEAM WITH A SHARED ETHOS

The EYT/E is responsible for leading practice and co-constructing a shared ethos. A shared vision creates a shared commitment, where everyone is clear about their role and purpose. It makes the setting's expectations explicit and acts as a guide for people's behaviour. To create a shared ethos it is important to take the necessary time as a team to discuss and debate values, views and beliefs about children and families. Everyone in the team must be involved in building the principles that underpin the practice with children. The team has to work together to build an inclusive value-based ethos.

It takes time to build a team that is committed to learning about itself and how to maximise opportunities for children to learn. It helps for each member of the team to be able to express their views and feelings about their work with children. It is important to make conscious and explicit what may often be unconscious beliefs about how children learn best. Sigmund Freud (1856–1939) described the mind as an iceberg. Below the surface of every organisation can be fears, assumptions and feelings that a skilled EYT/E can safely bring to the surface. Once opinions and beliefs have been expressed they can be debated and discussed. Differences of opinion can be welcomed as an opportunity to explore where they have originated from and why. Agreements can be reached and a shared approach can be moulded by the whole team. This is very important because as Karen John (2017) explains, 'The iceberg metaphor suggests that it is not what can be seen above the surface of the water that will "sink" relationships, a project or an organisation, but the much larger unseen mass below the surface.'

It is helpful for the EYT/E to understand the stages that teams go through in their development. They can then recognise valuable moments when it is possible to move the team forward to become the most effective it can be.

Tuckman (1965) identified how teams generally go through four stages of development, described as: forming, storming, norming and performing. All of these stages are important and involve team members testing out what interpersonal behaviour is appropriate in the group. Conflict is an important part of the constant process of team building and should not be avoided. However, it must be respectful and if the EYT/E has worked with the team to establish clear, preferably written, boundaries this clear guidance will help the team be more effective. A written contract will make explicit the team's expectations of one another.

 Points for reflection

- What would you want in a team contract?
- How would you encourage everyone to feel safe enough to express their views?
- How do you encourage a shared sense of responsibility thus avoiding a blame culture?

The EYT/E can further promote team working directly with colleagues, other professionals and carers by utilising Belbin's (2005) theory about team roles at work. Belbin identified nine team roles, each of which will have strengths and weaknesses. They are plant, resource investigator, coordinator, shaper, monitor evaluator, team worker, implementer, completer and specialist. Successful teams have the right mix of people in them sharing the roles between them. Team role questionnaires can help develop a shared understanding of preferred roles and gaps within a team. This self-insight can lead to higher achievements. 'The mature team knows what it is good at, realises where its weaknesses lie, plays to its strengths and avoids engaging in activities where it cannot compete effectively' (Belbin, 2005: 48).

In order to ensure that the EYT/E can demonstrate that they shape, support and sustain the setting's policies and practices it is necessary for them to reflect on the process of developing these policies and practices. If the whole team feel that they count, are capable and connect with one another, they will have the courage to contribute. These crucial Cs were identified by Adlerian psychologists Betty Lou Bettner and Amy Lew (Lew and Bettner, 1990).

 —— **Ideas for practice** ──────────────────────────────

At meetings ask yourself:

- What is the nature of contributions made at meetings?
- Does everyone have a chance to speak? Do these views count?
- Are strong emotions recognised and contained so that everyone has the courage to contribute?
- Is there evidence that people feel capable?
- Are there opportunities to connect and get to know one another's preferred team roles?

SUPPORTING COLLEAGUES THROUGH CHANGE

Change is a constant in all our lives and especially so in the early years. Incessant changes to National Policy and the introduction of new initiatives can feel overwhelming. This can lead to individuals feeling exhausted. Eric Abrahamson (2004) named this malaise as *repetitive-change syndrome*. He described it as having two components:

1. Initiative overload: the tendency of organisations to launch more change initiatives than anyone could reasonably handle.
2. Change-related chaos: the continuous state of upheaval that results when so many waves of initiatives have worked through an organisation that hardly anyone knows which change they are implementing or why, leading to a loss of organisational memory.

In order to deploy staff effectively it is necessary to recognise the impact that change can have on the team. The EYT/E needs to be well versed in the theory of change management as it helps them manage the interpersonal world at work. Knowing that change causes recognisable patterns in one's own behaviour and that of others can help lessen anxieties and ensure appropriate support is given when it is most needed. John Fisher developed a process of transition model showing the emotions that may occur during the change process (Fisher, 2003, revised 2012). People experience these feelings at different times and for differing lengths of time. It is important to know and understand each individual team member's likely reactions to change and to talk this through with them. A plan to support colleagues through any transition is important. Bridges (2009) suggests that to support people to prepare for a new change it helps to give them a purpose, a picture, a plan and a part to play.

As well as understanding the emotions at play during the management of change there are also several stages that can be planned for. Kotter (2012 [1996]) suggests eight steps to consider when managing change. These are:

1. Establishing a sense of urgency
2. Creating the guiding coalition
3. Developing a vision and strategy
4. Communicating the change vision
5. Empowering broad-based action
6. Generating short-term wins
7. Consolidating gains and producing more change
8. Anchoring new approaches in the culture

In early years settings this means exploring the need for change and sharing an understanding of how the change will benefit the children's progress. It can help to visit other settings to see this impact and to share this information with the parents and children. It will be necessary to share updates in regular displays, newsletters and on the website to demonstrate the changes taking place and the difference they are making.

All of these theories require the EYT/E to communicate clearly and sensitively. Communication is critical to the success of any team. They must demonstrate that they can communicate in a calm, assertive and sensitive manner with parents and staff. They must role-model expected healthy norms of behaviour, so that the children observe how issues are addressed and resolved. Peter Elfer (1996: 30) says in *Key Times*: 'it is difficult to sustain close and responsive relationships with young children without an organisational culture that expects and supports a process of reflection on the emotional dimensions of practice' (quoted in Manning-Morton and Thorp, 2003: 34).

Leading supervision, performance management, appraisal and CPD is critical. It provides an opportunity for the EYT/E to ask questions of the staff they manage, with an attitude of appreciation, curiosity, commitment and not knowing the answer. John (2017) acknowledges that: 'An effective supervision policy and structure within early years settings demonstrate a commitment to positive working relationships, foster open communication among managers and other staff and promote good practice.'

Supervision provides a time to explore with individual team members, their key children's behaviour, how they work with the child and family. It provides a safe place to explore attitudes, responses and to consider what is going well and what to do differently.

Performance management is focused on reaching appraisal targets and demonstrating the impact the individual's work is having on the outcomes, attainment and progress of the children.

Professional development is about developing a future career path, identifying relevant training and ensuring individuals have the appropriate knowledge and skills to carry out their professional role.

Sometimes the EYT/E will have to have difficult conversations about professional relationships, deployment of staff, or attitude and behaviours within the team. It is really important that these conversations are seen by both parties as a learning opportunity where a joint problem is shared. It is not helpful to see these conversations as a means to getting your own way. You do need to understand the viewpoint of the other person. You need to gain information about the situation and you may start to see the problem through a different lens. Douglas Stone, Bruce Patton and Sheila Heen of the Harvard negotiation project (1999) call these difficult conversations 'learning conversations'. They suggest that it is more effective to work as partners, sharing perspectives, understanding the emotions involved, agreeing what options exist to resolve the matter and confirming how communication will be kept open as you both move forward.

It is important to remain in adult mode at work, especially when working with young children. Staff and parents may want you to take on a parental role, so that they do not have to take responsibility for their actions. Rodd (2006) suggests that the EYT/E in the initial stages of their careers may have a more authoritarian and paternalistic relationship with parents. She suggests that maturity brings a broader perspective and a better view for collaborative working with parents.

 **Case study 12.1**

Sally, a Deputy Manager of a nursery, describes how she undertakes her wider professional responsibilities

I am the deputy of a private nursery that is part of a large chain. It provides childcare and early education from 3 months to 5 years of age from 7.30am to 6.30pm. I make a positive contribution to the life of the nursery by going that extra mile, with parents and staff. I feel it's my job to notice when individuals are uncertain and struggling. It is important that I help people recognise what they don't know and motivate and encourage them to learn new skills. I don't want staff to just come to work to be paid, they must be child focused and always think what is the best for the child. I encourage staff to take up training opportunities, especially if their initial qualifications have been achieved online or I feel that the calibre of their training has not been deep enough. I have one-to-ones with my manager every 6 weeks and I carry out supervision with up to a dozen staff. We also have regular one-to-ones together and conversations when needed or wanted.

The staff team are powerful as a group and as a collective can at times be hard to manage. There can be groups of staff with strong attitudes. I find it helps to know everyone well individually and to deploy them according to their strengths, not in their friendship groups. I set up staff groups and ask them to collaborate on projects, such as designing a water wheel with the children. If I must have a difficult conversation with a member of staff, for example about punctuality, it's essential that I manage my own feelings. I remind myself that we expect children to be able to negotiate and solve problems, therefore I cannot let my personal feelings of frustration get in the way. We should reach a resolution that benefits the children.

I work to develop effective relationships with the team by having an open-door policy, having daily conversations and always greeting everyone first thing and saying goodbye at the end of the day. I must be approachable and open to discussing my actions and the nursery's policies and procedures. This helps avoid people making assumptions and these conversations help clarify good child-centred practice. Once a month we have a staff meeting after work for about 2 hours. We will review policies and discuss the company's latest quality assurance audit. Everyone has something to say at these meetings and we also encourage email discussions as well.

It's important to respond to feedback from the team. At times, it can be helpful for staff to feed back to someone from outside the organisation. This has resulted in useful feedback for the management team in my setting. Recently the team have told us that they would like to see us in the rooms more often. My manager and I are going to organise some office swaps so that when we are in the room the staff can be released to carry out administration tasks, such as drawing up the rota. We will get an insight into each other's roles. We are also working on a better feedback and action loop along the lines of 'you told us this, so we have done that'. It's work in progress but will help communication between management and staff.

Parents expect a lot and they pay a great deal for our services. I have learnt about how important it is to build a relationship right from the start. Over the years I have witnessed poor management practice and I have learnt from this about how I wanted to do it very differently. I tell parents a bit about myself and reassure them that I have their child's best interests at heart. I make sure when I am showing new parents around that everyone in the team stops to say hello and introduce themselves; these little things really matter. We regularly organise events for parents so that they can build up networks of support amongst themselves too.

In the future, I would like to visit more nurseries. I think it would be very helpful for everyone's professional development to visit more settings especially ones that are in a different socio-economic situation.

I have learnt not to agree to do everything. I have had to balance this and take on what I can do and to reach out for help when I need to learn new things. I have over time built up a network of support with other deputies and managers and can ring them for advice.

(Continued)

I have learnt so much over the past 5 years as I have progressed in my career. There have been times when my vision of how best to work with children has been at odds with the setting. I have taken responsibility for this and helped to shape changes to policy and practice. I have worked hard to develop high-quality and congruent relationships with parents and staff. I have just taken on the role of SENCO to improve what we offer and ensure each child gets the best start in life. I could possibly start to reach outside of my setting, to work with other nurseries, in a mentoring role, and I am confident that I will continue my professional development and could become a manager in the future.

 Points for reflection

- Are you and those you supervise clear about the value of supervision?
- Can you explain the difference between performance management and supervision?
- How are you ensuring that your setting meets the requirements of the EYFS and offers appropriate provision, properly managed and supervised, for children in its care?

SHAPING AN INCLUSIVE AND INTEGRATED CULTURE

The EYT/E is part of a wide network of professionals from other services. Each service will have its own culture, training and beliefs about how children learn and develop. This can lead to differences of opinion and a lack of understanding about each other's approaches. The EYT/E must ensure effective professional relationships so that they can draw on advice and specialist support when it is needed and so will need to address difficulties if and when they arise.

It can be far from simple to organise multiprofessional team work and collaboration. Some of the barriers include:

1. Time pressures, to take advantage of all the documentation and advice about integrated working
2. Unclear strategic management
3. Different physical locations
4. Different budget streams
5. Brief encounters with part-time colleagues who themselves feel overwhelmed
6. Different professional experiences, knowledge, skills and vocabulary
7. Different line management and supervision arrangements
8. Different pay and conditions
9. Apparent polarities of opinion with no time to debate and clarify approaches
10. Lack of strategic support or vision to create the necessary circumstances for relationship building

(Vaggers, 2014)

The most important first step to working together is to agree why you are collaborating in the first place and what advantages it provides. This may seem obvious but it can be surprising how little attention is given to this in the busy day-to-day work in early years settings. If the EYT/E is able to find time to have a conversation with the speech and language therapist or Health Visitor to discuss what each party is hoping to achieve and what they value about working together this can help create an ethos of *collaborative advantage.*

Collaborative advantage is 'a world in which it is possible to feel inspired' (Huxham and Vangen, 2006: 3). It creates energy, access to resources, a shared risk, efficiency, coordination and seamlessness; it prevents repetition, omission, divergence, conflicting activities. It creates opportunities for learning, dissemination and addresses moral issues that will only be alleviated through a multi-organisational response (2006: 7).

Often collaboration leads to *collaborative inertia* where neither party is clear what they can achieve by working together and would prefer to carry on working in isolation. Collaborative inertia is mired in difficulties, in communicating and gaining agreement to act, differences between parties on organisational purpose, procedures and structures, professional languages, accountabilities, and power (Huxham and Vangen, 2006).

Building positive relationships with partner colleagues will help the EYT/E to shape and implement local and national policies. It will support their work during integrated reviews and 2-year-old provision and progress checks and team around the child meetings.

Angela Anning's (2001) research showed that it was important for professionals from different disciplines to spend time getting to know who each other were and what they did and not enough focus has been spent on this: 'However, little attention has been given to two significant aspects of operationalising integrated services. The first is the challenge for workers of creating new professional identities in the emergent communities of practice (who I am). The second is for workers to articulate and share their personal and professional knowledge in order to create new versions of knowledge (what I know) for new ways of working.'

Relational leadership is fundamental to undertaking wider professional responsibilities. Deborah Ancona and her colleagues (2007) described recent shifts in thinking about relational leadership: 'Traditional images of leadership didn't assign much value to relating. Flawless leaders shouldn't need to seek counsel from anyone outside their tight inner circle, the thinking went and they were expected to issue edicts rather than connect on an emotional level. Times have changed, of course, and in this era of networks, being able to build trusting relationships is a requirement of effective leadership' (p. 3). She advocated the following three methods to do this:

1. Enquire
2. Advocate
3. Connect

By employing these methods to build professional relationships an EYT/E can learn and share their beliefs about how children learn best and optimise opportunities for their development. Weaving these social webs and interactions can be done in many ways including through corridor chats, staff meetings and joint training. West-Burnham, Farrer and Otero (2007) observed leaders who created social capital; they then identified conditions that promoted social dialogue, these were:

1. Hospitality
2. Participation
3. Mindfulness
4. Humility
5. Mutuality
6. Deliberation
7. Appreciation
8. Hope
9. Autonomy

This is a helpful list to reflect on when things appear stuck or difficult.

 —— **Ideas for practice** ————————————————

Think about the systems in place and the leadership culture in your EY setting and consider how it enables you to:

- Provide a welcoming ethos and a deliberate intent to develop shared knowledge of one another's perspectives?
- Identify a child's development needs and to ask for specialist help as early as possible?
- Put in place opportunities to exchange professional opinions and learn about different professional cultures?

GOOD AUTHORITY

'Good authority is leadership that inspires and contains ambition and anxiety' (John, 2012). It requires a democratic approach to leadership where each member of the team takes responsibility for the vision of the setting. It creates a sense of pride in being part of the team; people cooperate and are confident in their practice.

Michael Fullan (1998) identified that self-confidence is important for deployment of self. Deployment of self directs one's attention towards one's own professional development. It is necessary for persistence, integrity and perpetual learning. The EYT/E who knows and recognises their strengths and compensates for their weaknesses is able to lead effectively with good authority. Warren Bennis and Burt Nanus (1997) describe this as positive self-regard. They explain that with a positive sense of self-regard it is possible to be accepting of oneself and others, trusting one's own self and trusting others, even if the risk is great. This positive self-regard will in turn lead to colleagues experiencing increased motivation and confidence.

 Points for reflection

- How do you recognise your strengths and compensate for weaknesses?
- How do you encourage feedback from colleagues so that it is respectful and useful?

Good authority is necessary to work effectively with parents. It is important to work *in dialogue* with parents. Pen Green Centre in Corby explains what this means:

> Our understanding is that to engage in dialogue, we have to be humble, to identify with other humans and not to be so defensive about our knowledge that we cannot listen to or hear the views of the parents. (Arnold and Cummings, 2013)

An EYT/E with good authority and a positive self-regard will be humble and authentic when in dialogue with parents. They will seek to understand as well as to be understood. In order to build trusting relationships with parents and colleagues it is important to trust yourself and others. Warren Bennis (1989) identified in his book on becoming a leader four critical ingredients that generate and sustain trust. They are constancy, congruity, reliability and integrity. These are key characteristics for undertaking wider professional responsibilities.

Trusting your own judgement and that of others is a critical leadership process. All professionals leave an impression in all their day-to-day encounters. They need to nourish and maintain a stable and resilient sense of self in order to nourish and build the confidence of the people around them. As American author and poet Maya Angelou wrote: 'People will forget what you said. People will forget what you did. But people will never forget how you made them feel' (Kelly, 2003: 263). If staff, parents and professional partners are left with the feeling of being trusted and seen as capable, this will leave a lasting impression.

As mentioned in the introduction, an EYT/E cannot be a reluctant leader. In many early years settings there is often a very flat hierarchy; the EYT/E will be working alongside the team and they may not have a clearly designated leadership role. Despite this, in order to take responsibility for wider professional responsibilities, the EYT/E has to demonstrate how they lead the teaching and learning for maximum impact on the children's progress. This definition of teaching is helpful here:

> Teaching means systematically helping children to learn so that they are helped to make connections in their learning and are actively led forward, as well as helped to reflect on what they have already learnt ... although teaching can be defined simply, it is a complex process. (Foundation Years, 2012)

The EYT/E working with staff and parents must enable children to be agents of their own learning, within a rigorous environment. They must support their team to be reflective practitioners moving towards a common purpose with consistent practice grounded in collective values.

In any team, but particularly small teams, there can be an ever-present danger of collusion. This is where team members engage in behaviour that does not support the ethos and vision of the setting in order to gain acceptance, approval, recognition or security and to feel emotionally and psychologically safe. When working with good authority the EYT/E cannot ignore this 'elephant in the room'. They must tell themselves and the team what the truth of the matter is. This takes courage and integrity. Belinda Harris (2007), in her book about the emotional work of school leaders, wrote how leaders 'need to balance finding support in their environment and finding support from within themselves to create an inner sense of wholeness and completeness'. This requires a congruent fit between one's own values and that of the setting, as was discussed in the introduction of this chapter.

FINAL REFLECTIONS

There is a lack of training in leadership in the early years. Bertram and Pascal (2014) recommend that there should be 'investment in early years leadership at all levels, and across early education, social care and health services to champion and promote the importance of early years services and ensure the development and delivery of an integrated high-quality system'.

Despite this lack of opportunity, the early years EYT/E should engage in further professional development. This is a clear demonstration of your commitment to your wider professional responsibilities. Exploring and learning about how to build an effective team, how to manage change, develop integrated working and good authority helps the EYT/E articulate the complexities of the role.

> We know now that there is no single, simple way to teach because there is no simple way to learn and the EYT/E's task in the twenty-first century classroom is becoming increasingly complex and sophisticated. (MacGilchrist et al., 2004: 72)

The early years EYT/E's role is sophisticated and their leadership role is a complex one. Exploring the open horizon of wider professional responsibilities is an opportunity to learn new skills and demonstrate existing expertise.

 **Key points**

- Reflect on your wider professional role and access CPD on leadership and management.
- Observe managers and senior leaders and reflect on their leadership strategies and behaviours.
- Develop support networks where you can share experiences and expertise with others in similar roles.
- Visit other high-quality EY settings and/or arrange staff swaps to benefit from seeing practice in other settings.
- Ask your line manager and other colleagues for feedback on what it is about your role that you do well and what could you develop.
- Develop a trusting dialogue with parents, staff and professional partners where you seek to understand as well as to be understood.

FURTHER READING

Ancona, D., Malone, T.W., Orlikowski, W.J. and Senge, P.M. (2007) 'In praise of the incomplete leader', *Harvard Business Review*, 85 (2): 92–100 (Reprint R0702E, pp. 1–9).

This text explores the importance of relationships in the workplace.

Cheminais, R. (2009) *Effective Multi-Agency Partnerships*. London: Sage.

This text provides an in-depth overview about the complexity of relationships within multi-agency partnerships.

Harris, B. (2007) *Supporting the Emotional Work of School Leaders*. London: Paul Chapman.

This book examines the rarely considered emotional impact of leadership.

USEFUL WEB RESOURCES

Joseph A. Raelin Northeastern University – We the Leaders: In Order to Form a Leaderful Organization: available at:

http://citeseerx.ist.psu.edu/viewdoc/download?doi=10.1.1.617.5494&rep=rep1&type=pdf

This web link features an article which endeavours to develop an emerging paradigm of leadership known as 'leaderful practice'. Leaderful practice constitutes a direct challenge to the conventional view of leadership.

'Collusion, Culture and Bad Management'
www.management-issues.com/opinion/6423/collusion-culture-and-bad-management

This article by Peter Vajda explores the importance of ethical behaviours in the workplace.

Fisher's Personal Transition Curve

www.csu.edu.au/__data/assets/pdf_file/0006/949533/fisher-transition-curve-2012.pdf

This management tool can be used to help manage change and focus on the beneficial outcomes for children.

'A Theoretical Framework: The individual psychology of Alfred Adler'

www.adleriansociety.co.uk/phdi/p3.nsf/imgpages/0939_KarenJohn-ASIIPConf-April2011.
    pdf/$file/KarenJohn-ASIIPConf-April2011.pdf

This conference paper from Karen John examines both individual and humanistic psychology in a belief that an individual is the best in determining his or her own needs, desires, interests and growth.

 **Online resources**

Visit https://study.sagepub.com/education to find a selection of scholarly journal articles chosen to support each chapter.

APPENDIX 1.1

TEACHERS' STANDARDS. (EARLY YEARS) FROM SEPTEMBER 2013. NATIONAL COLLEGE FOR TEACHING AND LEADERSHIP

TEACHERS' STANDARDS (EARLY YEARS)

An Early Years Teacher must:

1. **Set high expectations which inspire, motivate and challenge all children.**

   1.1 Establish and sustain a safe and stimulating environment where children feel confident and are able to learn and develop.

   1.2 Set goals that stretch and challenge children of all backgrounds, abilities and dispositions.

   1.3 Demonstrate and model the positive values, attitudes and behaviours expected of children.

2. **Promote good progress and outcomes by children.**

   2.1 Be accountable for children's progress, attainment and outcomes.

   2.2 Demonstrate knowledge and understanding of how babies and children learn and develop.

   2.3 Know and understand attachment theories, their significance and how effectively to promote secure attachments.

   2.4 Lead and model effective strategies to develop and extend children's learning and thinking, including sustained shared thinking.

   2.5 Communicate effectively with children from birth to age five, listening and responding sensitively.

   2.6 Develop children's confidence, social and communication skills through group learning.

   2.7 Understand the important influence of parents and/or carers, working in partnership with them to support the child's well-being, learning and development.

3. Demonstrate good knowledge of early learning and EYFS.

3.1 Have a secure knowledge of early childhood development and how that leads to successful learning and development at school.

3.2 Demonstrate a clear understanding of how to widen children's experience and raise their expectations.

3.3 Demonstrate a critical understanding of the EYFS areas of learning and development and engage with the educational continuum of expectations, curricula and teaching of Key Stage 1 and 2.

3.4 Demonstrate a clear understanding of systematic synthetic phonics in the teaching of early reading.

3.5 Demonstrate a clear understanding of appropriate strategies in the teaching of early mathematics.

4. Plan education and care taking account of the needs of all children.

4.1 Observe and assess children's development and learning, using this to plan next steps.

4.2 Plan balanced and flexible activities and educational programmes that take into account the stage of development, circumstances and interests of children.

4.3 Promote a love of learning and stimulate children's intellectual curiosity in partnership with parents and/or carers.

4.4 Use a variety of teaching approaches to lead group activities appropriate to the age range and ability of children.

4.5 Reflect on the effectiveness of teaching activities and educational programmes to support the continuous improvement of provision.

5. Adapt education and care to respond to the strengths and needs of all children.

5.1 Have a secure understanding of how a range of factors can inhibit children's learning and development and how best to address these.

5.2 Demonstrate an awareness of the physical, emotional, social, intellectual development and communication needs of babies and children, and know how to adapt education and care to support children at different stages of development.

5.3 Demonstrate a clear understanding of the needs of all children, including those with special educational needs and disabilities, and be able to use and evaluate distinctive approaches to engage and support them.

5.4 Support children through a range of transitions.

5.5 Know when a child is in need of additional support and how this can be accessed, working in partnership with parents and/or carers and other professionals.

6. **Make accurate and productive use of assessment.**

    6.1 Understand and lead assessment within the framework of the EYFS framework, including statutory assessment requirements (see annex 1).

    6.2 Engage effectively with parents and/or carers and other professionals in the on-going assessment and provision for each child.

    6.3 Give regular feedback to children and parents and/or carers to help children progress towards their goals.

7. **Safeguard and promote the welfare of children, and provide a safe learning environment.**

    7.1 Know and act upon the legal requirements and guidance on health and safety, safeguarding and promoting the welfare of the child.

    7.2 Establish and sustain a safe environment and employ practices that promote children's health and safety.

    7.3 Know and understand child protection policies and procedures, recognise when a child is in danger or at risk of abuse, and know how to act to protect them.

8. **Fulfil wider professional responsibilities.**

    8.1 Promote equality of opportunity and anti-discriminatory practice.

    8.2 Make a positive contribution to the wider life and ethos of the setting.

    8.3 Take a lead in establishing a culture of cooperative working between colleagues, parents and/or carers and other professionals.

    8.4 Model and implement effective education and care, and support and lead other practitioners including Early Years Educators.

    8.5 Take responsibility for leading practice through appropriate professional development for self and colleagues.

    8.6 Reflect on and evaluate the effectiveness of provision, and shape and support good practice.

    8.7 Understand the importance of and contribute to multi-agency team working.

ANNEX 1: EARLY YEARS FOUNDATION STAGE STATUTORY ASSESSMENT GUIDANCE AS SPECIFIED AT STANDARD 6

Section 2 – Assessment

    2.1 Assessment plays an important part in helping parents, carers and practitioners to recognise children's progress, understand their needs, and to plan activities and support. Ongoing assessment (also known as formative assessment) is an integral part of the learning and development process. It involves practitioners observing children to understand their level of achievement, interests and learning styles, and to then shape learning experiences for each child reflecting those observations. In their interactions with children, practitioners should respond to their own day-to-day observations about children's progress, and observations that parents and carers share.

2.2   Assessment should not entail prolonged breaks from interaction with children, nor require excessive paperwork. Paperwork should be limited to that which is absolutely necessary to promote children's successful learning and development. Parents and/or carers should be kept up-to-date with their child's progress and development. Practitioners should address any learning and development needs in partnership with parents and/or carers, and any relevant professionals.

Progress check at age two

2.3   When a child is aged between two and three, practitioners must review their progress, and provide parents and/or carers with a short written summary of their child's development in the prime areas. This progress check must identify the child's strengths, and any areas where the child's progress is less than expected. If there are significant emerging concerns, or an identified special educational need or disability, practitioners should develop a targeted plan to support the child's future learning and development involving other professionals (for example, the provider's Special Educational Needs Co-ordinator) as appropriate.

2.4   Beyond the prime areas, it is for practitioners to decide what the written summary should include, reflecting the development level and needs of the individual child. The summary must highlight: areas in which a child is progressing well; areas in which some additional support might be needed; and focus particularly on any areas where there is a concern that a child may have a developmental delay (which may indicate a special educational need or disability). It must describe the activities and strategies the provider intends to adopt to address any issues or concerns. If a child moves settings between the ages of two and three it is expected that the progress check would usually be undertaken by the setting where the child has spent most time.

2.5   Practitioners must discuss with parents and/or carers how the summary of development can be used to support learning at home. Practitioners should encourage parents and/or carers to share information from the progress check with other relevant professionals, including their health visitor, and/or a teacher (if a child moves to school-based provision at age three). Practitioners must agree with parents and/or carers when will be the most useful point to provide a summary. It should be provided in time to inform the Healthy Child Programme health and development review at age two whenever possible (when health visitors gather information on a child's health and development, allowing them to identify any developmental delay and any particular support from which they think the child/family might benefit). Taking account of information from the progress check (which reflects ongoing, regular observation of children's development) should help ensure that health visitors can identify children's needs accurately and fully at the health review. Providers must have the consent of parents and/or carers to share information directly with other relevant professionals, if they consider this would be helpful.

Assessment at the end of the EYFS – the Early Years Foundation Stage Profile (EYFSP)

2.6 In the final term of the year in which the child reaches age five, and no later than 30 June in that term, the EYFS Profile must be completed for each child. The Profile provides parents and carers, practitioners and teachers with a well-rounded picture of a child's knowledge, understanding and abilities, their progress against expected levels, and their readiness for Year 1. The Profile must reflect: ongoing observation; all relevant records held by the setting; discussions with parents and carers; and any other adults whom the teacher, parent or carer judges can offer a useful contribution.

2.7 Each child's level of development must be assessed against the early learning goals (see Section 1). Practitioners must indicate whether children are meeting expected levels of development, or if they are exceeding expected levels, or not yet reaching expected levels ('emerging'). This is the EYFS Profile.

2.8 Year 1 teachers must be given a copy of the Profile report together with a short commentary on each child's skills and abilities in relation to the three key characteristics of effective learning (see paragraph 1.10). These should inform a dialogue between Reception and Year 1 teachers about each child's stage of development and learning needs and assist with the planning of activities in Year 1.

2.9 Schools must share the results of the Profile with parents and/or carers, and explain to them when and how they can discuss the Profile with the teacher who completed it. For children attending more than one setting, the Profile must be completed by the school where the child spends most time. If a child moves to a new school during the academic year, the original school must send their assessment of the child's level of development against the early learning goals to the relevant school within 15 days of receiving a request.

   If a child moves during the summer term, relevant providers must agree which of them will complete the Profile.

2.10 The Profile must be completed for all children, including those with special educational needs or disabilities. Reasonable adjustments to the assessment process for children with special educational needs and disabilities must be made as appropriate. Providers should consider whether they may need to seek specialist assistance to help with this. Children will have differing levels of skills and abilities across the Profile and it is important that there is a full assessment of all areas of their development, to inform plans for future activities and to identify any additional support needs.

APPENDIX 1.2

EARLY YEARS EDUCATOR (LEVEL 3): QUALIFICATIONS CRITERIA. NATIONAL COLLEGE FOR TEACHING AND LEADERSHIP (2013)

Section i: Summary of qualifications content and assessment criteria for Level 3 Early Years Educator

A: Qualification content

All Level 3 Early Years Educator qualifications will require candidates to demonstrate an in-depth understanding of early years education and care, including that they can:

1. Support and promote children's early education and development
2. Plan and provide effective care, teaching and learning that enables children to progress and prepares them for school
3. Make accurate and productive use of assessment
4. Develop effective and informed practice
5. Safeguard and promote the health, safety and welfare of children
6. Work in partnership with the key person, colleagues, parents and/or carers or other professionals

Full details of required qualification content are shown in Section ii on the following pages.

B: Accreditation

All Level 3 Early Years Educator qualifications must meet the national requirements set by Ofqual for valid, reliable assessment[1] and awarding procedures. They must also be regulated by Ofqual onto the Qualifications & Credit Framework or National Qualifications Framework.

---

[1]Skills for Care & Development working collaboratively with Awarding Organisations has developed assessment principles as guidance that complement Ofqual requirements. These can be downloaded from the Skills for Care & Development website.

Section ii: Minimum qualification content requirements for Level 3 Early Years Educator

1. Support and promote children's early education and development

1.1 Understand the expected patterns of **children's development** from birth to 5 years, and have an understanding of further development from age 5 to 7.
Children's development patterns to include:

- cognitive
- speech, language and communication development
- literacy and numeracy
- physical
- emotional
- social
- neurological and brain development

1.2 Understand the significance of attachment and how to promote it effectively.
1.3 Understand a range of underpinning theories and philosophical approaches to how children learn and develop, and their influence on practice.
1.4 Analyse and explain how children's learning and development can be affected by their stage of development and individual circumstances.
1.5 Understand the importance of promoting diversity, equality and inclusion, fully reflecting cultural differences and family circumstances.
1.6 Understand the importance to children's holistic development of:

- speech, language and communication
- personal, social and emotional development
- physical development

1.7 Understand systematic synthetic phonics in the teaching of reading, and a range of strategies for developing early literacy and mathematics.
1.8 Understand the potential effects of, and how to prepare and support children through, **transitions and significant events** in their lives.

Transitions and significant events include:

- moving to school
- starting and moving through day care
- birth of a sibling
- moving home
- living outside of the home
- family breakdown
- loss of significant people
- moving between settings and carers

1.9 Understand the current early education curriculum requirements.
1.10 Promote equality of opportunity and anti-discriminatory practice.

2. Plan and provide effective care, teaching and learning that enables children to progress and prepares them for school

2.1 Plan and lead activities, purposeful play opportunities and educational programmes which include the learning and development areas of current early education curriculum requirements.

To include:

- communication and language (extending vocabulary, language structure, and dialogue, for example)
- physical development
- personal, social and emotional development
- literacy
- mathematics
- understanding the world
- expressive arts and design

2.2 Ensure plans fully reflect the stage of development, individual needs and circumstances of children.
2.3 Provide learning experiences, environments and opportunities appropriate to the age, stage and needs of individual and groups of children.
2.4 Encourage children's participation, ensuring a balance between adult-led and child-initiated activities.
2.5 Engage in effective strategies to develop and extend children's learning and thinking, including sustained shared thinking.
2.6 Support and promote children's speech, language and communication development.
2.7 Support children's group learning and socialisation.
2.8 Model and promote positive behaviours expected of children.
2.9 Support children to manage their own behaviour in relation to others.
2.10 Understand when a child is in need of additional support.
2.11 Plan and provide activities to meet additional needs, working in partnership with parents and/or carers and other professionals, where appropriate.

3. Make accurate and productive use of assessment

3.1 Understand how to assess within the current early education curriculum framework using a range of assessment techniques.
3.2 Carry out and record observational assessment accurately.

3.3 Identify the needs, interests and stages of development of individual children.

3.4 Make use of formative and summative assessment, tracking children's progress to plan next steps and shape learning opportunities.

3.5 Discuss children's progress and plan next stages in their learning with the key person, colleagues, parents and/or carers.

4. Develop effective and informed practice

4.1 Demonstrate a good command of the English language in spoken and written form.

4.2 Explain the importance of continued professional development to improve own skills and early years practice.

4.3 Engage in continuing professional development and reflective practice to improve own skills, practice, and subject knowledge (for example, in English, mathematics, music, history, or modern foreign languages).

5. Safeguard and promote the health, safety and welfare of children

5.1 Know the legal requirements and guidance on health and safety, security, confidentiality of information, safeguarding and promoting the welfare of children.

5.2 Identify and act upon own responsibilities in relation to health and safety, security, confidentiality of information, safeguarding and promoting the welfare of children.

5.3 Plan and carry out physical care routines suitable to the age, stage and needs of the child.

5.4 Understand why health and well-being is important for babies and children and promote healthy lifestyles.

5.5 Understand how to respond to accidents and emergency situations.

5.6 Demonstrate skills and knowledge for the **prevention and control of infection**.

Prevention and control of infection including:

- hand washing
- food hygiene
- dealing with spillages safely
- safe disposal of waste
- using correct personal protective equipment
- knowledge of common childhood illnesses and immunisation
- exclusion periods for infectious diseases

5.7 Carry out risk assessment and risk management in line with policies and procedures.

5.8 Understand safeguarding policies and procedures, including child protection, recognise when a child is in danger or at risk of **abuse**, and know how to act to protect them.

Types of **abuse** including:

- domestic
- neglect
- physical
- emotional
- sexual abuse

5.9 Maintain **accurate and coherent records and reports** and share information, only when appropriate, to ensure the needs of all children are met.

Records and reports include:

- medication requirements
- special dietary needs
- planning
- observation and assessment
- health, safety and security
- accidents
- daily registers

6. Work in partnership with the key person, colleagues, parents and/or carers or other professionals

6.1 Work co-operatively with colleagues and other professionals to meet the needs of babies and children and enable them to progress.

6.2 Work in partnership with parents and/or carers to help them recognise and value the significant contributions they make to the child's health, well-being, learning and development.

6.3 Encourage parents and/or carers to take an active role in the child's play, learning and development.

APPENDIX 2

EYFS (2017A) STAFF: CHILD RATIOS — ALL PROVIDERS (INCLUDING CHILDMINDERS)

STAFF: CHILD RATIOS — ALL PROVIDERS (INCLUDING CHILDMINDERS)

3.28 Staffing arrangements must meet the needs of all children and ensure their safety. Providers must ensure that children are adequately supervised and decide how to deploy staff to ensure children's needs are met. Providers must inform parents and/or carers about staff deployment, and, when relevant and practical, aim to involve them in these decisions. Children must usually be within sight and hearing of staff and always within sight or hearing.

3.29 Only those aged 17 or over may be included in ratios (and staff under 17 should be supervised at all times). Students on long-term placements and volunteers (aged 17 or over) and staff working as apprentices in early education (aged 16 or over) may be included in the ratios if the provider is satisfied that they are competent and responsible.

3.30 The ratio and qualification requirements below apply to the total number of staff available to work directly with children[34]. Exceptionally, and where the quality of care and safety and security of children is maintained, changes to the ratios may be made. For group settings providing overnight care, the relevant ratios continue to apply and at least one member of staff must be awake at all times.

EARLY YEARS PROVIDERS (OTHER THAN CHILDMINDERS)

3.31 For children aged under two:

- there must be at least one member of staff for every three children
- at least one member of staff must hold a full and relevant level 3 qualification, and must be suitably experienced in working with children under two
- at least half of all other staff must hold a full and relevant level 2 qualification
- at least half of all staff must have received training that specifically addresses the care of babies

- where there is an under two-year-olds' room, the member of staff in charge of that room must, in the judgement of the provider, have suitable experience of working with under two's

3.32 For children aged two: there must be at least one member of staff for every four children[35]

- at least one member of staff must hold a full and relevant level 3 qualification
- at least half of all other staff must hold a full and relevant level 2 qualification

3.33 For children aged three and over in registered early years provision where a person with Qualified Teacher Status, Early Years Professional Status, Early Years Teacher Status or another suitable level 6 qualification is working directly with the children[36]:

- there must be at least one member of staff for every 13 children
- at least one other member of staff must hold a full and relevant level 3 qualification

3.34 For children aged three and over at any time in registered early years provision when a person with Qualified Teacher Status, Early Years Professional Status, Early Years Teacher Status or another suitable level 6 qualification is not working directly with the children:

- there must be at least one member of staff for every eight children
- at least one member of staff must hold a full and relevant level 3 qualification
- at least half of all other staff must hold a full and relevant level 2 qualification

3.35 For children aged three and over in independent schools (including in nursery classes in free schools and academies), where a person with Qualified Teacher Status, Early Years Professional Status, Early Years Teacher Status or another suitable level 6 qualification, an instructor[37], or another suitably qualified overseas trained teacher, is working directly with the children:

- for classes where the majority of children will reach the age of five or older within the school year, there must be at least one member of staff for every 30 children
- for all other classes there must be at least one member of staff for every 13 children[38]
- at least one other member of staff must hold a full and relevant level 3 qualification

3.36 For children aged three and over in independent schools (including in nursery classes in academies), where there is no person with Qualified

Teacher Status, Early Years Professional Status, Early Years Teacher Status or another suitable level 6 qualification, no instructor, and no suitably qualified overseas trained teacher, working directly with the children:

- there must be at least one member of staff for every eight children
- at least one member of staff must hold a full and relevant level 3 qualification
- at least half of all other staff must hold a full and relevant level 2 qualification

3.37 For children aged three and over in maintained nursery schools and nursery classes in maintained schools[39]:

- there must be at least one member of staff for every 13 children[40]
- at least one member of staff must be a school teacher as defined by section 122 of the Education Act 2002[41]
- at least one other member of staff must hold a full and relevant level 3 qualification[42]

3.38 Reception classes in maintained schools and academies are subject to infant class size legislation.[43] The School Admissions (Infant Class Size) Regulations 2012 limit the size of infant classes to 30 pupils per school teacher[44] (subject to permitted exceptions) while an ordinary teaching session is conducted. 'School teachers' do not include teaching assistants, higher level teaching assistants or other support staff. Consequently, in an ordinary teaching session, a school must employ sufficient school teachers to enable it to teach its infant classes in groups of no more than 30 per school.

3.39 Some schools may choose to mix their reception classes with groups of younger children (nursery pupils, non-pupils or younger children from a registered provider), in which case they must determine ratios within mixed groups, guided by all relevant ratio requirements and by the needs of individual children within the group. In exercising this discretion, the school must comply with the statutory requirements relating to the education of children of compulsory school age and infant class sizes. Schools' partner providers must meet the relevant ratio requirements for their provision.[45]

ENDNOTES

34 Ofsted may determine that providers must observe a higher staff:child ratio than outlined here to ensure the safety and welfare of children.

35 In a maintained school or non-maintained special school, where the two-year-olds are pupils, staff must additionally be under the direction and supervision of a qualified or nominated teacher when carrying out specified work (as laid out in the Education

(Specified Work) (England) Regulations 2012). Specified work broadly encompasses lesson (or curriculum) planning, delivering lessons, assessing the development, progress and attainment of pupils and reporting on the latter. The headteacher must be satisfied that the staff have the skills, expertise and experience needed to carry out the work and determine the appropriate level of direction and supervision.

36 We expect the teacher (or equivalent) to be working with children for the vast majority of the time. Where they need to be absent for short periods of time, the provider will need to ensure that quality and safety is maintained.

37 An instructor is a person at the school who provides education which consists of instruction in any art or skill, or in any subject or group of subjects, in circumstances where: (a) special qualifications or experience or both are required for such instruction; and (b) the person or body of persons responsible for the management of the school is satisfied as to the qualifications or experience (or both) of the person providing education.

38 Subject to any permitted exceptions under The Schools Admissions (Infant Class Sizes) Regulations.

39 Where schools have provision run by the governing body (under section 27 of the Education Act 2002) for three- and four-year-olds who are not pupils of the school, they can apply: a 1:13 ratio where a person with a suitable level 6 qualification is working directly with the children (as in paragraph 3.33); or a 1:8 ratio where a person with a suitable level 6 qualification is not working directly with children but at least one member of staff present holds a level 3 qualification (as in paragraph 3.34).

40 Where children in nursery classes attend school for longer than the school day or in the school holidays, in provision run directly by the governing body or the proprietor, with no teacher present, a ratio of one member of staff to every eight children can be applied if at least one member of staff holds a full and relevant level 3 qualification, and at least half of all other staff hold a full and relevant level 2 qualification.

41 See also the Education (School Teachers' Prescribed Qualifications, etc) Order 2003 and the Education (School Teachers' Qualifications) (England) Regulations 2003.

42 Provided that the person meets all relevant staff qualification requirement as required by The School Staffing (England) Regulations 2009.

43 Academies are required by their funding agreements to comply with the School Admissions Code and the law relating to admissions although the Secretary of State has the power to vary this requirement where there is demonstratable need.

44 As defined by section 122 of the Education Act 2002. 2 S.I. 2012/10.

45 The Specified Work Regulations 2012 allow a non-teacher to carry out the work of the teacher ("specified work") where the non-teacher is assisting or supporting the work of the teacher, is subject to the teacher's direction and supervision as arranged with the headteacher, and the headteacher is satisfied that that person has the skills, expertise and experience required to carry out the specified work.

REFERENCES

Abrahamson, E. (2004) 'Managing change in a world of excessive change', The University of Western Ontario, Ontario: Ivey Publishing. Available at https://iveybusinessjournal. com/publication/managing-change-in-a-world-of-excessive-change-counterbalancing-creative-destruction-and-creative-recombination/ (accessed 14 November 2017).

Allen, G. (2011) *Early Intervention: The Next Steps*. London: Cabinet Office.

Ancona, D., Malone, T.W., Orlikowski, W.J. and Senge, P.M. (2007) 'In praise of the incomplete leader', *Harvard Business Review*, 85 (2): 92–100. Reprint R0702E (pp. 1–9).

Anning, A. (2001) 'Knowing who I am and what I know: developing new versions of professional knowledge in integrated service settings'. Paper presented to the British Educational Research Association Annual Conference, University of Leeds, 13–15 September 2001.

Arnold, C. (2010) *Understanding Schemas and Emotion in Early Childhood*. London: Sage.

Arnold, C. and Cummings, A. (2013) 'Engaging in a dialogue with parents about their children's learning', in M. Whalley, C. Arnold, R. Orr and the Pen Green Centre Team, *Working with Families in Children's Centres and Early Years Settings*. London: Hodder Education.

Asmussen, K., Feinstein, M.J. and Chowdry, H. (2016) *Foundations for Life: What Works to Support Parent-Child Interaction in the Early Years*. Early Intervention Foundation, Evidence. Available at www.eif.org.uk/wp-content/uploads/foundationsforlife/EIF_ Foundations-for-Life.pdf (accessed 15 November 2017).

Ballard, P.B. (1929) *The Practical Infant Teacher*. London: Pitman.

Bandura, A. (1977) *Social Learning Theory*. New York: General Learning Press.

Bassot, B. (2016) *The Reflective Practice Guide: An Interdisciplinary Approach to Critical Reflection*. Abingdon: Routledge.

Belbin, M. (2005) *Team Roles at Work*. Oxford: Elsevier/Butterworth–Heinemann.

Bennis, W. (1989) *On Becoming a Leader*. Reading, MA: Addison–Wesley.

Bennis, W. and Nanus, B. (1997) *Leaders' Strategies for Taking Charge*. London: Harper Business.

Bertram, T. and Pascal, C. (APT/CREC 2010) Accounting Early for Lifelong. Centre for Research in Early Childhood Learning. Available at www.crec.co.uk/AcE.pdf

Bertram, T. and Pascal, C. (2014) *Early Years Literature Review*. Birmingham: Centre for Research in Early Childhood. Available at the Early Education website: www.early-education.org.uk

Blakemore, S.J. and Frith, U. (2005) *The Learning Brain: Lessons for Education*. London: Wiley-Blackwell.

Bodrova, E. (2008) Make-believe play versus academic skills: a Vygotskian approach to today's dilemma of early childhood education. *European Early Childhood Education Research Journal* 16 (3). Available at www.tandfonline.com/doi/ abs/10.1080/13502930802291777 (accessed 16 November 2017).

Bolton, G. (2010) *Reflective Practice*. London: Sage.

Bowlby, J. (1988) *A Secure Base: Clinical Applications of Attachment Theory*. Hove: Brunner–Routledge.

Bridges, W. (2009) *Managing Transitions*. Boston: Da Capo Press.

Britto, P. (2014) 'How children's brains develop – new insights', https://blogs.unicef.org/blog/how-childrens-brains-develop-new-insights (accessed 4 August 2017).

Broadhead, P., Howard, J. and Wood, E. (2010) *Play and Learning in the Early Years from Research to Practice*. London: Sage.

Brock, A. and Rankin, C. (2008) *Communication, Language and Literacy from Birth to Five*. London: Sage.

Brotherson, S. (2009) *Understanding Brain Development in Young Children*. Bright Beginnings, NDSU Extension Service, North Dakota State University.

Bruce, T. and Spratt, J. (2011) *Essentials of Literacy from 0–7*, 2nd edn. London: Sage.

Bruner, J. (1983) *Child's Talk: Learning to Use Language*. New York: W.W. Norton.

Bruner, J. (1996) *The Culture of Education*. Cambridge, MA: Harvard University Press.

Bruner, J. (1999) *The Process of Education*, rev. edn. Cambridge, MA and London: Harvard University Press.

Callanan, Meg, Anderson, Margaret, Haywood, Sarah, Hudson, Ruth and Speight, Svetlana – NatCen Social Research (2017) *Study of Early Education and Development: Good Practice in Early Education*. DFE-RR553. London: Department for Education/NatCen Research. Available at www.gov.uk/government/publications/good-practice-in-early-education (accessed 6 November 2017).

Campbell-Barr, V. and Leeson, C. (2016) *Quality and Leadership in the Early Years: Research, Theory and Practice*. London: Sage.

Children and Families Act 2014. Norwich: TSO. Available at www.legislation.gov.uk/ukpga/2014/6/pdfs/ukpga_20140006_en.pdf (accessed 29 October 2017).

Clark, A. and Moss, P. (2017 [2006]) *Listening to Young Children: The Mosaic Approach*, 3rd edn. London: NCB.

Claxton, G. (2002) *Building Learning Power*. Bristol: Henleaze House.

Costley, C., Elliott, G. and Gibbs, P. (2010) *Doing Work Based Research*. London: Sage.

Curtis, S.J. and Boultwood, M.E.A. (1977) *A Short History of Educational Ideas*, 5th edn. London: University Tutorial Press.

Curtis, W., Ward, S., Sharp, J. and Hankin, L. (2014) *Education Studies – an Issues Based Approach*, 3rd edn. London: Sage.

Dalli, C., White, J., Rockel, J. and Duhn, I. (2011) *Quality Early Childhood Education for Under-Two-Year-Olds: What Should It Look Like? A Literature Review*. Report to the Ministry of Education. Wellington, New Zealand.

David, T., Goouch, K., Powell, S. and Abbott, L. (2003) *Birth to Three Matters: A Review of the Literature Compiled to Inform the Framework to Support Children in Their Earliest Years*. Department for Education and Skills Research Report No. RR444. Nottingham: DfES Publications.

Delafield-Butt, J.T. and Trevarthen, C. (2015) 'The ontogenesis of narrative: from moving to meaning', *Frontiers in Psychology*, 6: 1157. Published online 2 September 2015. doi: 10.3389/fpsyg.2015.01157. Available at www.ncbi.nlm.nih.gov/pmc/articles/PMC4557105 (accessed 29 October 2017).

Denscombe, M. (2017) *The Good Research Guide*, 6th edn. Open University Press, McGraw-Hill Education.

Department for Children, Schools and Families (DCSF) (2006) *Every Child Matters: Childcare Act 2006*. Available at http://webarchive.nationalarchives.gov.

uk/20100408173848/http://www.dcsf.gov.uk/everychildmatters/earlyyears/childcare/childcareact2006/childcareact/ (accessed 29 October 2017).

Department for Children Schools and Families (DCSF) (2007) *The Children's Plan: Building Brighter Futures*. Available at http://webarchive.nationalarchives.gov.uk/20130323053911/https://www.education.gov.uk/publications/eOrderingDownload/Childrens_Plan_Summary.pdf (accessed 17 April 2018).

Department for Children, Schools and Families (DCSF) (2008a) *A Review of Services for Children and Young People (0–19) with Speech, Language and Communication Needs*. The Bercow Report. Nottingham: DCSF Publications.

Department for Children, Schools and Families (DCSF) (2008b) The National Strategies | Early Years. *Early Years Quality Improvement Support Programme (EYQISP)*. Nottingham: DCSF Publications Available at http://webarchive.nationalarchives.gov.uk/20130404005529/https://www.education.gov.uk/publications/eOrderingDownload/DCSF-00669-2008.pdf (accessed 27 October 2017).

Department for Children, Schools and Families (DCSF) (2008c) The National Strategies | Early Years. *Every Child a Talker: Guidance for Early Language Lead Practitioners* (First Instalment). Nottingham: DCSF Publications. Available at www.foundationyears.org.uk/files/2011/10/ecat_guidance_for_practitioners_12.pdf (accessed 7 November 2017).

Department for Children, Schools and Families (DCSF) (2008d) *Principles into Practice Cards*. Available from http://webarchive.nationalarchives.gov.uk/20130321061516/https://www.education.gov.uk/publications /eOrderingDownload/DCSF-00012-2007.pdf (accessed 7 November 2017).

Department for Education (DfE) (2013a) *More Great Childcare: Raising Quality and Giving Parents More Choice*. London: DfE. Available at www.gov.uk/government/publications/more-great-childcare-raising-quality-and-giving-parents-more-choice (accessed 7 November 2017).

Department for Education (DfE) (2013b) *Early Years Outcomes: A Non-Statutory Guide for Practitioners and Inspectors to Help Inform Understanding of Child Development Through the Early Years*. DFE-00167-2013. London: DfE. Available at www.foundationyears.org.uk/files/2012/03/Early_Years_Outcomes.pdf (accessed 7 November 2017).

Department for Education (DfE) (2013c) *Use of Reasonable Force in Schools*. DFE-00295-2013. Available at www.gov.uk/government/uploads/system/uploads/attachment_data/file/444051/Use_of_reasonable_force_advice_Reviewed_July_2015.pdf (accessed 29 October 2017).

Department for Education (DfE) (2014a) *Early Years: Guide to the 0–25 SEND Code of Practice*. DFE-00563-2014. London: DfE. Available at www.gov.uk/government/publications/send-guide-for-early-years-settings (accessed 7 November 2017).

Department for Education (DfE) (2014b) *The Equality Act 2010 and Schools: Departmental Advice for School Leaders, School Staff, Governing Bodies and Local Authorities*. London: DfE. Available at www.gov.uk/government/uploads/system/uploads/attachment_data/file/315587/Equality_Act_Advice_Final.pdf (accessed 29 October 2017).

Department for Education (DfE) (2015) *The Prevent Duty: Departmental Advice for Schools and Childcare Providers*. London: DfE. Available at www.gov.uk/government/publications/protecting-children-from-radicalisation-the-prevent-duty (accessed 29 October 2017).

Department for Education (DfE) (2015, updated 2017) *Working Together to Safeguard Children*. DFE-00130-2015. London: DfE. Available at www.gov.uk/government/publications/working-together-to-safeguard-children–2 (accessed 29 October 2017).

Department for Education (DfE) (2016) *Keeping Children Safe in Education: Statutory Guidance for Schools and Colleges*. DFE-00140-2016. London: DfE. Available at www.gov.uk/government/publications/keeping-children-safe-in-education–2 (accessed 29 October 2017).

Department for Education (DfE) (2017a) *Statutory Framework for the Early Years Foundation Stage: Setting the Standards for Learning, Development and Care for Children from Birth to Five*. Available at www.gov.uk/government/uploads/system/uploads/attachment_data/file/596629/EYFS_STATUTORY_FRAMEWORK_2017.pdf (accessed 7 November 2017).

Department for Education (DfE) (2017b) *Early Years Workforce Strategy*. DFE-00077-2017. London: DfE. Available at www.gov.uk/government/uploads/system/uploads/attachment_data/file/596884/Workforce_strategy_02-03-2017.pdf (accessed 6 November 2017).

Department for Education (DfE) (2017c) Open consultation – Working Together to Safeguard Children: revisions to statutory guidance (25 October – 31 December 2017). Available at www.gov.uk/government/consultations/working-together-to-safeguard-children-revisions-to-statutory-guidance (accessed 29 October 2017).

Department for Education (DfE) (2017d) Primary Assessment in England. Government consultation response. Available at www.gov.uk/government/uploads/system/uploads/attachment_data/file/644871/Primary_assessment_consultation_response.pdf (accessed 6 November 2017).

Department for Education and Department of Health (DfE/DH) (2011) *Supporting Families in the Foundation Years*. London: DfE/DH. Available at www.gov.uk/government/uploads/system/uploads/attachment_data/file/184868/DFE-01001-2011_supporting_families_in_the_foundation_years.pdf (accessed 7 November 2017).

Department for Education and Department of Health (DfE/DH) (2015) *Special Educational Needs and Disability Code of Practice: 0–25 years*. DFE 00205-2013. London: DfE. Available at www.gov.uk/government/publications/send-code-of-practice-0-to-25 (accessed 7 November 2017).

Department for Education and Skills (DfES) (2000) *Curriculum Guidance for the Foundation Stage*. London: Qualifications and Curriculum Authority.

Department for Education and Skills (DfES) (2003) *Every Child Matters: Change for Children*. Green Paper. Norwich: TSO.

Department for Education and Skills (DfES) (2004) Choice for Parents, the Best Start for Children: A Ten-year Strategy for Childcare. Nottingham: DfES

Department for Transport (2017) Child car seats: the law. Available at www.gov.uk/child-car-seats-the-rules. See link to 'New child car seat rules' (Feb 2017) (accessed 29 October 2017).

Disclosure and Barring Service (DBS) (2012, updated 2017) *DBS Check Detailed Guidance*. Available at www.gov.uk/government/publications/dbs-identity-checking-guidelines (accessed 29 October 2017).

Dowling, M. (2013) *Young Children's Thinking*. London: Sage.

Driscoll, J. (2007) *Practising Clinical Supervision: A Reflective Approach for Healthcare Professionals*, 2nd edn. Edinburgh: Bailliere Tindall Elsevier.

Duffy, B. (2006) *Supporting Creativity and Imagination in the Early Years* (Supporting Early Learning). Maidenhead: McGraw–Hill/Open University Press.

Early Arts (2017) Creativity in early brain development. 30 March 2017. https://earlyarts.co.uk/blog/creativity-in-early-brain-development (accessed 6 August 2017).

Early Education (2012) *Development Matters in the Early Years Foundation Stage (EYFS)*. London: Early Education.

Education and Skills Act 2008. Norwich: TSO. Available at www.legislation.gov.uk/ukpga/2008/25/pdfs/ukpga_20080025_en.pdf (accessed 29 October 2017).

Elfer, P., Goldshmied, E. and Selleck, D.Y. (2011) *Key Persons in the Early Years: Building Relationships for Quality Provision in Early Years Settings and Primary Schools.* London: Routledge.

Elliott, A. (2006) 'Early childhood education: pathways to quality and equity for all children', *Australian Education Review*, 50: 1–75.

Field, F. (2010) *The Foundation Years: Preventing Poor Children Becoming Poor Adults.* London: Cabinet Office.

Finnegan, J. and Lawton, K. (2016) *Lighting Up Young Brains: How parents, carers and nurseries support children's brain development in the first five years.* London: Save the Children UK. Available at www.savethechildren.org.uk/content/dam/global/reports/education-and-child-protection/lighting-up-young-brains.pdf (accessed 8 November 2017).

Fisher, J. (2003) *The Process of Transition* (revised 2012). Available at www.businessballs. com/change-management/personal-change-stages-john-fisher-162/ (accessed 8 November 2017).

Foundation Years (2012) Principles for early years education. www.foundationyears.org. uk/files/2012/10/Curriculum-guidance-for-the-foundation-stage-Principles-for-early-years-education.pdf (accessed 16 November 2017).

Foundation Years (2014) The SEND reforms. www.foundationyears.org.uk/files/2014/07/The-SEND-reforms-1-pager.pdf (accessed 16 November 2017).

Fullan, M. (1998) *What's Worth Fighting for in Headship.* Maidenhead: Open University Press.

Gibbs, G. (1988) *Learning by Doing: A Guide to Teaching and Learning Methods.* Oxford: Further Educational Unit, Oxford Polytechnic.

Goddard, C. and Temperley, J. (2011) *Transforming Early Years: Different, Better, Lower Cost Services for Children and Their Families.* Summary of findings from the Transforming Early Years Programme January 2010 – July 2011. Available at www.nesta.org.uk/sites/default/files/transforming_early_years.pdf (accessed 15 November 2017).

Goddard Blythe, S. (2000) *Early Learning in the Balance: Priming the First ABC. Support for Learning.* Oxford: Blackwell.

Goddard Blythe, S. (2011) 'Physical foundations of learning', in R. House (ed.), *Too Much, Too Soon: Early Learning and the Erosion of Childhood.* Stroud: Hawthorn Press. pp. 131–46.

Goouch, K. (2010) *Towards Excellence in Early Years Education: Exploring Narratives of Experience.* Abingdon: Routledge.

Goouch, K. and Lambirth, A. (2010) *Teaching Early Reading and Phonics: Creative Approaches to Early Literacy.* London: Sage.

Goouch, K. and Lambirth, A. (2017) *Teaching Early Reading and Phonics: Creative Approaches to Early Literacy*, 2nd edn. London: Sage.

Gopnik, A. (2009) *The Philosophical Baby: What Children's Minds Tell Us about Truth, Love and the Meaning of Life.* London: Vintage.

Goswami, U. (2015) *Children's Cognitive Development and Learning.* York: Cambridge Primary Review Trust.

Government Equalities Office and Equality and Human Rights Commission (2010) Equality Act 2010: Guidance. Available at www.gov.uk/guidance/equality-act-2010-guidance (accessed 8 November 2017).

Graue (2006) *The Answer Is Readiness – Now What Is the Question?* Journal of Early Education and Development, Volume 17, 2006, pages 43–46 – Issue 1. Abstract available at www.tandfonline.com/doi/abs/10.1207/s15566935eed1701_3

Gray, D. (2014) *Doing Research in the Real World*, 3rd edn. London: Sage.

Green, J. and Collie, F. (1916) *Pestalozzi's Educational Writings*. London: Edward Arnold.

Griggs, Julia and Bussard, Loraine – NatCen Social Research (2017) *Study of Early Education and Development (SEED): Meeting the needs of children with special educational needs and disabilities in the early years*. DFE-RR554. London: Department for Education/NatCen Research. Available at www.foundationyears.org.uk/files/2017/01/SEED-Meeting-the-needs-of-children-with-SEND-in-the-early-years.pdf (accessed 7 November 2017).

Groeneveld, M.G., Vermeer, H.J., van IJzendoorn, M.H. and Linting, M. (2010) 'Children's wellbeing and cortisol levels in home-based and center-based childcare', *Early Childhood Research Quarterly*, 25: 502–14.

Hardy, Kathy (n.d.) 'Children's art: It's the process, not the product that counts', *Early Childhood Newsletter*, www.theallianceforec.org/library.php?c=1&news=36 (accessed 10 November 2017).

Harms, T., Clifford, R.M. and Cryer, D. (2005) *Early Childhood Environment Rating Scale (ECERS-R)*, 3rd rev. edn. New York: Teachers College Press.

Harms, T., Clifford, R.M. and Cryer, D. (2006) *Infant/Toddler Environment Rating Scale*. New York: Teachers College Press.

Harris, B. (2007) *Supporting the Emotional Work of School Leaders*. London: Paul Chapman Publishing.

Herculano-Houzel, S. (2009) 'The human brain in numbers: a linearly scaled-up primate brain', *Frontiers in Human Neuroscience*, 3: 31.

Hillman, J. and Williams, T. (2015) *Early Years Education and Childcare: Lessons from Evidence and Future Priorities*. London: Nuffield Foundation. Available at www.nuffieldfoundation.org/sites/default/files/files/Early_years_education_and_childcare_Nuffield_FINAL.pdf (accessed 15 November 2017).

HM Government (2015) *Information Sharing Advice for Practitioners Providing Safeguarding Services to Children, Young People, Parents and Carers*. DFE-00128-2015. Available at www.gov.uk/government/uploads/system/uploads/attachment_data/file/419628/Information_sharing_advice_safeguarding_practitioners.pdf (accessed 29 October 2017).

Hodgson, J. Buttle, H., Conridge, B., Gibbons, D. and Rob J. (2013) Phonics instruction and early reading: professional views from the classroom. NATE. Available at https://ukla.org/downloads/NATE_Phonics_and_early_reading_report.pdf (accessed 17 April 2018).

Home Office (2017) *An Employer's Guide to Right to Work Checks*. Available at www.gov.uk/government/uploads/system/uploads/attachment_data/file/638349/Employer_s_guide_to_right_to_work_checks_-August_2017.pdf (accessed 29 October 2017).

Hope, C. (2017) 'Children denied chance to develop "resilience" by too strict health and safety rules, warns Ofsted chief', The Telegraph [online], 5 August 2017. Available at www.telegraph.co.uk/news/2017/08/05/children-denied-chance-develop-resilience-strict-health-safety (accessed 29 October 2017).

Hopkins, R., Stokes, L. and Wilkinson, D. (2010) *Quality, Outcomes and Costs in Early Years Education: Report to the Office for National Statistics*. London: NIESR.

House, R. (ed.) (2011) *Too Much Too Soon – An Erosion of Childhood*. Stroud: Hawthorn Press.

Huxham, C. and Vangen, S. (2006) *Managing to Collaborate: The Theory and Practice of Collaborative Advantage*. London: Routledge.

Iona School and Nursery (2015) Prevent Duty Policy. Available at www.theionaschool.org. uk/wp-content/uploads/2012/02/Prevent-Duty-policy.pdf (accessed March 2017).

Isaacs, S. (1930) *Intellectual Growth in Young Children*. London: Routledge.

Isaacs, S. (1929) *The Nursery Years: The Mind of the Child from Birth to Six Years*. London: Routledge & Kegan Paul.

Isaacs, S. (2013 [1937]) *The Educational Value of the Nursery School*. London: British Association for Early Childhood Education.

Jackson, B. and Jackson, S. (1979) *Childminder: A Study in Action Research*. London: Routledge and Kegan Paul.

John, K. (2012) *ASIIP Year Book*. London: ASIIP.

John, K. (2017) 'Holding the baby: leadership that inspires and contains ambition and anxiety', in K. John, L. Klavins, C. Parker, J. Vaggers, M. Whalley and P. Whitaker, *Democratizing Early Years Leadership: Applying Systems and Psychological Theories and Research in Practice*. Hove: Routledge (in press).

Katz, Lilian (2011) 'Current perspectives on the early childhood curriculum', in R. House (ed.), *Too Much, Too Soon: Early Learning and the Erosion of Childhood*. Stroud: Hawthorn Press. pp. 118–30.

Kelly, B. (2003) *Worth Repeating: More than 5000 Classic and Contemporary Quotes*. Grand Rapids: Kregel.

Klatte, I.S. and Roulstone, S. (2016) 'The practical side of working with parent–child interaction therapy with preschool children with language impairments', *Child Language Teaching and Therapy*, 32 (3).

Knickmeyer, R.C., Gouttard, S., Kang, C., Evans, D., Wilber, K., Smith, J.K., Hamer, R.M., Lin, W., Gerig, G. and Gilmore, J.H. (2008) 'A structural MRI study of human brain development from birth to 2 years', *Journal of Neuroscience*, 28 (47): 12176–82. Available at www.jneurosci.org/content/28/47/12176 (accessed 15 November 2017).

Knowles, G. and Holmstrom, R. (2012) *Understanding Family Diversity and Home–School Relations*. Abingdon: Routledge.

Kolb, David A. (2015) *Experiential Learning: Experience as the Source of Learning and Development*. New York: Pearson FT Press.

Kotter, J. (2012 [1996]) *Leading Change*. Cambridge, MA: Harvard Business Review Press.

Kuzawa, W.C., Chugani, T.H., Grossman, I.L., Lipovich, L., Muzik, O., Hof, R.P., Wildman, E.D., Sherwood, C.C., Leonard, R.W. and Lange, N. (2013) 'Metabolic costs and evolutionary implications of human brain development', *PNAS*, 111: 36.

Laevers, F. (ed.) (1994) *Defining and Assessing Quality in Early Childhood Education*. Belgium: Laevers University Press.

Learning through Landscapes (n.d.) www.ltl.org.uk/childhood/nature.php (accessed 28 October 2017).

Lew, A. and Bettner, B. (1990) *A Parent's Guide to Understanding and Motivating Children*. Pennsylvania: Connexions Press.

Litjens, I. and Taguma, M. (2010) Revised Literature Overview for the 7th Meeting of the Network on Early Childhood Education and Care. Paris: OECD.

MacGilchrist, B., Myers, K. and Reed, J. (2004) *The Intelligent School*. London: Sage.

Malaguzzi, L. (1993) *Your Image of the Child: Where Teaching Begins* (trans. B. Rankin, L. Morrow and L. Giardini, 1994). Available at www.reggioalliance.org/downloads/malaguzzi:ccie:1994.pdf (accessed 16 November 2017).

Manning-Morton, J. and Thorp, M. (2003) *Key Times for Play: The First Three Years (Debating Play)*. Maidenhead: McGraw-Hill.

Manning-Morton, J. and Thorp, M. (Contributor) (2015) *Two-Year-Olds in Early Years Settings: Journeys of Discovery*. Maidenhead: Open University Press.

Marmot, M. (2010) *Fair Society, Healthy Lives*. The Marmot Review. Available at www.instituteofhealthequity.org (accessed September 2012).

Mathers, S., Ranns, H., Karemaker, A., Moody, A., Sylva, K., Graham, J. and Siraj-Blatchford, I. (2011) *Evaluation of the Graduate Leader Fund: Final Report*. Research Report DFE-RR144. London: DfE. Available at www.gov.uk/government/uploads/system/uploads/attachment_data/file/181480/DFE-RR144.pdf (accessed 18 November 2017).

Mathers, S., Singler, R. and Karemaker, A. (2012) *Improving Quality in the Early Years: A Comparison of Perspectives and Measures*. Oxford: University of Oxford and A+ Education. Available at www.education.ox.ac.uk/wordpress/wp-content/uploads/2010/08/2.-Improving-quality-in-the-early-years.pdf (accessed 8 November 2017).

Maxwell, K.L. and Clifford, L.M. (2004) School Readiness Assessment. Research in Review: Young Children. NAEYC.

Mckinnon, E. (2013) *Using Evidence for Advocacy and Resistance in Early Years Services: Exploring the Pen Green research approach*. Abingdon, Oxen: Routledge.

Miller, L. and Pound, L. (2011) *Theories and Approaches to Learning in the Early Years*. London: Sage.

Ministry of Education, New Zealand Government (1996, revised 2017) Te Whāriki. www.education.govt.nz/early-childhood/teaching-and-learning/te-whariki (accessed 27 October 2017).

Montessori Schools Association (2008) Guide to the Early Years Foundation Stage in Montessori settings, retrieved from http://m.cotswoldmontessori.co.uk/upload/Guide%20to%20EYFS%20in%20Montessori%20Settings.pdf (accessed 9th November 2017).

Moss, P. (2008) 'Forward', in A. Paige-Smith and A. Craft, *Developing Reflective Practice in the Early Years*. Maidenhead: Open University Press.

Moyles, J. (2006) *Effective Leadership and Management in the Early Years*. Maidenhead: Open University Press/McGraw–Hill Education.

Moyles, J., Adams, S. and Musgrove, A. (2002) *SPEEL: Study of Pedagogical Effectiveness in Early Learning*. Department for Education and Skills Research Report No. 363. Nottingham: DfES Publications.

Mukherji, P. and Dryden, L. (2014) *Foundations of Early Childhood – Principles and Practice*. London: Sage.

Munro, E. (2011) *The Munro Review of Child Protection: Final Report: A Child-Centred System*. Cm 8062. Norwich: TSO. Available at www.gov.uk/government/uploads/system/uploads/attachment_data/file/175391/Munro-Review.pdf (accessed 28 September 2017).

Musgrave, J. (2017) *Supporting Children's Health and Wellbeing*. London: Sage.

National Audit Office, Comptroller and Auditor General (2016) Entitlement to Free Early Education and Childcare. Department for Education. Available at www.nao.org.uk/wp-content/uploads/2016/03/Entitlement-to-free-early-education-and-childcare.pdf (accessed 8 November 2017).

National College for Teaching and Leadership (NCTL) (2013) *Teachers' Standards (Early Years) From September 2013*. Available at www.gov.uk/government/uploads/system/uploads/attachment_data/file/211646/Early_Years_Teachers__Standards.pdf (accessed 6 November 2017).

National Skills Academy for Social Care (2014) *The Leadership Qualities Framework*. London: Department of Health. Available at www.skillsforcare.org.uk/Leadership-management/Leadership-Qualities-Framework/Leadership-Qualities-Framework.aspx (accessed 7 November 2017).

National Society for the Prevention of Cruelty to Children (NSPCC) (2009) Child Protection Fact Sheet: The definitions and signs of child abuse. Available at www.ncl.ac.uk/studentambassadors/assets/documents/NSPCCDefinitionsandsignsofchildabuse.pdf (accessed 29 October 2017).

Nursery World (2017) 'Changes to early years goals and Profile planned'. Available at www.nurseryworld.co.uk/nursery-world/news/1162225/changes-to-early-years-goals-and-profile-planned (accessed 10 November 2017).

Nutbrown, C. (2012) *Foundations for Quality: The Independent Review of Early Education and Childcare Qualifications. Final Report*. Runcorn: Department for Education. Available at www.gov.uk/government/uploads/system/uploads/attachment_data/file/175463/Nutbrown-Review.pdf (accessed 7 November 2017).

OECD (Organisation for Economic Co-operation and Development) (2017a) *Encouraging Quality in Early Childhood Education and Care (ECEC)*. Research Brief: Qualifications, Education and Professional Development Matter. Paris: OECD Publishing. Available at www.oecd.org/education/school/49322232.pdf (accessed 29 July 2017).

OECD (Organisation for Economic Co-operation and Development) (2017b) *Early Learning Matters*. Paris: OECD Publishing. Available at www.oecd.org/edu/school/Early-Learning-Matters-Project-Brochure.pdf (accessed 14 November 2017).

OECD (Organisation for Economic Co-operation and Development) (2017c) Education at a Glance 2017: OECD Indicator. Paris: OECD Publishing. Available at http://dx.doi.org/10.1787/eag-2017-en (accessed 8 November 2017).

OECD (Organisation for Economic Co-operation and Development) (2017d) *Encouraging Quality in Early Childhood Education and Care (ECEC)*. Research Brief: Parental and Community Engagement Matters. Paris: OECD Publishing. Available at www.oecd.org/education/school/49322478.pdf (accessed 8 November 2017).

Ofsted (2013) *Achieving and Maintaining High-Quality Early Years Provision: Getting It Right the First Time*. Manchester: Ofsted.

Ofsted (2015, updated 2017) *Early Years Inspection Handbook*. Manchester: Ofsted. Available at www.gov.uk/government/publications/early-years-inspection-handbook-from-september-2015 (accessed 29 October 2017).

Ofsted (2015a) *Teaching and Play in the Early Years – A Balancing Act?* Manchester: Ofsted. Available at www.gov.uk/government/publications/teaching-and-play-in-the-early-years-a-balancing-act (accessed 9 November 2017).

Ofsted (2015b) *The Common Inspection Framework: Education, Skills and Early Years*. Manchester: Ofsted. Available at www.gov.uk/government/publications/common-inspection-framework-education-skills-and-early-years-from-september-2015 (accessed 9 November 2017).

Ofsted (2015c) Early Years Self-Evaluation Form Guidance. Available at www.gov.uk/government/publications/early-years-online-self-evaluation-form-self-and-guidance-for-providers-delivering-the-early-years-foundation-stage/early-years-self-evaluation-form-guidance (accessed 9 November 2017).

Ofsted (2016) *Inspecting Safeguarding in Early Years, Education and Skills Settings*. Main changes in the revised version August 2016. Available at www.gov.uk/government/

uploads/system/uploads/attachment_data/file/547390/Inspecting_safeguarding_in_early_years_education_and_skills_settings_change_document_Aug_2016.pdf (accessed 29 October 2017).

Ofsted (2017) Guidance: Early Years Inspections: Myths. Available at www.gov.uk/government/publications/common-inspection-framework-education-skills-and-early-years-from-september-2015 (accessed 9 November 2017).

Ofsted and Disclosure and Barring Service (2014, updated 2017) Disclosure and Barring Service (DBS) Checks: Childcare Providers. Ofsted's position on Disclosure and Barring (DBS) checks for childcare providers who register with Ofsted. Available at www.gov.uk/government/publications/disclosure-and-barring-service-dbs-checks-for-childcare-providers-who-register-with-ofsted (accessed 9 November 2017).

Osgood, J., Elwick, A., Robertson, L., Sakr, M. and Wilson, D. (2016) TACTYC Occasional Paper No. 9 – Early Years Training and Qualifications in England: Issues for Policy and Practice. Centre for Education Research and Scholarship, Middlesex University. Available at http://tactyc.org.uk/wp-content/uploads/2016/06/Occasional-Paper-9-V5-PDF.pdf (accessed 9 November 2017).

Oussoren, R. (2017) *Write Dance*, 3rd edn. London: Sage.

PACEY (Professional Association for Childcare and Early Years) (2013) *What Does 'School Ready' Really Mean?* Bromley: PACEY.

PACEY (Professional Association for Childcare and Early Years) (2017) Fundamental British values in the Early Years. Available at www.pacey.org.uk/news-and-views/pacey-blog/2015/september-2015/fundamental-british-values-in-the-early-years/ (accessed 9 November 2017).

Page, J. (2011) 'Do mothers want professional carers to love their babies?', *Journal of Early Childhood Research*, 9 (3): 310–23.

Pascal, C. and Bertram, T. (2008) *Accounting Early for Lifelong Learning*. Birmingham: Amber Publications.

Pascal, C. and Bertram, T. (2010) 'Introducing child development', in T. Bruce (ed.), *Early Childhood*, 2nd edn. London: Sage.

Pianta, R.C., Cox, M.J., and Snow, K.LB., (2007) School Readiness and the Transition to Kindergarten in the Era of Accountability - Education. The University of Michigan: Brookes Publishing.

Pound, L. (2011 *Influencing Early Childhood Education: Key Figures, Philosophies and Ideas*. Maidenhead: Open University Press.

Pugh, G. and Duffy, B. (2006) *Contemporary Issues in the Early Years*, 4th edn. London: Sage.

Raelin, J.A. (2005) 'We the Leaders: in order to form a leaderful organization,' *Journal of Leadership and Organizational Studies*, 12(1): 18–31.

Reardon, D. (2013) *Achieving Early Years Professional Status*, 2nd edn. London: Sage.

Reed, M. and Canning, N. (2012) *Reflective Practice in the Early Years*, 2nd edn. London: Sage.

Roberts, R. (2010) *Wellbeing from Birth*. London: Sage.

Robertson, F. (2017) *Equality and Inclusion in Early Years: A Guide to Understanding Equality, Inclusion and Poverty for All Those Working with Children and Young People*. Haddington: East Lothian Council. Available at www.eastlothian.gov.uk/download/downloads/id/6854/equality_in_early_years (accessed 16 November 2017).

Robson, C. (2011) *Real World Research*, 3rd edn. Oxford: Blackwell.

Rodd, J. (2006) *Leadership in Early Childhood*, 3rd edn. Maidenhead: Open University Press.

Schön, D.A. (1983) *The Reflective Practitioner: How Professionals Think in Action.* London: Temple Smith.

Science Daily (2017) 'Phonics works: Sounding out words is best way to teach reading, study suggests', 20 April 2017. Available at www.sciencedaily.com/releases/2017/04/170420094107.htm (accessed 10 November 2017).

SEED (2015, updated 2017) Study of Early Education and Development (SEED): Research about the current childcare and early education model in England. Available at www.gov.uk/government/collections/study-of-early-education-and-development-seed (accessed 7 November 2017).

Sharpe, C. (2004) *Developing Young Children's Creativity: What Can We Learn from Research?* NFER. Available at www.nfer.ac.uk/publications/55502/55502.pdf (accessed 30 October 2017).

Sheridan, S., Giota, J., Han, Y.M. and Kwon, J.Y. (2009) 'A cross-cultural study of preschool quality in South Korea and Sweden: ECERS evaluations', *Early Childhood Research Quarterly*, 24: 142–56.

Siraj, I., Kingston, D. and Melhuish, E. (2015) *Assessing Quality in Early Childhood Education and Care: Sustained Shared Thinking and Emotional Well-being (SSTEW) Scale for 2–5-Year-Olds Provision.* London: IoE Press/Stoke-on-Trent: Trentham Books.

Siraj-Blatchford, I., Sylva, K., Muttock, S., Gilden, R. and Bell, D. (2002) *Researching Effective Pedagogy in the Early Years (REPEY).* London: Department for Education and Skills/Institute of Education, University of London.

Standards and Testing Agency (2016) Guidance: Phonics screening check: structure and content of the check. (Updated 24 April 2017). Available at www.gov.uk/government/publications/phonics-screening-check-sample-materials-and-training-video/phonics-screening-check-structure-and-content-of-the-check (accessed 16 November 2017).

Steiner, R. (1928) Quoted in A. Renwick Sheen (n.d.) 'The change of teeth', *Child and Man*, 1 (6). Retrieved from www.waldorflibrary.org/images/stories/articles/teeth.pdf (accessed 9 November 2017).

Steiner Waldorf Schools Fellowship (n.d.) 'What is Steiner education?' www.steinerwaldorf.org/steiner-education/what-is-steiner-education (accessed 18 November 2017).

Steiner Waldorf Foundation (2009) Guide to the Early Years Foundation Stage in Steiner Waldorf Early Childhood Settings, retrieved from www.foundationyears.org.uk/files/2011/10/Guide_to_the_EYFS_in_Steiner_Wardorf_settings1.pdf (accessed 9th November 2017).

Stiles, J. and Jernigan, L. (2010) 'The basics of brain development', *Neuropsychology Review* 20: 327–48. Available at www.ncbi.nlm.nih.gov/pmc/articles/PMC2989000 (accessed 15 November 2017).

Stone, D., Patton, B. and Heen, S. (1999) *Difficult Conversations: How to Discuss What Matters Most.* New York: Penguin.

Sylva, K., Melhuish, E., Sammons, P., Siraj-Blatchford, I. & Taggart, B. (2004) *The Effective Provision of Pre-school Education (EPPE) Project: Findings from Pre-school to end of Key Stage 1.* Nottingham: Department for Education and Skills.

Sylva, K., Melhuish, E., Sammons, P., Siraj-Blatchford, I. and Taggart, B. (2008) *Effective Pre-school and Primary Education 3–11 Project (EPPE 3–11). Final Report from the Primary Phase: Pre-school, School and Family Influences on Children's Development during Key Stage 2.* DCSF-RR061. London: Department for Children, Schools and Families.

Sylva, K., Melhuish, E., Sammons, P., Siraj-Blatchford, I. and Taggart, B. (2010) *Early Childhood Matters: Evidence from the Effective Pre-school and Primary Education Project.* Abingdon: Routledge.

Sylva, K., Melhuish, E., Sammons, P., Siraj-Blatchford, I., Taggart, B., Toth, K., and Welcomme, W. (2012) *Effective Pre-school, Primary and Secondary Education 3–14 Project (EPPSE 3–14). Final Report from the Key Stage 3 Phase: Influences on Students' Development From age 11–14.* Research Report DFE-RR202. London: Department for Education.

Sylva, K., Siraj-Blatchford, I. and Taggart, B. (2010) *ECERS-E: The Early Childhood Environment Rating Scale Curricular Extension to ECERS-R.* London: IoE Press/ Stoke-on-Trent: Trentham Books. Available at www.ucl-ioe-press.com/books/ early-years-and-primary-education/ecers-e-the-early-childhood-environment-rating- scale-curricular-extension-to-ecers-r (accessed 9 November 2017).

Taylor, H. and Harris, A. (2013) *Learning and Teaching Mathematics 0–8.* London: Sage.

Technology and Play (2015) *Exploring Play and Creativity in Pre-Schoolers' Use of Apps.* Final Project Report. Available at www.techandplay.org/reports/TAP_Final_Report.pdf (accessed 18 November 2017).

Tickell, Dame Clare (2011) *The Early Years: Foundations for Life, Health and Learning.* London: Department for Education.

Trevarthen, C. (1995) 'The child's need to learn a culture', *Children and Society*, 9 (1): 5–19.

Tuckman, B. (1965) 'Developmental sequence in small groups', *Psychological Bulletin*, 63: 384–99.

UNICEF (2012) *School Readiness: A Conceptual Framework.* New York: United Nations Children's Fund. Available at www.unicef.org/education/files/Chil2Child_ ConceptualFramework_FINAL(1).pdf (accessed 29 October 2017).

United Nations (1989) Convention on the Rights of the Child. New York: United Nations. Available at www.unicef.org.uk/what-we-do/un-convention-child-rights (accessed 9 November 2017).

United Nations (2013) Convention on the Rights of the Child, Committee on the Rights of the Child General comment No. 17 (2013): The right of the child to rest, leisure, play, recreational activities, cultural life and the arts (Article 31). Available at www. iccp-play.org/documents/news/UNGC17.pdf (accessed 16 November 2017).

University of Oxford, Department of Education (2017) Effective Pre-school, Primary and Secondary Education: EPPE/EPPSE 3–14. www.ucl.ac.uk/ioe/research/featured-research/ effective-pre-school-primary-secondary-education-project (accessed April 2017).

Vaggers, J. (2014) 'How can children's centre leaders best enable integrated working to flourish?' Unpublished thesis University of Leicester. Available at https://lra.le.ac.uk/ bitstream/2381/32454/1/2015VAGGERSJPHD.pdf (accessed 9 November 2017).

Weisman, D.L. (2012) 'An essay on the art and science of teaching', *The American Economist*, 57 (1): 111–25. Available at http://journals.sagepub.com/doi/abs/10.1177/0 56943451205700109?journalCode=aexb (accessed 9 November 2017).

West-Burnham, J., Farrar, M. and Otero, G. (2007) *Schools and Communities Working Together to Transform Children's Lives.* London: Bloomsbury.

Weston, P. (2002) *The Froebel Education Institute: The Origins and History of the College.* University of Surrey Roehampton.

Whitbread, N. (1972) *The evolution of the nursery-infant school: a history of infant and nursery education in Britain, 1800–1970.* International Library of Social Policy. Original from, the University of Michigan. Digitized, Apr 25, 2007. Routledge and Kegan Paul.

Whitebread, D. (2015) '"Our classroom is like a little cosy house": organising the Early Years classroom to encourage self-regulated learning', in D. Whitebread and P. Coltman (eds), *Teaching and Learning in the Early Years*, 4th edn. Abingdon: Routledge.

Whitebread, D. and Bingham, S. (2011) 'School Readiness: A Critical Review of Perspectives and Evidence'. TACTYC: Occasional Paper No. 2. Available at http://tactyc.org.uk/occasional-paper/occasional-paper2.pdf (accessed 9 November 2017).

Whitebread, D. with Basilio, M., Kuvalja, M. and Verma, M. (2012) *The Importance of Play: A Report on the Value of Children's Play with a Series of Policy Recommendations*. Brussels: Toy Industries of Europe. Available at www.importanceofplay.eu/IMG/pdf/dr_david_whitebread_-_the_importance_of_play.pdf (accessed 28 October 2017).

Workman, B. (2007) 'Casing the joint: Explorations by the insider-researcher for preparing work-based projects', *Journal of Workplace Learning*, 19 (3): 146–60.

Yared, Teshome Yaya and Taha, Hassan Yousif (2014) 'The role of multicultural art education in a cultural diversified society'. University of Gothenburg. Available at https://gupea.ub.gu.se/handle/2077/38262 (accessed 30 October 2017).

INDEX

Note: Figures and Tables are indicated by page numbers in bold print, photographs by page numbers in italics. The letter "*b*" after a page number indicates bibliographical information in a Further Reading section.

Abrahamson, Eric 208
Abrahamson, I. 114*b*
abuse:
   allegations 176
   categories 173–4
   definitions 176
   see also safeguarding
Accounting for Lifelong Learning Skills (AcE)
   project 113
action research 68, **69**
Alliance for Early Childhood 162
Ancona, D. et al 213, 217*b*
Angelou, Maya 215
Anning, Angela 213
Anthroposophy 44
Arnold, C. 148, 151*b*
Arnold, C. and Cummings, A. 215
assessment:
   Assessment at the end of the EYFS - the Early
      Years Foundation Profile (EYFSP) 223
   Assessment and Planning Cycle 101, 104,
      105, 108
   Early Years Foundation Stage Statutory
      Assessment Guidance as Specified at
      Standard 6 221–2
   formative and summative 105–8
   and observation 42–3, 81, 108–110, 111
      methods 109
   progress check **106–7**
   for SEND 193–4, 196–7
attachment theory 142
autism (case study) 177

Ballard, P.B.: *The Practical Infant Teacher* 47
Bandura, A. 44
Barber, J. 95*b*
Barrington, F. 184*b*
Bassot, R. 66, 75*b*
behaviour 146–8
   boundaries 147
   and stress 148
   understanding children's emotional
      states 148

Belbin, M. 208
beliefs and values 60–61, 147
   of teams 206, 207
   see also diversity
belonging, sense of 192
benefits of pre-school education 81, 87
Bercow Report 120
bilingualism 120
Blakemore, S.J. and Frith, U. 127, 130, 131, 133*b*
Blythe, Goddard 157, 158–9
Bolton, G. 62, 65, 75*b*
Bowlby, John 55, 142
brain development 26–7, 44, 130, 158–9
   and appropriate expectations 158–9
   and creativity 155
Briggs, M. and Davis, S. 165*b*
Bristol Every Child a Talker (BECAT) 109
British values 180
Broadhead, P. et al 114*b*
Brock, A. and Rankin, C. 133*b*
Bronfenbrenner's ecological environment
   model 138, 139
Bruce, T. 165*b*
Bruce, T. and Spratt, J. 134*b*
Bruner, Jerome 21, 54

Callanan, M. et al, *Study of Early Education and
   Development: Good Practice in Early Education
   (SEED)* 1, 2, 3, 13, 60, 61, 79, 118, 201–2
   good planning practice 111
Campbell-Barr, V. and Leeson, C. 84, 96*b*
change 208–212
   change management: steps 209
   change related chaos 208
   emotions during change 209
   initiative overload 208
   repetitive change syndrome 208
Cheminais, R. 217*b*
child-centred learning 45, 46
childcare 51–2
Childcare Act (2006) 4, 170
childminders 51–2
   staff-child ratios 229

Children and Families Act (2014) 174, 188, 193
children's observation skills 23, 41
children's rights 174, 188–9
   see also inclusion and anti-discrimination
Choice for Parents, the Best Start for Children: A
   Ten-year Strategy for Childcare 4
Clark, A. and Moss, P. 109, 161
Claxton, Guy 45
Coalition government (2010-2015) 5
cognitive development 121–2, 123–4, 125
   see also brain development
collaborations of professionals:
   barriers 212
   collaborative advantage 213
   collaborative inertia 213
   reasons for 213
communication and language (CL) 25, 118–33
   building blocks of language development **126**
   case study 23–5
   communication-friendly environments
      130–33
   following a recipe *122*
   impairments and intervention 120
   key elements of good practice 118
   listening 110, 120, 124–7, 132
   perspectives of language acquisition 120–21
   reading and writing 128–30, 132–3
   research, reviews and reports **119**
   talking 110, 120, 127–8, 132
contact and exchange principle 27
continuous professional development 78
   group supervision 149–50
   see also wider professional responsibilities
Coram, Captain Thomas 39–40
Coram's Fields *40*
Counter-Terrorism and Security Act (2015)
   170, 180
creativity:
   and brain development 155
   of children with paint *140*
   creative developmental approach 154–5
   in the environment 161
   exploring a gallery *163*–4
   from children's ideas 154
   and language development 131
   and physical development 157–8
   and play on a sandy beach *159*–60
   prime and specific areas of learning 155–6
   providing creative experiences 155
   in Steiner schools 45
critical evaluation, need for 67
curriculum:
   knowledge of 2
   and play 100

self-guided 47
Te Whariki (Woven Mat) 52–3
Curtis, W. et al 46, 56*b*, 165*b*

DCSF, *Children's Plan, The: Building Brighter*
   Futures 4
Delafield-Butt, B.T. and Trevarthen, C. 124
Denscombe, M. 68, 69, 75*b*
Development Matters (Early Education) 110
Dewey, John 54
DfES, *Every Child Matters: Change for Children* 4
diet 45
direct exploration/experience 41, 43, 45, 48
dispositions 154–5
diversity 162, 190–92
documentary analysis 71
Dowling, M. 124, 125
Duffy, B. 157, 166*b*

Early Childhood Education and Care (ECEC)
   pioneers and key educationalists 36–55
   political, economic, social and technological
      demands (PEST) **55**
Early Intervention Foundation 139
Early Learning Goals (ELGs) 101, **102–3**
Early Years Foundation Stage (EYFS)
   25, 101, 142
   'prime' and 'specific' areas 101, **102–3**,
      155–6
Early Years Foundation Stage Profile
   (EYFSP) 105
Early Years Initial Teacher Training 7
Early Years Outcomes 110
Early Years Professional Status (EYPS) 7, 19
Early Years qualifications criteria 67
Early Years Teacher Status (EYTS) 7
Edgington, M. 31*b*
Education Health Care (EHC) Plans 194
Elfer, Peter 209
emotional abuse 173
English as a second language 121
environment and creativity 161
Equality Act (2010) 2, 174, 188
equality of opportunity 190–92
Essex County Council enabling environment
   audit 88
ethical issues:
   ICT 71
   practice-based inquiry (PBI) 68, 71, 72, 75
   see also safeguarding
ethos 30, 60–61, 138, 147, 188, 207–8
Experiential Education (EXE) 49–51
      ten action points 50
extremism and terrorism 180–81

feelings 155
Female Genital Mutilation 178
financial restraints 4–5
Fisher, John 209
Forest School learning 161
Freud, Anna 54
Freud, Sigmund 207
Froebel, Friedrich 3, 18, 37–9
  environmental features 38–9
  Mother Songs, Games and Stories 37

Gandini, L. et al 166*b*
Germany 37
Giardiello, P. 56*b*
Gibbs' reflective cycle **64**
good practice: significant elements 20
Goouch, K. 18, 25
Goouch, K. and Lambirth, A. 29, 31*b*, 130, 134*b*
Gopnik, A. 124
government support/publications 4–6, 101
Guardian, The 51

Hallet, E. 14*b*
Harms, T. et al *Early Childhood Environment
  Rating Scale* 79, 84
Harris, B. 216, 217*b*
health and safety 181
hearing loss 120, 121
Hevey, Denise 51
high-quality teaching:
  and features of leadership 80
  long-term benefits 81, 87
  Ofsted descriptors 78, 81
  Ofsted inspections 82–5
    outcomes 83–4
  outcomes 81
  outdoor learning in an urban setting *82*
  and professional development 78
  research studies 79, 86–7
  and skills/abilities of EYT/Es 79
  see also quality improvement (QI); reflective
    practice
HighScope approach 48–9
Hodkinson, A. 203*b*
home to nursery transition 142, 147
Hopkins, R. et al 81, 82, 88
House, R. 57*b*, 166*b*
Hunt, Abigail 163, 164

'image of the child' 61
inclusion and anti-discrimination 189–90, 190–92
  see also diversity
Infant Toddler Environment Rating Scale
  (ITERS-R, Harms et al) 79, 84

Information Communication Technology (ICT)
  70–71, 74–5
  children working together on a computer **74**
  ethical issues 71
inspections 82–5
  outcomes 83–4
  paperwork required 85
  points for reflection 83
  preparing for 84–5
  safeguarding 170
iPads 43
Isaacs, Susan 18, 41–3
  Educational Value of the Nursery School, The 43
  Intellectual Growth in Young Children 42
  Nursery Years, The 42

Jackson B. and Jackson, S. 51
John, Karen 207, 209, 214

Katz, Lilian 154, 158, 160
  principles of teaching 156, 158
Keeping Children Safe in Education 170, 176
key educationalists **54–5**
Key Person approach 60
kindergarten 37
Klein, Melanie 54
knowledge and understanding 154
Kolb's learning cycle **62**
Kotter, J. 209

Labour government (1997-2010) 4
Laevers, Ferre 3, 49–51, 91, 109
Laevers, Ferre et al, Leuven Well-being and
  Involvement Scale 141
Lancashire County Council Self-evaluation tool 89
language *see* communication and language (CL)
leadership:
  and change 208–212
  democratic approach 214
  developing relationships 211
  elements of showing leadership 206
  features of QI leadership 80
  feedback 211
  good authority 214–16
  Leadership Qualities Framework 67
  motivation 211–12
  multiprofessional teamwork 212–14
  relational 213–14
  self-confidence 214–15
  and supervision 148–50, 209–210
  training for 216
Leadership Qualities Framework 67
learning/development areas: providing
  opportunities **28**

life skills/everyday activities 2, 27
Linden, J. and Webb, J. 184*b*
Lindon, J. and Trodd, L. 76*b*
listening 124–7
    listening to the 'voice of the child' *126*
    types 125
literature review 71
London Foundling Hospital 39

Macmillan sisters 3, 18, 43–4
Making Children's Learning Visible (MCLV) 61
Malaguzzi, Loris 47–8
    *Your Image of the Child: Where Teaching
        Begins* 125
Malting House School 41, 43
Manning-Morton, J. and Thorp, M. 145, 147, 151*b*
mathematics 27, 157
Mathers, S. et al 4, 5, 84, 88, 93
    *Evaluation of the Graduate Leader Fund - Final
        Report* 5–6
    Improving Quality in the Early Years 79, 85
Miller, L. and Hever, D. 14*b*
Montessori, Maria 41, 45–7
    compared with Steiner **46–7**
'More Great Childcare' 6
Mosaic Approach 109, 161
Moyles, J. et al 10, 11, 21–2
Mukherji, P. and Dryden, L. 57*b*
Musgrave, J. 151*b*

nappy changing 145
National Childminding Association (NCMA) 51
National College for Teaching and Leadership
    (NCTL) 7, 19
National Curriculum Key Stage 1 and 2 18, 25
national standards 25
neglect of children 173
networks of support 211, 213–14
New Zealand 52–3
Northern Ireland 18
Nutbrown Review 5, 6, 7, 19, 203*b*

observation 42–3, 49–50, 81, 108–110, 111
    methods 109
    of play 148
    see also assessment; children's observation
        skills
Ofsted:
    *Achieving and Maintaining High-Quality Early
        Years Provision* 80
    Early Years Inspection Handbook 29–30, 81, 83–4
    Early Years Inspections: Myths 82
    inspections 82–5, 178–9
    safeguarding 175, 178–9

Self-Evaluation Guidance for Early Years 60
*Teaching and Play in the Early Years - a
    Balancing Act?* 20
Oliver, Jamie 45
'One Hundred Languages of Children' (poem) 122
Open-Air Nursery School and Training Centre,
    London 44
Oussoren, R. 166*b*
outcomes and quality of early years education 81
Owen, Robert 36

PACEY 113, 114
Page, Jools 144
Palaiologou, I. 75*b*, 115*b*
Parent-Child Interaction Therapy 120
parent-child relationship 138, 147
parents:
    communication with 201–2, 211
    and record keeping 199–200
Pascal, T. and Bertram, C. 109, 113, 216
pedagogy:
    and brain development 26–7
    case study: language session 23–5
    children cooking *20*
    contact and exchange principle 27
    definitions 21
    fostering love of reading **30**
    good practice: elements 20
    practice: descriptors 21–2
    prime areas of learning/development and
        providing opportunities **28**
    principles:
        definitions 22
        elements 29
    professional dimensions 22
    within national framework 25
Peer, L. and Reid, G. 203*b*
Pen Green Centre for Children and
    Families 215
    Making Children's Learning Visible (MCLV) 61
performance management 210
Personal, Social and Emotional Development
    (PSE) 25, 28, 44, 83, 101, 102, 139
    and brain development 155–6
    and safety 177
    see also relationships; safeguarding
Pestalozzi, Johann Heinrich 40
Phillips, Nicola 51, 52
physical environment 181–2
physical abuse 173
physical activities 36
physical contact and closeness 145
physical development 25, 28, 157–8
Piaget, Jean 41, 54

planning 24, 27, 42, 101, 104, 110–112
  effective learning characteristics 108
  good planning practice (SEED) 111
  linking prime and specific areas to Early
      Learning Goals **102–3**
  practice-based inquiry (PBI) 68–9, 70–71
  proformas 112
  short- and long-term 112
  Special Educational Needs and Disability
      (SEND) 197
  systems 112
  see also assessment
play:
  in Coram's Field *40*
  and curriculum 100
  environment 50–51, 100
  heuristic materials *38*
  importance of 37, 43, 100
  learning through play *159*–60
  observation of 148
  outdoor 43, 44
  planning 110
  purposeful play - mark making with natural
      materials *104*
  scaffolding academic skills 111
  socio-dramatic play outdoors *42*
  and teaching 20
political, economic, social, technological (PEST)
      factors **55**
positive self-regard 215
Pound, L. 57*b*
practice-based inquiry (PBI) 67–75
  action research 68, **69**
  case study: Information Communication
      Technology (ICT) resources 70–71, 73,
      74–5, *74*
  confidentiality 72
  drivers of change **69**
  evaluation 74–5
  feedback 72, 75
  Fishbone diagram (cause and effect analysis) **72**
  informed consent 72
  leading change 73
  methodology 71–2
    baseline audit 71
    documentary analysis 71
    literature review 71
    practice forums 72
  outcomes 73–4
  planning 68–9, 70–71, 73
  resistance to change 73
  structure 68
principles of teaching (Katz) 156, 158
process vs. product 162

professional dimensions of pedagogy 22
Pugh, G. and Duffy, B. 14*b*
Pyke, Geoffrey 41

Qualified Teacher Status 7
Quality Audit Tool **11**
quality of early years provision
  case study: ITERS-R Audit 92–3
  continuous improvement ('Kaizen') 94
  dimensions of quality:
    activities 91
    interaction 92
    language and reasoning 91
    personal care routines 91
    programme structure 92
    provision for parents and staff 92
    space and furnishings 91
  leadership gurus 94–5
  Ofsted findings 8
  and outcomes 81
  quality improvement (QI) tools:
    Bristol Standard 90
    ECERS-R (Harms et al) 91, 92
    Essex County Council enabling
        environment audit 88
    ITERS-R (Harms et al) 91, 92
    Lancashire County Council Self-evaluation
        tool 89
    National Quality Improvement Network
        (NQN) 90
    National Strategies 89
    National Strategies: Early Years: Every Child
        a Talker 90
    Ofsted Early Years Inspection Handbook 90
    Professor Ferre Laevers: Process-Orientated
        Monitoring System 91
  SSTEW scales 94
  structural and process factors 88
  see also high-quality teaching; quality
      improvement (QI)

reading and writing 128–30
  fostering love of **30**, 130
  phonics 128–30
  'Standards and Testing Agency alien words'
      on display *129*
Reardon, D. 84
Reception year 25
record keeping 199–200
  for EHC needs assessment 200
Reed, M. and Canning, N. 14*b*, 96*b*
reflective practice 12, 60–66
  beliefs and values 60–61
  models 61–4

Driscoll's 'What?' model **63**
Gibbs' reflective cycle **64**
Kolb's learning cycle **62**
'reflection-in-action' and 'reflection-on-action' 61–2
reflective mirror metaphor 64, **65–6**
Reggio Children 134*b*
Reggio Emilia approach 3, 47–8, 162
Reid, J. and Burton, S. 184*b*
relationships:
  Key Person EYFS Principles into Practice
    Card **143**
  key person relationships 142
  professional love 144
  secure attachment relationships 142, 143
  *Sustained Shared Thinking and Emotional
    Well-being scale (STSEW)* 84, 86, 94,
    119, 123, 141–2
*Researching Effective Pedagogy in the Early Years
  (REPEY)* 86
Rights Respecting Schools Award (RRSA) 188
risk assessment 181
Roberts, R. 139, 140, 147, 151*b*
Roberts-Holmes, G. 76*b*
Robertson, Fiona 191–2
Roulstone, C. and Sharynne, M. 134*b*

safeguarding:
  accidents, injuries and medicines 183
  allegations of abuse 176
  categories of abuse 173–4
  checks before recruitment 175
  designated safeguarding lead (DSL) 174
  Disclosure and Barring Service 175
  disqualification by association 175–6
  information sharing 178
  key policies 171–2
  legislation 170
  Local Area Designated Officer (LADO) 172, 176
  Local Safeguarding Children Board (LSCB)
    170, 178
  Multi-Agency Safeguarding Hubs 178
  outings 183
  physical environment 181–2
  Prevent Duty 180–81
  principles 170
  restraint (positive handling) 176–7
  safer recruitment 175–6
  Single Central Record 175
  and Special Educational Needs (SEN) 177
    case study 177
  staff-child ratios 180, 181
  statutory safeguarding duties 170–71
  teaching children 176–7

terrorism 180
visitors 182
scaffolding 111
Scandinavian Forest School 161
Schön, Donald 61, 62
School Meals Act (1906) 43
school readiness 25, 45, 112–14
Schweizer, S. 57*b*
Scotland 18, 36
selective mutism 121
self-confidence 214–15
self-expression 42
settings for teaching 21
  purpose and values of 206
  reflecting on the setting 206
sexual abuse 173
Sharpe, C. 166*b*
Siraj, I. et al:
  Effective Pre-school, Primary Project, (EPPSE)
    86–7
  *Effective Pre-school, Primary and Secondary
    Education (EPPE/EPPSE)* 86
  *Effective Provision of Pre-School Education
    (EPPE)* 3, 4, 8, 10, 86, 87
  *Researching Effective Pedagogy in the Early Years
    (REPEY)* 86
  *Sustained Shared Thinking and Emotional Well-
    being scale (STSEW)* 84, 86, 94, 119, 123,
    141, 151*b*
Siraj-Blatchford, I. et al 21, 92, 123
skills/skilfulness 154
Slaughter, E. 96*b*
SMART targets 150
social context 110
social world 43
Special Educational Needs and Disability
    (SEND) 188, 189, 193–9
  assessment 193–4, 196–7
  case study: autism 177
  case study: learning difficulties and ASD 199
  definitions 198–9
  graduated approach 196–8
  health services 194
  planning 197
  role in supporting SEND 195
  SEND Code of Practice 193–4, 196
  settings 195–6
staff-child ratios 180, 181
  all providers (including childminders) 229
  all providers (other than childminders)
    229–32
stammering 120
Steiner, Rudolph 18, 44–5
  compared with Montessori **46–7**

Stone, Douglas et al 210
Study of Pedagogical Effectiveness in Early
    Learning (SPEEL) 10, 21–2
supervision 148–50, 209–210
    case study: group supervision 149–50
    practitioners working alongside each
        other *149*
    see also leadership
Supporting Families in the Foundation Years' 5
Switzerland 41
Sylva, K. et al, *Effective Provision of Pre-School
    Education* (EPPE) 3, 4, 8, 10, 13, 86, 87,
    92, 123
symbolic languages 47, 48

'tacit knowledge' 61
talking 110, 120, 127–8, 132
targets 25
Taylor, H. and Harris, A. 32*b*
Te Whariki ('Woven Mat') 52–3
'teacher' as name 18
Teacher's Standards (Early Years) 67
teachers-learner partnership 48, 49
teaching: definition 215–16
teamwork:
    building teams 207–8, 216
    collusion 216
    communication 209
    conflict 207
    differences of opinion 207, 210
    ethos 207
    leadership 206, 207
    'learning conversations' 210
    multiprofessional collaboration 212–14
    roles 208
Technology and Play Report 43
thinking skills 123–4, 125
Tickell, Dame Clare 5
title Early Years Teacher/Educator (EYT/E) 18
training and qualifications 5–8, 10
    case study 1.1 6–7
    and developmental progress 10, 12–13
    Early Years Educator (Level 3): Qualifications
        Criteria 224–8
    graduate Early Years programme under
        CWDC and Teaching Agency **9**
    for leadership 216
    Teachers' Standards (Early Years) 219–21

trainee teacher engaged in pedagogical
    practice *10*
variations in other countries 18–19
variations in UK 18

UK: variations in EYT/E 18
UN Convention on the Rights of the Child
    (UNCRC) 100, 174, 188–9
unconscious learning 45
UNICEF 113, 188

voice 121
Vygotsky, Lev 43, 54

Wales 18
Waller, T. and Davis, G. 31*b*
well-being:
    children's behaviour 146–8
    concept of well-being 138
    definitions 139
    emotions and relationships 138, 139, 141–4, **143**
    of EY staff 148–50
    models of well-being 139, 140
        belonging and boundaries (Roberts) 139
        ecological environment model
            (Bronfenbrenner) 138, 139
    routines 145
    starting school: case study 145–6
Weston, P. 57*b*
Whally, Margy 3
Whitebread, D. 30
Whitebread, D. and Bingham, S. 112
Whitebread, D. and Coltman, P. 32*b*
Whitehead, M.R. 134*b*
wider professional responsibilities:
    case study: deputy manager of a nursery
        210–212
    definition 206
    good authority 214–16
    leadership through change 208–212
    leading a team 207–8
    multiprofessional teamwork and
        collaboration 212–14
Winnicott, Donald 54
work-based projects *see* practice-based inquiry (PBI)
Workman, B. 68
Wright, S. 166*b*
Write Dance (WD) 162